The Innkeepers'
REGISTER

Country Inns of 🏮 *North America*
1993-1994

Edited by Diane Graves

Trillium House 9/93

INDEPENDENT INNKEEPERS' ASSOCIATION
Marshall, Michigan
Founded in 1972 by Norman T. Simpson

Cover Art by Maureen Reed
Commentary by Virginia Rowe

For further information, call Independent Innkeepers' Association,
800-344-5244

Contents

Special Features by Virginia Rowe

INTRODUCTION

We hope you enjoy this 5th edition of the *Innkeepers' Register*. Each year we make additions and improvements to better serve our special traveling guests. We welcome your suggestions on additional information or changes which would be of benefit in helping you select inns to visit.

Traveling via the country inn circuit is a unique and delightful experience. Each inn is different, providing varied experiences and regional attractions. At the same time, each is alike in that guests are assured personal attention, good service, and pleasant surroundings. Country inns provide an ambiance that cannot be imitated in other hospitality facilities.

Bob Lenz, President
Asa Ransom House, Clarence, New York

Norman D. Kinney,
Executive Director
Independent Innkeepers'
Association
Marshall, Michigan

For planning your next trip, we would like to pass along a suggestion that some guests have recommended. Since each area is unique and offers so many interesting attractions, a two-evening stay is a worthwhile suggestion. The reasoning is that with a guest's arrival mid or late afternoon and departure the next day to travel to the next destination, he has less than one day to enjoy the individuality of the inn and the area. Most Innkeepers are very happy to suggest local adventures; many have brochures and personal recommendations.

With these comments, we proudly offer you this prestigious collection of more than 250 of the finest inns available anywhere. Happy traveling!

" . . . the best at what we do."

from our Mission Statement
INDEPENDENT INNKEEPERS' ASSOCIATION

PREFACE

*We are an association of independent innkeepers dedicated to
providing our guests with a unique hospitality experience by
being the best at what we do. . . individually and collectively.*

*Through mutual involvement, we work together to educate,
promote, and support each other in our continuing efforts to set
standards for our profession.*

— IIA MISSION STATEMENT

These are the goals and objectives of the Independent Innkeepers'
Association, which has evolved from the tiny group gathered together in
1966 by Norman T. Simpson. Renowned as the "father of country inns," his
book, *Country Inns and Back Roads*, was the first of its kind in contemporary
times. He held informal dinners for the innkeepers who were featured in
the first early editions. Then, as the number of inns grew, it became clear
that country innkeepers felt isolated and out of contact with like-minded
people in the hospitality industry. Hotel and motel organizations offered
little of value to keepers of country inns. Their appreciation and need for
gathering together with other innkeepers was immediately obvious.

The opportunity to discuss mutual problems and find solutions, and
the discovery that their failures and triumphs were shared by others, gave
rise to the idea of a network of fine country inns in which was implicit the
sense of responsibility to each other and their shared values and standards
in serving the public.

At first there were annual meetings, which would take place at one or
another of the inns in this book. Then, the need for smaller, more focused
sessions resulted in several regional meetings in various parts of the
country throughout the year.

By 1972, Norman formally established this loose collection of inns as
the Independent Innkeepers' Association. The innkeepers in this group
came from all walks of life, many of them having left successful careers and
lucrative opportunities to experience the joys and tribulations of innkeeping. An important quality in each of them was not only a deep sense of
commitment to their inns, but also an enthusiasm and desire to be involved
with other innkeepers who shared their goals and standards and who
wanted to work together for the common good.

The feeling of fellowship and family is a strong bond rooted in the
shared purpose of maintaining what is finest and best in the true tradition
and spirit of American innkeeping.

Today, five years after Norman Simpson's death, the board of directors
and the membership are continuing and expanding the work he began. In
this ever-increasingly competitive arena, we will hold to the standards of
personal hospitality, which he defined and which are so important to us and
our many guests who look for both professional excellence and a genuine
feeling of friendly welcome.

Accreditation Program

In accordance with our stated purpose of maintaining the highest standards of innkeeping, the Independent Innkeepers' Association requires member participation in a quality assurance program. This program provides for mandatory periodic inspection of every inn by Quality Consultants, Inc., of Greenwich, Rhode Island, specialists who have been retained to give an impartial evaluation of each inn.

Staff members of Quality Consultants are personally trained to provide thorough, unbiased and honest evaluations and do so in an unobtrusive and timely manner. The evaluation visit is for two consecutive nights, whenever possible, to permit the evaluator to get a full picture of the operation of the inn. The visits, of course, are unannounced.

The evaluation begins with the first telephone call placed by the consultants who subsequently visit the facility and report on both the highlights of their stay and any areas which may be of concern. Only upon completion of the checkout procedure do they identify themselves and go over the rough draft of their findings. A formal typed report is mailed to the innkeeper and to the IIA office within 7 days of the visit.

Following are a few of the many issues on which member inns are rated:

Basic Requirements

Warm welcome by innkeepers or staff
Architecturally attractive facility
Buildings (inside & out) well maintained
Safety of guests insured (inside & out)
Sitting room for guests only
Impeccable housekeeping throughout inn
A pleasant dining experience or fine dining available nearby
Excellent lighting in guest rooms
Bathrooms well furnished with large, quality towels and adequate shelf space, clothes hooks, etc.

Special Or Personal Touches

Fresh cut flowers or well-tended houseplants
Soft music in dining and common rooms
Quality paintings, artwork, artifacts or memorabilia
Historical references or other material of interest
Comfortable, well-maintained outdoor seating
Books, area maps, magazines, games, bulletin boards and various other materials for guests' amusement
Quality amenities, refreshments

Another important and valuable adjunct to our accreditation program involves our encouragement of guest evaluations, through card inserts in the back of our book. We are interested in hearing from our guests and will appreciate receiving evaluations of the IIA inns you have visited.

The IIA continues to work with members to support and encourage them in improving their properties and maintaining the high standards which make our members the leaders in their field.

Some Criteria For Membership In The IIA

These are a few of the criteria used in evaluating the eligibility of an inn for membership in the IIA. Other more stringent criteria are also used; however, these are the most basic requirements.

- Inn is owner-operated or the innkeeper/manager is highly committed to the spirit of personal hospitality. Staff shows genuine interest toward guests.

- The innkeeper has owned/run the inn for a minimum of three years, or, if from a background of successful innkeeping, two years.

- Inn building is architecturally interesting and attractive with appropriately groomed grounds, tasteful, comfortable and inviting interior furnishings and at least one common room for houseguests only. Guest rooms are attractively and completely furnished for comfort of guests.

- Housekeeping and maintenance is excellent, with immaculate guest rooms and bathrooms.

- Breakfast and dinner should be a pleasant eating experience. If the evening meal is not provided on the premises, fine dining must be readily available in the immediate area (preferably within walking distance).

The IIA Gift Certificate

A Lovely Gift for Someone Special

The gift of an overnight stay or a weekend at a country inn can be one of the most thoughtful and appreciated gifts you can give your parents or children, dear friends, or valued employees for Christmas, a birthday, an anniversary, or any special occasion. Innkeepers and other employers are discovering this is an excellent way of rewarding their employees, while at the same time giving them some much needed rest and relaxation.

An IIA gift certificate means that you can give the gift of a stay at any one of over 250 member inns from Kennebunkport, Maine to Southern California; from Quebec, Canada to Key West, Florida; from Martha's Vineyard, Massachusetts to Seaview, Washington. We have inns in the Blue Ridge Mountains, on ranches in the western desert, near state parks and forests and nature preserves, in restored villages in historic districts, on lakes and by the sea. Choose your pleasure.

An IIA gift certificate is good for two years and may be purchased through the IIA office by personal check or Mastercard or Visa. With each gift certificate we send along a brand new copy of the *Innkeepers' Register*. For further information call **800-344-5244**.

A five dollar ($5) postage and handling fee will be added to all gift certificate purchases.

WHAT IS A COUNTRY INN?

When Norman Simpson first began writing about country inns, he was often asked to explain the term, and at first his answer would be, "a country inn is an inn in the country." Although all country inns were not then (or now) in the country, he felt that the word "country" was still operative. He said, "country implies an escape from urban pressures and demands, and not only conjures up euphoric bucolia but a welcome innocence associated with the American past. In many ways country inns are personified by some 19th-century attitudes concerning reliability, sincerity, warmheartedness, and a genuine desire to be of service. Each inn is original and unique, reflecting not only the old-time American ideal of rugged individualism, but also the personalities and tastes of the innkeeper-owners, who are more than likely on hand to make their guests feel personally welcome, comfortable, and at ease."

Although there were a number of specifics Norman looked for in an inn, his "bottom line" was always the people who ran it. One of his favorite expressions in referring to country inns was "personal hospitality," meaning the strong feeling of involvement and commitment on the part of the innkeeper, and a hospitable friendliness that came out of a genuine liking for people.

Among his personal set of requirements, beyond cleanliness, good housekeeping, maintenance, attractive furnishings with individuality, excellent service, and good food, were the little indications that the comfort and needs of the guests were being met: adequate lighting and an extra pillow for reading in bed, interesting reading material in guest rooms, generous-sized, thick towels, adequate shelf space in the bathroom, and all the special and personal touches, such as plantings, fresh flowers, music, paintings and artwork, and various and sundry articles of interest, that create the feeling of a "home away from home." He approved of the quiet afforded by the absence of television and telephones in guest rooms. He expected an inn to have at least one hospitable parlor or sitting room where guests could meet and talk in a convivial atmosphere.

He had a strong conviction that anything of a business or commercial nature should be kept to a bare minimum, and above all, the real thing, as opposed to the ersatz, should be used in furnishings as well as foods. If reproductions of antique furniture were used, they should be excellent reproductions, and if, God forbid, anything plastic was discovered, it had better be virtually invisible and of superior quality. Food should be fresh and made from scratch.

He felt that country inns should reflect their regions, and he was particularly happy when he found an inn that was rooted in its community with all the local color and flavor of the area.

A convivial place to meet new people, to have good conversation, to make friends, to relax or to be active—ultimately, to feel "at home." For Norman Simpson, these were the attributes of a good country inn.

by Virginia Rowe

KEY TO SYMBOLS

	ENGLISH	FRENCH	GERMAN	JAPANESE	SPANISH
	number of rooms; rates and rate plan for 2 people number of suites; rates and rate plan for 2 people credit cards accepted	nombre de chambres, les prix pour deux personnes, plan de repas; nombre d'apparte-ments, les prix pour deux personnes, plan de repas les cartes de crédit acceptées	Anzahl der Zimmers; Tarif-und Tarifplan Anzahl der Zimmerflüchte; Tarif-und Tarifplan Kreditkarten angenommen	部屋数：宿泊料金と料金別プランスイート数：宿泊料金と料金別プランクレジットカード通用	número de habitaciones; tarifas y tablas de tarifas para dos personas número de apartamentos; tarifas y tablas de tarifas para dos personas tarjetas de crédito que aceptamos
	baths—private/shared	salle de bains et WC privés ou communs	Bäder privat/geteilt	バス付 / 共同バス	habitaciones con baño / sin baño
	open/close	période de fermeture ou ouverture	offen: geschlossen	営業中 / 休業 ― シーズン	temporado — fecha en que se abre / fecha en que se cierra
	children and pets acceptability, inquire for rates	les enfants admis? chiens admis? renseignez-vous sur les tarifs	Kinder und Haustiere erlaubt; nach Tarifen erkundigen	子供とペット可、別料金	reglamentos para niños y animales domésticos (pídase tarifas)
	recreation and attractions on premises or in area	les sports et les divertissements à l'hôtel ou l'environs	Erholung und Sehenswürdigkeiten; an Ort und Stelle oder in der Gegend	当地のレクレーション・催し物	atracciones y diversiones / en los terrenos o cercanos
	meals available; wine & liquor available	repas offerts et bar sur place	Speise und Spirituosen erhältlich	食事と飲食可	comida y licores en venta / no se venden
	smoking acceptability	zone fumeur ou non fumeur	Rauchen erlaubt/ begrenzt/verboten	喫煙可	se puede fumar / no se puede fumar
	special features, i.e., wheelchair access; conference facilities	accés pour fauteuil roulant; capacité pour séminaires	Sondermerkungen; Rollstuhl Zugang, z.B. Konferenzräume	特別施設　会議室車イス出入口	a notar: acceso para sillas de ruedas, facilidades para conferencias
MAP	Modified American Plan	Breakfast & dinner included in rate demi-pension Frühstück und Abendessen im Preis einbegriffen 特別アメリカプラン ― 朝・夕食付 la tarifa incluye cena y desayuno			
AP	American Plan	3 meals included in rate pension complète (3) drei Mahlzeiten im Preis inbegriffen アメリカプラン ― 3食付 la tarifa comprende desayuno, almuerzo y cena			
EP	European Plan	no meals included in rate les repas ne sont pas compris Keine Mahlzeiten im Preis inbegriffen ヨーロッパプラン ― 食事なし la tarifa no incluye comida alguna			
B&B	Bed & Breakfast	Breakfast included in rate le petit déjeuner est compris Frühstück einbegriffen 朝食付 la tarifa incluye el desayuno			

RESERVATION AND RATE INFORMATION

Rates listed herein represent a general range of rates for two people for one night at each inn, and should not be considered firm quotations. The rates cover both high and low seasons; tax and gratuities are usually not included. It is well to inquire as to the availability of various special plans and packages. Please be aware that reservation and cancellation policies vary from inn to inn. Listed recreation and attractions are either on the premises or nearby. For more detailed information, ask for inn brochure.

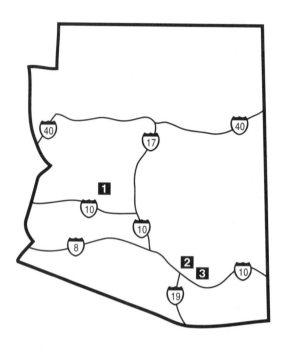

1. Rancho de Los Caballeros, Wickenburg
2. Lodge on the Desert, Tucson
3. Tanque Verde, Tucson

THE LODGE ON THE DESERT

	33 Rooms, $54/$129 B&B 7 Suites $68/$173 B&B
	Visa, MC, Amex, Diners, CB, Discov.
	All Private Baths
	Open year-round
	Children Welcome Pets by prior arrangement
	Heated Swimming Pool, Croquet, Golf, Tennis, Racquet ball, Shuffleboard, Ping-pong
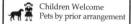	Continental Breakfast, Lunch, Dinner; AP & MAP available 11/1-6/1
	Wine & Liquor available
	Smoking accepted
	Conference Facilities (40)
	Wheelchair Access (7 Rooms)

2 The feeling of old Mexico and of the Southwest is everywhere in the adobe-colored casas grouped around intimate patios at this Mexican hacienda-style resort-inn. Magnificent mountain and desert views, spacious lawns, and colorful gardens belie the proximity of fine residences and nearby downtown Tucson, with all its cultural and recreational attractions.

From I-10 take Speedway exit, 5 mi. (E) to R. turn (S) at Alvernon Way. .8 mi. to Lodge on L. bet. 5th & Broadway.

TEL. 602-325-3366 or
800-456-5634;
FAX 602-327-5834
306 N. Alvernon Way,
P.O. Box 42500
Tucson, AZ 85733
Schuyler & Helen Lininger,
Innkeepers

RANCHO DE LOS CABALLEROS

 74 Rooms, $110/$162 AP
12 Suites, $150/$205 AP
No Credit Cards

 All Private Baths

 Closed Mid-May to Oct. 1

Children Welcome
No Pets

 18 Hole Golf, Riding,
Tennis, Heated Pool,
Skeet & Trap Shooting,
Cookouts, Sq. Dancing

 All Meals AP
Wine & Liquor Available

Smoking Accepted

 Conference Facilities (275)

Wheelchair Access

In Wickenburg, Take U.S. 60 two mi.
(W) of light, turn L. (S) on Vulture
Mine Road. Continue two mi. to ranch
sign & entrance.

TEL. 602-684-5484

1551 S. Vulture Mine Rd.
Wickenburg, AZ 85390

Dallas C. Gant, Jr.,
Innkeeper

1 A green jewel in the desert, with an 18-hole championship golf course, tennis courts, trail rides and other planned activities for adults and children, this rambling ranch-resort has been run by the same family since its inception in 1948. Individual bungalows and terraces, poolside buffet lunches, and evening cookouts brighten winter vacations.

TANQUE VERDE RANCH

 44 Rooms, $200/$310 AP
16 Suites, $230/$350 AP

Visa, MC, Amex

 All Private Baths

Open Year-round

Children & Families
welcome; No Pets

 Riding (115 horses), 5
Tennis Courts, Health
Spa, Pool

All Meals AP (incl.
activities)

Wine & Liquor Available

Smoking Accepted

 Conference Facilities (120)

Wheelchair Access (56
Rooms)

In Tucson, take Speedway Blvd. (E) to
dead end at ranch.

TEL. 602-296-6275

14301 E. Speedway Blvd.,
Tucson, AZ 85748

Robert Cote, Innkeeper

3 In a spectacular setting of desert and mountains, this 125-year-old ranch evokes the spirit of the Old West. Horseback riding, guided nature hikes, bird study programs, as well as a modern health spa, tennis, in-door and outdoor pools, selective menus, and a casual, relaxed atmosphere mean good times for lucky guests. It has a 4-star rating by Mobil.

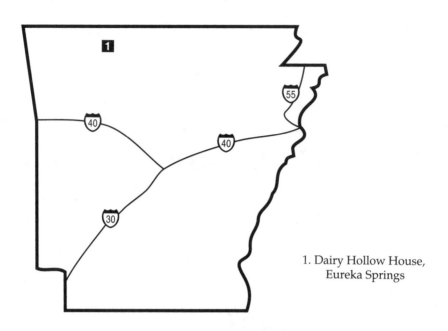

1. Dairy Hollow House,
   Eureka Springs

DAIRY HOLLOW HOUSE

3 Rooms, $125/$155 B&B
3 Suites, $135/$165 B&B
Visa, MC, Amex, Diners, Discov.
All Private Baths

Open Year-round

Children Welcome
No Pets

Galleries, Shops, Canoe floats, Fishing, Water-skiing, Golf, Tours, Lake Swimming, Local Theater

Breakfast; *Prix-fixe* Dinner Mid-March-New Year's Eve, Feb.-mid-March Weekends only. BYOB

Smoking outside only

(Restaurant) Conference Facilities (30-40)

Wheelchair Access

1 Thrice named Best Inn of the Year, this easy going inn offers guests niceties galore; flower-filled rooms, fireplaces, Jacuzzis, antiques. Bountiful breakfasts are delivered daily in a basket to the 1880's Farmhouse or newer Main House. Exceptional *Nouveau' Zarks* cuisine is fresh and seasonal. Hike or float the Ozarks or explore Eureka Springs, a lively Victorian-era arts community.

Exit Hwy. 62 onto "Historic Loop/Old 62B" (Spring St.) for 1.2 mi. past shops downtown; 2nd house on R. past Grotto Spring. Office on lower level on far side.

TEL. 501-253-7444
800-562-8650

515 Spring St.
Eureka Springs, AR 72632
Ned Shank & Crescent
Dragonwagon, Innkeepers

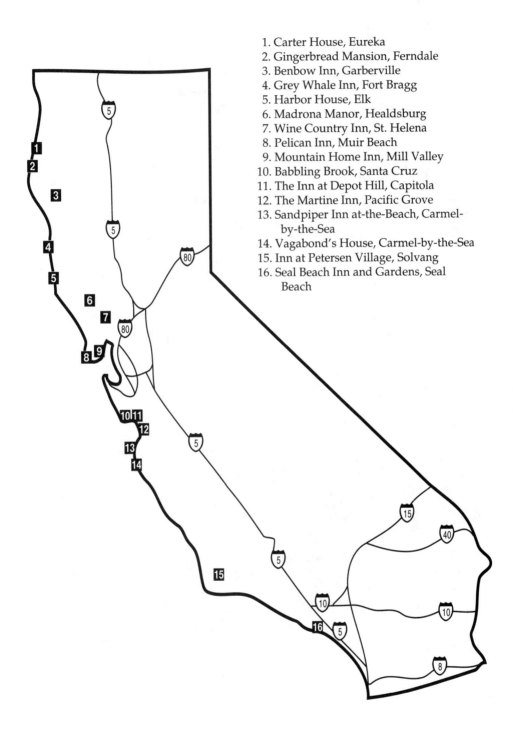

1. Carter House, Eureka
2. Gingerbread Mansion, Ferndale
3. Benbow Inn, Garberville
4. Grey Whale Inn, Fort Bragg
5. Harbor House, Elk
6. Madrona Manor, Healdsburg
7. Wine Country Inn, St. Helena
8. Pelican Inn, Muir Beach
9. Mountain Home Inn, Mill Valley
10. Babbling Brook, Santa Cruz
11. The Inn at Depot Hill, Capitola
12. The Martine Inn, Pacific Grove
13. Sandpiper Inn at-the-Beach, Carmel-by-the-Sea
14. Vagabond's House, Carmel-by-the-Sea
15. Inn at Petersen Village, Solvang
16. Seal Beach Inn and Gardens, Seal Beach

THE BABBLING BROOK

	12 Rooms, $85/$135 B&B
	Visa, MC, Amex, Discov
	All Private Baths 2 Jet Baths
	Open Year-round
	Appropriate for Children over 12; No Pets in guest rooms
	Tennis Courts, Swimming nearby, Beaches, Parks, Boardwalk, Shopping, Narrow-gauge Railroad, Winery
	Breakfast, Afternoon tea Wine and Cheese
	No Smoking
	Wheelchair Access

10 Historic waterwheel, falls and brook in an acre of redwoods and pines surround this secluded inn. Built in 1909 on the foundation of a 1790 gristmill and 2000-year-old Indian fishing village, it's on the National Register of Historic Places. Rooms have private entrances, decks overlooking the gardens, most have fireplaces. Gazebo is popular for weddings. Top ten B&B for '92 by "InnOvations."

From Hwy. 17 take Half Moon Bay exit to Hwy. 1 (N). Continue on Mission St. to L. on Laurel at signal, 1 1/2 blks. down hill on R. From (S) on Hwy. 1, turn L. on Laurel, 1 1/2 blks. on R. From (N) on Hwy. 1 turn R. on Laurel St.

TEL. 408-427-2437; FAX 408-427-2457; 800-866-1131
1025 Laurel St.
Santa Cruz, CA 95060
Helen King, Innkeeper

BENBOW INN

	55 Rooms, $88/$260 EP
	Visa, MC
	All Private Baths
	Closed late Nov.-mid-Dec.; Jan- mid-April
	No Pets
	Golf Course, Lake Boating, Swimming, Sailing, Hiking Trails, Avenue of the Giants (redwoods), Bicycles, TVs & VCRs
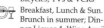	Breakfast, Lunch & Sun. Brunch in summer; Dinner Liquor & Wine Available
	No Smoking in dining room
	Conference Facilities (22)
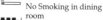	

3 In glorious redwood country, this 1926 English Tudor inn has been dispensing hospitality for many years. A variety of rooms, some with fireplaces, private entrances, or patios, are all handsomely furnished with antiques and fine prints. There are activities and recreation galore outside, while books, a classic film library, live entertainment and holiday events provide indoor diversion.

From S.F., follow Rte. 101 (N) 200 mi. and exit at Benbow

TEL. 707-923-2124

445 Lake Benbow Dr., Garberville, CA 95440

Chuck & Patsy Watts, Innkeepers

CARTER HOUSE/HOTEL CARTER

 24 Rooms, $69/$169 B&B
6 Suites, $169/$450 B&B

 Visa, MC, Amex

 Private & Shared Baths;
1 Jacuzzi

 Open Year-round

 Appropriate for Children;
No Pets

 Redwood Forests, Isolated Beaches, Unique
Shopping, Galleries,
Theater

 4-course Breakfast; Dinner
Wine & Cordials available

Smoking in Restricted
Areas

Conference Facilities (20)

Wheelchair Access (22
Rooms)

From Hwy. 101 (N) (5th St.) turn L. on
"L" St. From Hwy. 101 (S) (4th St.) turn
R. on "L" St. Inn is at 3rd & "L" Sts.

TEL. 707-445-1390
707-444-8062
FAX. 707-444-8062
1033 Third St.
Eureka, CA 95501
Mark & Christi Carter,
Innkeepers

1 A remarkably detailed re-creation of an 1884 San Francisco mansion, the inn sits at the gateway to Eureka's historic district. It offers guests exquisite decor, unrivaled hospitality, and what has been called "the best breakfast in California." Hotel Carter next door, another marvelous replica, offers more rooms (with telephones and TVs), a fine restaurant and conference facilities.

THE GINGERBREAD MANSION

 5 Rooms, $85/$140 B&B
4 Suites, $115/$185 B&B

 Visa, MC

 All Private Baths

 Open Year-round

 Appropriate for Children
over 10; No Pets

 Games, Library, Bicycles,
Engl. Garden, Redwood
Parks, Beach, Fishing,
Galleries, Unique Shops

 Breakfast,
Afternoon Tea & Cake

 No Smoking

Hwy. 101, 15 mi. south of Eureka, take
Ferndale exit. Continue over bridge 5
mi. to Main St. Turn L. at Bank of
America bldg. Go 1 block.

TEL. 707-786-4000
400 Berding St.,
P.O. Box 40
Ferndale, CA 95536-0040
Ken Torbert, Innkeeper

2 From its wonderfully intricate gingerbread architecture to its 20-foot high fuchsias in formal English gardens, this most-photographed Victorian inn is a showplace in the state historic landmark Victorian village. The feeling is elegant, warm, and light, with turn-down service, "his & her" bubble baths by the fire, bicycles, and even umbrellas for rainy days.

GREY WHALE INN

14 Rooms $80/$180 B&B
Off seas. 20% less Su.-Th.

Visa, MC, Discov, Enroute

All Private Baths; 1 Jacuzzi

Open Year-round

Appropriate for Children
over 12
No Pets

TV theater with VCR, rec.
room with pool table,
fishing, hiking, whale-
watching. Phones in rms.

Buffet Breakfast
Complimentary wines
for special occasions

No smoking inside

Conference Facilities (34)

4 The Mendocino Coast, with its dining, shopping, Skunk Train through the redwood forest, secluded ocean beaches, whale-watching, and state parks, is an ideal vacation spot. In this 4-story, 1915 redwood inn guests will find different features in every room: fireplace, sundeck, whirlpool, garden or ocean view. Buffet breakfast includes prizewinning sweet breads and hot entree.

Hwy. 101 to Cloverdale, then Hwy. 128 W. to Hwy. 1. Continue (N) to Fort Bragg (3 1/2 hrs. from S.F.). Or Hwy. 1 along the coast (5 hrs. from S.F.)

TEL. 707-964-0640
Res. 800-382-7244
615 No. Main Street
Fort Bragg, CA 95437
John & Colette Bailey,
Innkeepers

HARBOR HOUSE INN BY THE SEA

10 Rooms, $135/$240
MAP

No Credit Cards

All Private Baths

Open Year-round

Children over 15
No Pets

Private beach, Kayaking,
Wineries, Galleries, Golf,
Riding

Breakfast & Dinner
Wine & Beer available

No Smoking in dining
room

5 Dramatic ocean views, where massive rocks jut from the sea, benches along a winding wildflower-edged path down to a private beach, quiet moments for solitude and reflection—all of this and more at this gracious inn, built entirely of virgin redwood. Add a quality of old-fashioned comfort with fireplaces and superbly fresh cuisine for just a hint of the pleasures that await you.

From S.F., 3 hrs. (N) on Hwy. 101. In Cloverdale take Hwy. 128 (W) to Hwy. 1 (S) 5 mi. to Elk.

TEL. 707-877-3203

Box 369
5600 S. Highway One
Elk, CA 95432
Dean & Helen Turner,
Innkeepers

THE INN AT DEPOT HILL

4 Rooms, $155/$195 B&B
4 Suites, $195/$250 B&B

All Private Baths, some Jacuzzis

No Pets

Full Breakfast, Afternoon Tea or Wine, & Hors d' oeuvres, After Dinner Dessert

Smoking Permitted on Private Patios Only

Wheelchair Access (1 Room)

From Hwy. 1 take Capitola-Sognel exit to Bay Ave. towards the ocean. Bay becomes Monterey Ave. Inn is on the left after crossing the railroad tracks.

TEL. (408) 462-DEPOT (3376)
FAX (408) 462-3697
250 Monterey Ave.
Capitola-by-the-Sea
California 95010
Suzie Lankes, Innkeeper

11 Sophistication & elegance in a quaint Mediterranean-style, beachside resort. Buy a ticket to romance and illusion as you travel the world; Stay in Portofino, Stratford on Avon, Sissinghurst or Paris. Or come home to America in the contemporary Capitola beach or Railroad Baron room. All of our 8 suites are so varied that it will be difficult to decide where your journey will begin or end.

THE INN AT PETERSEN VILLAGE

40 Rooms, $95/$155 B&B
1 Suite, $210 B&B
Visa, MC, Amex

All Private Baths, 1 Jacuzzi

Open Year-round

Appropriate for children over 6; No Pets

Outdoor Summer Theatre, Wineries, Shops, Galleries, Restaurants, Horse-drawn Trolley Tours, Bicycling, Glider & Balloon rides

Breakfast, Cheese & Wine hour, European Buffet Wine Available

Smoking Accepted

Conference Facilities (40)

From Hwy. 101 take Rte. 246 for 2 mi. to Solvang

TEL. 805-688-3121
(In Calif: 800-321-8985)

1576 Mission Drive,
Solvang, CA 93463

The Petersen Family, Innkeepers

15 This European-style hotel overlooks an enclave of shops, arcades, and a courtyard that makes up Petersen Village, set in the heart of a Danish community in central California. On the 2nd and 3rd floors, tastefully decorated inner guest rooms circling the courtyard have views of trees, flowers, and the fountain, while those on the outer side look toward the Santa Inez mountains.

MADRONA MANOR

🛏	18 Rooms, 3 Suites, $120/ $290 B&B and MAP
💳	Visa, MC
🛁	All Private Baths
💡	Open Year-round
🐕	Children accepted Leashed Dogs, outer bldgs.
R	Swimming pool, Tennis, Golf, Antiquing, Wine tasting, Canoeing
🍽	B&B Sun.-Thurs. Full Breakfast; Dinner & Sun. brunch Wine & Beer available
🚬	Smoking in restricted areas
🏨	Conference Facilities (40)
♿	Wheelchair Access (1 rm)

6 This majestic Victorian manor, on the National Register of Historic Places, conveys a sense of homey elegance and gracious hospitality. Guests enjoy thick terry robes, unique and tantalizing cuisine, beautiful mountain views and surrounding Sonoma wine country. A new suite, with fireplace & sitting room, boasts a king bed, deck, marble bath and jacuzzi. We keep getting better!

Rte. 101 (N) to Central Healdsburg exit. At 3-way light, sharp L. on Mill St., 3/4 mi. to arch.

TEL. 707-433-4231
FAX 707-433-0703
800-258-4003
101 Westside Rd.
Healdsburg, CA 95448
John & Carol Muir
Innkeepers

THE MARTINE INN

🛏	19 Rooms, $119/$225 B&B 3 Suites, $245/$275 B&B
💳	Visa, MC, Amex
🛁	All Private Baths
💡	Open Year-round
🐕	No Children; No Pets
R	Sports activities nearby
🍽	Complimentary Breakfast Wine available
🚬	Smoking in guest rooms with fireplaces. No smoking in common rooms.
🏨	Conference Facilities (20)
♿	Wheelchair Access (1 rm.)

12 Come relax & enjoy breathtaking views of the Monterey Bay where seals, otters, and whales can be seen while staying at this romantic cliffside mansion. Your room may have a view of the crashing surf or a woodburning fireplace to snuggle up to that special person. Awake to a sumptuous breakfast awaiting you in the parlor.

Hwy. 1 to Hwy. 68 (Forest Ave.) to Pacific Grove. R on Ocean View Blvd. (15 blocks). Inn On right.

TEL. 408-373-3388
or 800-852-5568
FAX: 408-373-3896
255 Oceanview Blvd.
Pacific Grove, CA 93950
Marion & Don Martine &
Tracy Harris, Innkeepers

MOUNTAIN HOME INN

 10 Rooms, $127/$185 B&B

 Visa, MC

All Private Baths

 Open Year-round

 Appropriate for Children over 12
No Pets

 Hiking, Biking, Beaches, Wineries, Riding, San Francisco

 Comp. Breakfast Lunch & Dinner for the Public

No Smoking in Dining Areas

Conference Facilities (40)

Wheelchair access (1 rm.)

From Golden Gate Bridge, 4.1 mi. (N) Hwy. 1 exit L. at light for 2.6 mi. Turn R. onto Panoramic for .8 mi. At junction take high road. Continue 1.8 mi. to inn on R (last bldg. before wilderness)

TEL. 415-381-9000

810 Panoramic Hwy.
Mill Valley, CA 94941

Susan & Ed Cunningham, Innkeepers

9 The panoramic view of San Francisco Bay from this aerie on Mt. Tamalpais is breathtaking. Adjacent to a wonderful mountain and giant redwood wilderness, this multilevel, modern-rustic inn, built around four huge redwood trees, has many rooms with balconies and some with whirlpools or oak-burning fireplaces. Fresh fish is one of the specialties of the New American cuisine.

PELICAN INN

 7 Rooms, $135/$150 B&B

 Visa, MC

All Private Baths
Closed Christmas Day

 Open to overnight guests only on Mon.; Open to all on Public Holiday Mon.

Children welcome
No Pets

 Beachcombing, Hiking, Whale-watching

Full English complimentary Breakfast;
Lunch & Dinner
Wine & Beer available

Conference Facilities (40)

In S.F. 4.1 mi. north of Golden Gate Bridge, take Hwy. 1 exit. Go L. at light (Arco gas station) & continue 5 mi. on Hwy. 1 to inn.

TEL. 415-383-6000

10 Pacific Way
Muir Beach, CA 94965-9729

R. Barry Stock, Innkeeper

8 A scant 10 miles from Golden Gate Bridge, in the sea-blown fog of Muir Beach, among pine, alder honeysuckle, and jasmine, is half-timbered Pelican Inn, reminiscent of 16th-century Tudor England. A refuge between the ocean and the great redwoods, the inn's Inglenook fireplace, country cooking, British ales and antiques beckon guests to carefree feasting and relaxation.

SANDPIPER INN AT-THE-BEACH

🛏	14 Rooms, $100/$175 B&B
💳	Visa, MC
🛁	All Private Baths
💡🔥	Open Year-around
🐕	Appropriate for Children Over 12; No Pets
R	Pebble Beach golf, Tennis, Point Lobos St. Park, 17-Mile Drive, Fine Dining, Boutiques, Galleries, Big Sur, Monterey Bay Aquar.
☕	Breakfast Complimentary beverage
🚬	Smoking in restricted areas
🍴	
♿	

13 Only 60 yds. from Carmel's wide beach, with unique ocean views across the bay to Pebble Beach. Early California architecture is complemented by country antiques, gardens & patio. Comfortable lounge has a cathedral ceiling & fireplace. Rooms are individually decorated, some with fireplaces. A romantic getaway in a beautiful, quiet residential area with warm, restful ambiance.

Hwy. 1, R. at Ocean Ave. (W) thru Carmel 1 mi. L. at Scenic Rd. (S) .8 mi. to end of beach at Martin Way (S).

TEL. 408-624-6433
FAX 408-624-5964

2408 Bay View Ave.
Carmel by-the-sea, CA 93923

Graeme & Irene Mackenzie
Innkeepers

THE SEAL BEACH INN AND GARDENS

🛏	10 Rooms, $108/$155 B&B 13 Suites, $155/$175 B&B
💳	Visa, MC, Amex, Diners, Discovery, JCB
🛁	All Private Baths
💡🔥	Open Year-round
🐕	No Pets
R	Pool, Tennis, Boating, Golf, Swimming, Bicycles
☕	Buffet Breakfast, Catered Meals, Advance Reservation
🚬	No Smoking Inside
🍴	Conference Facilities (24)
♿	

16 Massed flowers, lush plants, and glowing color make the brick courtyard of this Mediterranean-style inn a fairyland, with ornate streetlights, canopies, fountains and objects d'art. Serving Los Angeles and Orange County, 35 min. south of L.A. Airport and 10 min. from Long Beach Airport in a charming Seaside Village nearby all Southern California business & tourist attractions.

Hwy. 405 Fwy., Seal Beach Blvd. exit, turn L. for 2.7 mi. R. on Pacific Coast Hwy. for .7 mi. L. on 5th St.

TEL. 310-493-2416
FAX 310-799-0483

212 5th Street
Seal Beach, CA 90740

Marjorie Bettenhausen
Schmaehl & Harty
Schmaehl, Innkeepers

VAGABOND'S HOUSE INN

11 Rooms, $79/$135 B&B

Visa, MC, Amex

All Private Baths

Open Year-round

Appropriate for Children over 11
Pets accepted

Carmel beach, 17-Mile Drive, Golf, Tennis, Big Sur, Monterey Bay Aquarium

Breakfast
Cream Sherry

Turn off Hwy. 1 to Ocean Ave., (W) to town center. R. onto Dolores for 2.5 blocks to inn.

TEL. 408-624-7738 or 800-262-1262

P.O. Box 2747
Dolores & 4th
Carmel, CA 93921
Honey Spence, Innkeeper

14 The stone courtyard here is an almost magical experience, with the great oak and cascading waterfalls, surrounded by vines, ferns, and gorgeous flowers. Tuffy, the watch cat, suns on a doorstep. Around the courtyard are unique rooms with fireplaces. All the natural beauty and fascinating shops of Carmel are just around the corner.

THE WINE COUNTRY INN

21 Rooms, $97/$154 B&B
3 Suites, $168/202 B&B

Visa, MC, Amex

All Private Baths

Closed mid-to-late Dec.

Not Appropriate for Children
No Pets

Pool & Jacuzzi, Wineries, Tennis, Golf, Hiking

Breakfast

Smoking Accepted

Wheelchair Access

From S.F. take I-80 (N) to Napa exit. Follow Hwy. 29 (N) 18 mi. to St. Helena & 2 mi. beyond to Lodi Lane. Turn R. for 1/3 mi. to inn.

TEL. 707-963-7077

1152 Lodi Lane,
St. Helena, CA 94574

Jim Smith, Innkeeper

7 Perched on a small hill, overlooking the manicured vineyards and nearby hills of the Napa Valley, this inn is known for its casual and quiet atmosphere. The intimate rooms boast family-made quilts, private balconies, fireplaces and pine antiques. Famous restaurants and wineries tours round out the Napa Valley experience.

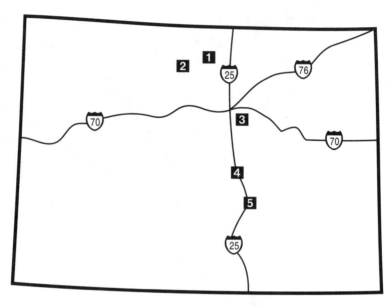

1. The Lovelander Bed & Breakfast
   Inn, Loveland
2. River Song, Estes Park
3. Castle Marne, Denver
4. Hearthstone Inn, Colorado Springs
5. Abriendo Inn, Pueblo

ABRIENDO INN

6 Rooms, $54/$89 B&B
1 Suite, $85 B&B

Visa, MC, Amex, Diners

All Private Baths

Open Year-round

Children over 7
Welcome; No Pets

Museums, Nature, Bike
Trails, Historic Walking
Tour, Rafting, Fishing,
Boutiques, Galleries, Shops

Breakfast, afternoon
Cheese & Crackers, and
Beverages; BYOB

Smoking permitted on
veranda and grounds

5 Make this classic mansion your home while visiting Pueblo. Experience the comfortable elegance of the beautiful Foursquare architecture. Feel like you belong here at the Abriendo Inn as you stroll the park-like grounds, view the surrounding neighborhood and walk through nearby Historic Union Ave. district. Along with ambiance, there is the privacy of in-room phones & TV.

I-25 to Exit 97-B Abriendo Ave. 1 Mile from exit on left side of street

TEL. (719) 544-2703
FAX (719) 542-1806

300 West Abriendo Avenue
Pueblo, CO 81004

Kerrelyn M. Trent,
Innkeeper

CASTLE MARNE

 7 Rooms, $80/$120 B&B
2 Suites, $135/$215 B&B

 Visa, MC, Amex

 All Private Baths

 Open Year-round

 Unsuitable for Children
Under 10; No Pets

 Croquet, Game Rm, City
Park w/Tennis, Running
Paths, Golf, Zoo, Museum,
Botanic Gardens, Shopping, Historic Sites

 Full Breakfast
Afternoon Tea

Smoke-Free Inn

From airport take Martin Luther King Blvd. or I-70 (W) to York St. (S) to R. on 16th Ave. to Race St. From I-25 (S) turn L. on Colfax Ave. to L. on Race St.

TEL. 303-331-0621;
800-92-MARNE;
FAX 303-331-0623

1572 Race St.,
Denver, CO 80206

Peiker Family, Innkeepers

3 Close to downtown and countless attractions, one of Denver's grandest historic mansions (National Register), designed by a renowned architect, is now a welcoming inn. Carefully preserved, hand-rubbed woods, the stained glass "Peacock Window," and ornate fireplaces blend with authentic period antiques and family heirlooms to create a charming Victorian Atmosphere.

HEARTHSTONE INN

 23 Rooms, $78/$130 B&B
2 Suites,

Visa, MC, Amex

23 Private Baths

 Open Year-round

Children Accepted
No Pets

Croquet, Puzzles, Games,
Walking, Golf, Tennis,
Rafting, Museums, Pikes
Peak, Jogging Trail, Air
Force Academy

Breakfast Daily;
Luncheons can be arranged for 20-48 persons

No Smoking

Conference Facilities (40)

 Wheelchair Ramp, 1
guest rm, Conference rm.

From I-25, Exit 143 (Uintah St.) (E) away from mountains 3 blocks to Cascade. Turn R. (S) 7 blocks to corner of Cascade & St. Vrain.

TEL. 719-473-4413, 800-521-1885; FAX 719-473-1322

506 No. Cascade Ave.
Colorado Sprgs, CO 80903

Dot Williams &
Ruth Williams, Innkeepers

4 Bright colors highlight this eye-catching Inn. Wonderful antiques, color-coordinated linens and unusual gourmet breakfasts make the Hearthstone Inn a restful, yet exciting change of pace. The friendly atmosphere and helpful staff aid you in meeting new people, or enjoying time on your own. Also, an ideal setting for executive conferences and retreats, utilizing the large meeting room.

COLORADO

THE LOVELANDER B&B INN

 9 Rooms, $79/$105 B&B
1 Suite, $104 B&B

 Visa, MC, Amex, Discov

 All Private Baths

Open Year-round

 Children over 10 wel-
come; No Pets

 Rocky Mountain Natl.
Park, Big Thompson
Canyon, Benson Sculp-
ture Park, Galleries

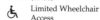 Breakfast
Wine Available

No Smoking

Conference Facilities
(15-30)

Limited Wheelchair
Access

1 Combining the essence of Victorian style with contemporary convenience, the Lovelander lies nestled in the Rocky Mountain foothills, a short drive from the breathtaking Rocky Mountain National Park. Beautifully appointed rooms, peaceful surroundings, gourmet breakfasts, and old-fashioned hospitality from the heart, create a haven for recreational and business travelers alike.

I-25, Exit 257B, to U.S. Hwy. 34 (W) for 5 mi. to Garfield Ave. Turn L. 10 blks. to 4th St., then R. to 2nd house on R.

TEL. 303-669-0798

217 W. 4th St.
Loveland, CO 80537

Marilyn & Bob Wiltgen;
Sandy Strauss, Innkeepers

RIVER SONG

3 Rooms, $85/$110 B&B
6 Suites, $110/$160 B&B

All Private Baths

Open Year-round

 Children over 12 in
carriage house; No Pets
(would disturb the deer)

 Private Hiking Trails,
Snowshoeing, XC Skiing,
Skating/Fishing Ponds,
Rocky Mtn. Natl. Park

 Breakfast; Gourmet
Candlelight Dinner by
advance res. BYOB

No Smoking

 Conference Facilities (16)

2 Imagine lying in a magnificent antique bed with the glaciers of the Rocky Mountain National Park looming just over the tops of your toes, or seeing the stars through the skylights above your brass bed, or thrill to feeding a gentle fawn outside your door, or being lulled to sleep by a melodious mountain stream. At RiverSong, time seems to stand still.

Please call for directions

TEL. 303-586-4666

P.O. Box 1910
Estes Park, CO 80517

Sue & Gary Mansfield,
Innkeepers

30

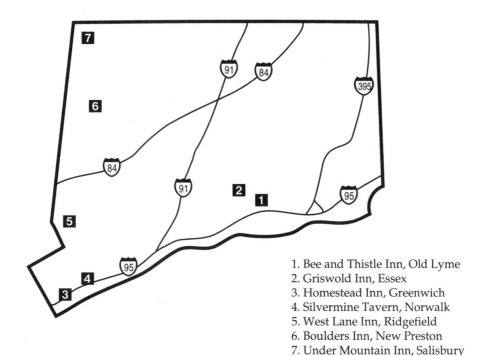

1. Bee and Thistle Inn, Old Lyme
2. Griswold Inn, Essex
3. Homestead Inn, Greenwich
4. Silvermine Tavern, Norwalk
5. West Lane Inn, Ridgefield
6. Boulders Inn, New Preston
7. Under Mountain Inn, Salisbury

BEE AND THISTLE INN

11 Rooms, $69/$125 EP
1 Cottage, $195 EP

Visa, MC, Amex, Diners

10 Private, 1 Shared Baths

Closed Jan. 5 to Jan. 24

Appropriate for Children Over 12; No Pets

Gardens, River, Golf, Museums, Art, Beach, Mystic

Breakfast, Lunch, Dinner; Sun. Brunch, English tea Wine & Liquor available

Smoking in Restricted Areas

Conference Facilities (20)

I-95 (S) Exit 70, turn R. off ramp to inn, 3rd bldg. on L. I-95 (N) Exit 70, turn L. off ramp to 1st light, R. to T in road, then L. to inn. 3rd bldg. on L.

TEL. 203-434-1667; 800-622-4946; FAX 203-434-3402

100 Lyme Street
Old Lyme, CT 06371

Bob & Penny Nelson, Innkeepers

1 In an unspoiled historic village on the Lieutenant River, sits this lovely 1756 inn. Its English gardens, sunlit porches, fireplaces, beautiful, carved staircase, canopied and 4-poster beds, antique quilts and furnishings reflect a gracious lifestyle. Widely commended for its cuisine, it has been voted the most romantic place to dine in Connecticut.

BOULDERS INN

🛏	17 Rooms, $125/$175 B&B $175/$225 MAP
💳	Visa, MC, Amex
🛁	All Private Baths
💡	Open Year-round
🐕👧	Children Under 12 by special arrangement; No Pets
R	Tennis, Beach, Boating, Hiking, Bicycles, Downhill & XC Skiing, Antiquing, Golf, Music Festival
🍽	Breakfast, Dinner, Sun. Brunch; B&B rates also Wine Liquor Available
🚭	Non-smoking Dining Room
🎪	Conference Facilities (35)
♿	Wheelchair Access

6 This 1895 Victorian mansion is in a spectacular setting at the foot of Pinnacle Mountain, where breathtaking sunsets over Lake Waramaug are enjoyed from the elegantly appointed living room, the glass-enclosed dining room, and most of the guest rooms and guest houses, many of which have fireplaces. The widely-renowned cuisine is also served on the outside terrace in summer.

Rte. 84(E) Exit 7 to Rte. 7(N) to New Milford. Take Rte. 202 to New Preston. L. on E. Shore Rd. (Rte. 45) to Lake Waramaug.

TEL. 203-868-0541

East Shore Rd. (Rte. 45)
New Preston, Ct 06777

Ulla & Kees Adema,
Innkeepers

THE GRISWOLD INN

🛏	14 Rooms, $80/$165 11 Suites, $85/$165
💳	Visa, MC, Amex
🛁	All Private Baths
💡	Dining Room Closed Christmas Eve/Day
🐕👧	Children Accepted Pets Accepted
R	Tennis, Golf, Swimming, Goodspeed Opera, Mystic Seaport
🍽	Breakfast, Lunch, Dinner; Famous Sunday Hunt Breakfast Wine & Liquor available
🚭	Non-smoking rooms available
🎪	Conference facilities (20)
♿	

2 A kaleidoscope of nostalgic images delights the eye here: myriad Currier & Ives steamboat prints and Antonio Jacobsen marine art, ship models, firearms, potbellied stove, to name a few. The superb New England cuisine features seafood, prime rib, meat pies, and the inn's own 1776 sausages. Lucius Beebe considered the Taproom the most handsome bar in America.

I-91 (S) to Exit 22 (S). Rte. 9 (S) to Exit 3 Essex. I-95 (N&S) to Exit 69 to Rte. 9 (N) to Exit 3 Essex.

TEL. 203-767-1776

36 Main St.
Essex, CT 06426

Victoria & William
Winterer, Innkeepers

THE HOMESTEAD INN

 17 Rooms, $127/$152 B&B
6 Suites, $152/$175 B&B

 All Major Credit Cards

 All Private Baths

 Open Year-round

 Children Accepted
No Pets

  R

 Breakfast, Lunch, Dinner,
Sun. Brunch
Wine & Liquor Available

 Smoking Accepted

Conference Facilities (20)

I-95 to Greenwich, Exit 3. From NYC: turn L. off ramp; from New Haven: turn R. off ramp, then L. at light onto Horseneck Ln. (just before RR overpass), to L. at Field Point Rd. Continue 1/4 mi. to inn on R.

TEL. 203-869-7500
420 Field Point Rd.
Greenwich, CT 06830
Lessie Davison & Nancy Smith, Innkeepers

3 Gracious, historic elegance, with a convivial atmosphere and the superlative talents of Parisian chef, Jacques Thiebeult, attract guests from far and wide. Set among noble trees in a beautiful, quiet residential area, the Homestead is only 45 minutes from New York City. Exquisitely decorated and appointed rooms and popular restaurant are much in demand, so please reserve early.

THE SILVERMINE TAVERN

10 Rooms, $80/$99 B&B

Visa, MC, Amex, Diners

All Private Baths

Closed Tuesday

Children Accepted
No Pets

Golf, Boating, Beach,
Tennis

Complimentary
Breakfast; Lunch, Dinner,
Sun. Brunch
Wine & Liquor Available

Non-Smoking Dining
Area

Conference Facilities (40)

I-95, Exit 15 or Merritt Pkwy., Exit 40A. Call for directions.

TEL. 203-847-4558

Perry Ave.
Norwalk, CT 06850

Frank Whitman, Jr.,
Innkeeper

4 A 1785 inn beside a millpond with swans and a waterfall — what could be more romantic? The Silvermine features Early American guest rooms, a treasure house of Early Americana and primitive paintings, and country dining at its best. New England dishes such as lobster pie and Indian pudding are just a few of the inducements here.

CONNECTICUT

UNDER MOUNTAIN INN

🛏	7 Rooms, $150/$180 MAP Special package rates
💳	Visa, MC
🛁	All Private Baths
🛎	Open Year-round
🐕	Appropriate for Children over 6; No Pets
☀R	Boating, Hiking, Alpine/ Nordic Skiing, Rafting, Antiquing, Music & Theater, Golf, Tennis, Fishing, Horsebk. Riding
🍷	Breakfast, Dinner, Afternoon Tea; Liquor & Wine available
🚭	Limited Smoking; No Pipes or Cigars
⊢🏠🏠⊣	Conference Facilities (15)
♿	

7 Enjoy British-flavored hospitality in an 18th century farmhouse, with a proper cup of tea, *The Manchester Guardian*, and a full English breakfast. Dinners could be bangers & mash, steak & kidney pie, or other English specialties cooked up by Manchester-born owner-chef Peter Higginson. A well-stocked library and cozy fireplaces vie with the lure of outdoors and many cultural attractions.

From Boston: Mass. Turnpike, Exit 2, (W) on 102, (S) on 7, (W) on 23 in Gt. Barrington, MA, S on 41. Inn is .7 mi. (S) of CT border. From NYC: (N) on Taconic Pkwy., (E) on 44, (N) on 41 for 4 mi. to inn.

TEL.203-435-0242
482 Undermountain Road
Salisbury, CT 06068
Peter & Marged
Higginson, Innkeepers

WEST LANE INN

🛏	20 rooms, $110/$165 B&B With Fireplaces st. at $145
💳	Visa, MC, Amex, Diners
🛁	All Private Baths
🛎	Open Year-round
🐕	Children Accepted No Pets
☀R	Golf, Tennis, XC Skiing, Swimming
🍷	Continental Breakfast & Light Lunch
🚬	Smoking Accepted
⊢🏠🏠⊣	Conference Facilities (18)
♿	Wheelchair Access (1 rm.)

5 Rich oak paneling, deep pile carpeting, and a cheery fire crackling on the hearth sets the tone of polished refinement at this luxurious inn. Framed by a stand of majestic old maples, a broad lawn, and flowering shrubs, it offers gracious hospitality and a quiet retreat from worldly cares, about an hour north of New York City.

From NYC & Westside Hwy. (N) to Sawmill River Pkwy. & Exit 43 (Katonah). Turn R. on Rte. 35 (E) 10 mi. to Ridgefield. Inn is on L. From Rte 90 & I-84, Exit 3 to Rte. 7 (S) to Rte. 35 and Ridgefield.

TEL. 203-438-7323

22 West Lane
Ridgefield, CT 06877
Maureen Mayer, Innkeeper

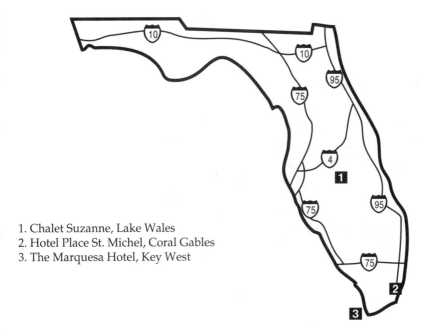

1. Chalet Suzanne, Lake Wales
2. Hotel Place St. Michel, Coral Gables
3. The Marquesa Hotel, Key West

CHALET SUZANNE

	26 Rooms, $105/$195 B&B 4 Suites, $125/$195 B&B
	Visa, MC, Amex, Discov. DC, CB, Personal Checks
	All Private Baths
	Restaurant Closed Mon. in Summer
	Children Welcome $20 Per Pet
R	Gardens, Pool, Lake, Airstrip, Central Florida attractions, Golf, Tennis nearby
	Breakfast, Lunch, Dinner; Special MAP Pkgs. Intimate Lounge
	Most Non-Smoking; Dining
	Conference Facilities (50)
	Wheelchair Access (2 rooms)

I-4 (W) from Orlando or I-4 (E) from Tampa to U.S. 27; (S), Exit 23 (Cypress Gardens) 18 mi. (S). Turn L. on County Rd. 17A for 1.5 mi. to inn on R.

TEL. 813-676-6011 or 800-433-6011
FAX. 813-676-1814
U.S. Hwy 27 & Co. Rd. 17A
3800 Chalet Suzanne Dr.
Lake Wales, FL 33853-7060
Hinshaw family, Innkeepers

1 "Fairy tales can come true . . ." This is a storybook inn with an around-the-world look to its cottages grouped at odd angles, its fountain courtyards, and fascinating furnishings. Awarded Uncle Ben's National Award — Ten Best Country Inns of 1991, the 4-star restaurant is famous for gourmet fare and caring attention. Chalet Suzanne is on the National Register of Historic Places.

FLORIDA
HOTEL PLACE ST. MICHEL

	27 Rooms, $99/$150 B&B 3 suites, $125/$150 B&B
	Visa, Amex, Diners
	All Private Baths
	Open Year-round
	Children - Yes Pets Not Accepted
R	Beaches, Golf, Tennis, Coral Rock Swimming Pool, Theaters, Galleries, Shopping, Jogging, Bike Trails, Fitness Ctr. Nearby
	Restaurant, French Deli, Sun. Brunch; Bar-Lounge, Wine & Liquor Available
	Non-Smoking Dining Area
	Conference Facilities (30)
	Wheelchair Access

2 Filled with antiques, this intimate European-style hotel (ca. 1926) in the heart of Coral Gables, offers superb service and comfort. Welcome baskets of fruit and cheese, complimentary continental breakfast, & the morning paper at your door. One of Florida's "top 10" small hotels, with award-winning restaurant. Major renovations in 1993.

I-95 (S), becoming U.S. 1 (S. Dixie Hwy.), continue (S) to Ponce de Leon Blvd., R. to corner of Alcazar Ave. & hotel.
TEL 305-444-1666
FAX 305-529-0074
162 Alcazar Ave.
Coral Gables, (Miami) FL 33134
Stuart N. Bornstein, Alan H. Potamkin, Innkeepers

THE MARQUESA HOTEL

	11 Rooms, $110/$200 EP 4 Suites, $145/$275 EP
	Visa, MC, Amex
	All Private Baths
	Open Year-round
	Children – Yes Pets not Accepted
R	Heated Pool, nearby Snorkeling, Fishing, Sailing, Historic attractions and homes
	Restaurant or Room service for Breakfast, Dinner; Poolside beverage service Wine & Liquor available
	Smoking permitted
	Conference Facilities (25)
	Wheelchair Access

3 In the heart of Key West's historic district, the Marquesa Hotel is a distinguished 1884 home, restored in 1988 to 4-diamond status, with floor-to-ceiling windows in the lobby, large bouquets of fresh flowers and a pool with a fountain. Room decor is a blend of traditional, classic and contemporary. The elegant restaurant presents a sophisticated and inventive menu.

U.S. 1, R. on No. Roosevelt Blvd., becomes Truman Ave. Continue to R. on Simonton for 5 blks. to Fleming. Turn R. to front of hotel.
TEL. 305-292-1919; 800-869-4631; FAX 305-294-2121
600 Fleming St.
Key West, FL 33040
Richard Manley, Erik de Boer, Owners; Carol Wightman, Manager

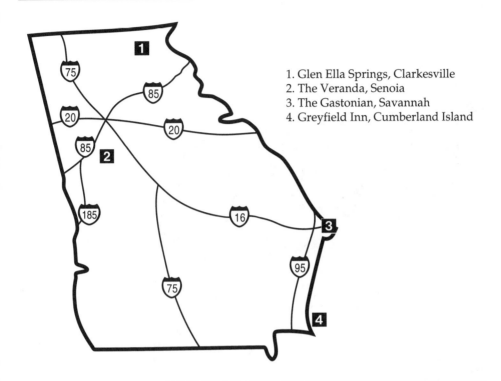

1. Glen Ella Springs, Clarkesville
2. The Veranda, Senoia
3. The Gastonian, Savannah
4. Greyfield Inn, Cumberland Island

THE GASTONIAN

10 Rooms, $98/$175 B&B
3 Suites, $150/$235 B&B

Visa, MC, Amex

All Private Baths, 6 Jacuzzis

Open Year-round

Appropriate for Children over 12; No Pets

Antiquing, Guided tours, Beaches, Biking, Fine Dining, Galleries, Museums, River Cruise & nearby Golf, Sea Fishing, Tennis.

Full Breakfast
Wine Available

No Smoking

Conference Facilities (25)

Wheelchair Access (1 room)

From I-16 exit at W. Martin Luther King Blvd. straight ahead with no turns, which becomes Gaston St. Continue to inn at 220 East Gaston St.

TEL. 912-232-2869;
800-322-6603;
FAX. 912-232-0710
220 E. Gaston St.
Savannah, GA 31401
Hugh & Roberta
Lineberger, Innkeepers

3 In the largest Historical Landmark District in the U.S., this 1868 inn is furnished with English antiques, offers beautiful gardens and sundeck with hot tub. All rooms have fireplaces, heat and A/C, Jacuzzi baths, showers, cable TV, fruit and wine — plus nightly turndown with sweets and cordials. Guests feast on a full, hot, sitdown Southern breakfast. Mobil ★★★★, AAA ◆◆◆◆.

GLEN-ELLA SPRINGS

🛏	14 Rooms $75/$135 B&B 2 Suites $135 B&B
💳	Visa, MC, Amex
🛁	All Private Baths
🛋	Open Year-round
👧🐕	Children Accepted No Pets
Ⓡ	Pool, Sundeck, Gift Shop, Meadows; Vegetable, Herb & Perennial Gardens. Near Hiking, Boating, Horse- back, Golf, Unique Village
🍽	Breakfast (guests only) Dinner by reservation BYOB
🚭	Smoking in some areas
⊢▦⊣	
♿	Wheelchair Access (5 Rooms)

1 This 1890 country inn, on the National Register, combines charm of the past with modern comfort and luxury. Completely renovated in 1987, each pine-paneled guest room is furnished with antiques and local reproductions, and has its own entrance onto a porch with rocking chairs and lovely views. Sophisticated Southern cuisine. One of Travel & Leisure's Top 10 for Summer '92.

Between Clarkesville and Clayton 1.5 mi. off U.S. 441.

TEL. 800-552-3479
706-754-7295
FAX 706-754-1560
Bear Gap Road
Rte 3, Box 3304
Clarkesville GA 30523
Bobby and Barrie Aycock,
Innkeepers

GREYFIELD INN

🛏	7 Rooms, $200 AP 2 Suites, $220 AP
💳	Visa, MC, Pers. Checks
🛁	1 Private, 3 Shared Baths
🛋	Open Year-round
👧🐕	Children Accepted No Pets
Ⓡ	Birdwatching, Hiking, Swimming, Shelling, Bik- ing, Fishing, Photography
🍽	Breakfast, Picnic Lunches, Dinner Wine & Liquor Available
🚭	Smoking Allowed in Bar
⊢▦⊣	Conference Facilities (18)
♿	

4 This turn-of-the-century mansion is on Cumberland Island, Georgia's largest and southernmost island. Miles of hiking trails traverse the island's unique ecosystems along with a beautiful, endless beach for shelling, swimming, sunning and birdwatching. Fine food, lovely original furnishings, and a peaceful, relaxing environment provide guests with a step back into another era.

Cumberland Island is accessible only by boat or plane; 2 ferry services provide transp. to island from Fernandina, FL or St. Mary's GA.

TEL. 904-261-6408
Cumberland Island, GA
P.O. Drawer N.
Fernandina Beach, FL 32034
Oliver & Mary Jo Ferguson,
Innkeepers

THE VERANDA

 9 Rooms $80/$100 B&B

 Visa, MC, Amex

 All Private Baths, 1 Whirlpool

 Open Year-round; Reservations necessary

 Children Accepted (inquire); No Pets

 Player Piano/organ, Library, Games, Kaleidoscopes, Historic Touring, Antiquing, Tennis & Golf nearby, Gift Shop.

 Full Breakfast; Dinner & Lunch by reservation only

Limited Smoking

 Conference Facilities (20)

Wheelchair Access (downstairs)

From Atlanta I-85 (S), Exit 12; L.(SE) on Hwy. 74 for 16.7 mi. R.(S) on Rockaway Rd. for 3.3 mi. At light turn L.(E) for 1 block to inn. Ask for brochure/map.

TEL. 404-599-3905
FAX 404-599-0806

252 Seavy St., Box 177
Senoia, GA 30276

Jan & Bobby Boal,
Innkeepers

 This elegantly restored turn-of-the-century inn on the National Register of Historic Places, comfortably furnished in period antiques, offers guests a quiet, relaxed Southern lifestyle. A treasury of books, games, puzzles, and the broad rocking-chair veranda, which gives the inn its name, as well as gourmet meals and lavish breakfasts are enjoyed by guests.

Rates are quoted for 2 people for 1 night and do not necessarily include service charges and state taxes. An asterisk after the rates indicates a per-person rate for AP and MAP plans. For more detailed information, ask the inns for their brochures.

AP — American Plan (3 meals included in room rate)

MAP — Modified American Plan (breakfast & dinner included in room rate)

EP — European Plan (meals not included in room rate)

B&B — Bed & Breakfast (breakfast included in room rate)

R — Represents recreational facilities and diversions either on the premises of an inn or nearby

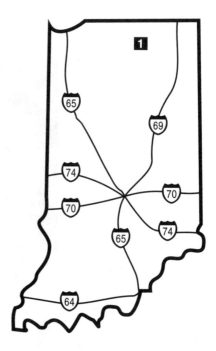

1. The Checkerberry Inn, Goshen

THE CHECKERBERRY INN

	11 Rooms, $104/$130 B&B
	3 Suite, $152/$400 B&B
	Visa, MC, Amex
	All Private Baths
	Closed January
	Well-behaved Children welcome; No Pets
	Tennis, Swimming Pool, Croquet on Premises, Golf, Lakes area nearby
	Lunch, Wed.-Sat., Dinner, Tues.-Sat. Beer & Wine Available
	Smoking Restricted
	Conference Facilities (28)
	Wheelchair Access (3 rooms)

1 Watch for Amish horses and buggies in this pastoral farmland. On a 100-acre wooded estate, the inn offers breathtaking views of unspoiled rolling countryside from individually decorated rooms. While away the hours enjoying fields of wildflowers, massive Beech trees, miles of country roads, and grazing horses in a nearby pasture. Imaginative meals and fine wines provide memorable dining.

Exit 107, Ind. toll road, (S) on State Rte. 13 to R. on State Rte. 4 to L. on County Rd. 37; 1 mi. to inn on R.

TEL. 219-642-4445

62644 CR 37
Goshen, IN 46526

John & Susan Graff,
Innkeepers
Shawna Koehler & Jane
Erickson, Asst. Innkeepers

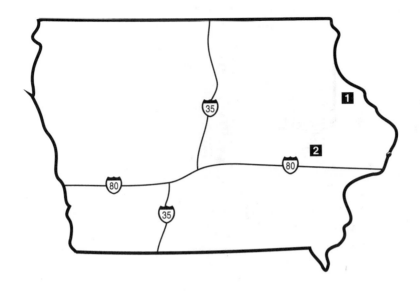

1. Redstone Inn/Stout House, Dubuque
2. Die Heimat Inn, Homestead

DIE HEIMAT COUNTRY INN

19 Rooms, $36.95/$62.95

Visa, MC, Discov.

All Private Baths

Open Year-around

Children Welcome
Well-behaved Pets
Accepted

Historic Amana Colonies,
Nature trail, Hiking, Golf,
Woolen Mills, Family-
style Dining, Furniture
Factories, Wineries,
Breakfast

Smoking restricted

Conference facilities (20-40)

I-80, Exit 225, (N) on Hwy. 151; (E) on Hwy. 6 to Homestead and inn at end of street. From Cedar Rapids: Hwy. 151(S) 20 mi. to Homestead.

TEL. 319-622-3937

Amana Colonies, Main St.
Homestead, IA 52236

Don and Sheila Janda,
Innkeepers

2 Die Heimat means "the homeplace" in German. This inn was once a communal kitchen of the Amana Colonies, which were originally settled by German immigrants who established their own religious and communal way of life. Walnut and cherry furniture made by Amana craftsmen, German heirloom antiques and beautiful quilts offer a glimpse into the past.

41

REDSTONE INN/STOUT HOUSE

🛏	21 Rooms, $65/$165 B&B
💳	Visa, MC, Amex, Diners
🛁	Mostly Private Baths
💡🕯	Open Year-round
🐕	Children Welcome No Pets
Ⓡ	Riverboat Rides & Casino, Cruises, Shopping, Antiquing, Downhill Skiing, Victorian Home Tour & Progressive Dinner.
☕🍸	Continental Breakfast, Afternoon Tea Wine & Liquor Available
🚭	No Pipes or Cigars
⊢╥╥╥⊣	Conference Facilities (25)
♿	

2 Two impressive mansions, the Queen Anne Victorian Redstone Inn and the Romanesque Stout House, offer elegant accommodations in downtown Dubuque. Rooms are individually decorated with period furnishings,some with whirlpools and fireplaces. Stained glass, mosaic tile, & oak-paneled library provide a handsome background for afternoon tea & refreshments.

From Hwys. 52, 151, 62 (N): Locust St. exit to 5th St. L. to 5th & Bluff Sts. From Hwy. 2j0 (W): 1st R. after Julien Dubuque Bridge. Locust St. to 5th St. & L. to Bluff St.

TEL. 319-582-1894

504 Bluff St.
Dubuque. IA 52001

Mary Kay Hurm,
General Manager

COUNTRY INN ARCHITECTURE

Country inns are probably more often found in Victorian buildings than in any one other style of architecture; however, that includes such a variation in styles as Queen Anne, Edwardian, Carpenter Gothic, and Italianate. Showy and flamboyant, these buildings have great eye-catching appeal with their cupolas, chimneys, gables, shingles, widow's walks, and capacious wraparound porches. The sometimes rather unusual combinations of exterior paint colors can be a little shocking to the modern eye, but were *de rigueur* for the Victorians. Understandably, as the country expanded westward in the 19th century, building followed the current architectural styles, and consequently there are more inns in Victorian buildings in the Midwest and Far West than in the East and South.

In New England will be found the more pristine and classic pre-Revolutionary, Federalist, and Georgian Colonial buildings. White clapboard or red brick, black shutters, two or more chimneys, "6 over 6" or "12 over 12" double-hung windows (infrequently with the original hand-blown wavy glass), and a fanlight over the door most often characterize the exterior of Colonial buildings. The very earliest have low, beamed ceilings and great fireplaces, sometimes with a blackened crane, that provide a cozy, welcoming setting for guests.

Beyond those two predominant styles, country inn architecture takes off in all directions. Rustic log houses with bark still covering the beams, 19th-century red brick mansions or brick factory buildings and small Midwestern hotels reflecting opulent early days, Greek Revival, English Tudor, Bavarian hip-roofed buildings with balconies, French Mediterranean, Spanish haciendas with flower-laden courtyards, classic, simple Shaker buildings — country inns offer hospitality in these and many other kinds of buildings. Many of them are listed on the National Register of Historic Places.

In the South, there are inns in "shotgun" or "single" houses, built sideways to the street with open piazzas along the side, for privacy, allowing cool breezes to blow through the house. Imposing Southern Colonial mansions with graceful 2-story Grecian pillars house several inns, although there are a few of these transplanted to other parts of the country, too. Some inns have been built in more contemporary styles, and these are usually found in very natural forest or mountain settings, utilizing local woods and stone and other materials.

A few buildings have been designed by famous architects, such as Cass Gilbert, Charles Bulfinch, and Walter Martens. Many American country inns are reminiscent of the country house hotels of Britain.
— by Virginia Rowe

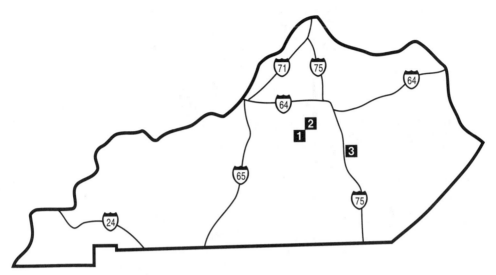

1. Beaumont Inn, Harrodsburg
2. Inn at Pleasant Hill, Shakertown
3. Boone Tavern Hotel, Berea

BEAUMONT INN

33 Rooms $70/$95 EP

Visa, MC, Amex, Discov

All Private Baths

Closed mid-Dec. to mid-March

Children Accepted
No Pets

Swimming Pool, Tennis, Shuffle-board, Golf, Fishing, Historic attractions

Breakfast/Dinner daily
Lunch, Tues.- Sun.

Non-smoking Rooms
available

Conference Facilities (25)

In Harrodsburg at intersection with U.S. 68, take U.S. 127 (S) to inn, at south end of town on east side of U.S. 127.

**TEL. 606-734-3381
800-352-3992**

638 Beaumont Dr.
Harrodsburg, KY 40330

The Dedman Family,
Innkeepers

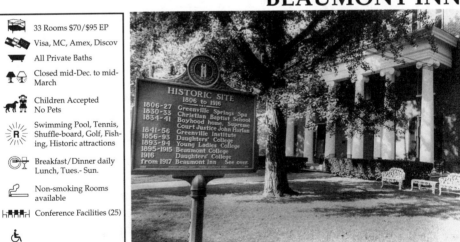

1 Owned and operated by 4 generations of the Dedman family, this country inn, on the National Register of Historic Places, was built in 1845 as a school for young ladies. In the heart of Bluegrass country, it is redolent of Southern history, brimming with beautiful antiques, fascinating memorabilia, and the food is traditional Kentucky fare. Over 30 varieties of trees grace the grounds.

BOONE TAVERN HOTEL

🛏	59 Rooms $57/$79
	All Private Baths
	Open Year-round
	Children Welcome Pets Accepted
R	Campus Tours, Appalachian Museum, Craft & Antique Shops, Danforth Chapel, and Planetarium
	Breakfast, Lunch & Dinner served daily Dress code for Dinner and Sunday Lunch
	We Kindly Request No Smoking
♿	Wheelchair Access (2 Rms)

3 Historic Boone Tavern Hotel is nestled within and owned by Berea College, which provides tours and attractions to guests. Berea proudly bears the title, "Arts and Crafts Capital of Kentucky" because of its many crafts and antique shops. The Hotel dining and meeting rooms offer superb southern cuisine, charming atmosphere, and friendly student service.

I-75 S. Lexington approx. 45 mi, Exit 76, L off ramp, follow U.S. 25 S. to 4th stop light, R. 1 block to Boone Tavern Hotel, or I-75 N. Knoxville, TN to Exit 76, R off ramp, follow U.S. 25 S. to 4th stop light, R 1 block to Boone Tavern Hotel

**TEL. 800-366-9358;
606-986-9358 or 986-7711**
Main and Prospect Street
Berea, KY 40403
Robert A. Stewart, Innkeeper

INN AT PLEASANT HILL

🛏	75 Rooms, $54/$100 EP 5 Suites, $100/$150 EP
	Visa, MC
	All Private Baths
	Closed Dec. 24 & 25
	Children Accepted No Pets
R	Village Touring, Riverboat
	Breakfast, Lunch, Dinner
	Non-Smoking Dining Rm.
	Conference Facilities (75)
♿	

2 Part of a restored Shaker community, originally established in 1805, the inn's rooms are located in 15 of the 30 original buildings clustered along a country road on 2,700 acres in Bluegrass country. Rooms are simply and beautifully furnished with examples of Shaker crafts. Meals are hearty and home-made, and tours, demonstrations, and cultural events abound.

From Lexington, U.S. 68 (W) 25 mi. and R. to village. From Harrodsburg, U.S. 68 (E) 7 mi. Turn L. to village.

TEL. 606-734-5411

3500 Lexington Rd.
Harrodsburg, KY 40330

Ann Voris, Innkeeper

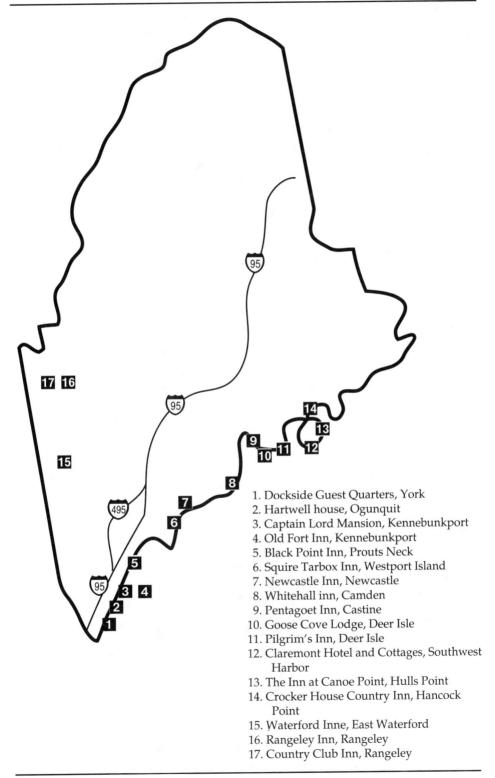

1. Dockside Guest Quarters, York
2. Hartwell house, Ogunquit
3. Captain Lord Mansion, Kennebunkport
4. Old Fort Inn, Kennebunkport
5. Black Point Inn, Prouts Neck
6. Squire Tarbox Inn, Westport Island
7. Newcastle Inn, Newcastle
8. Whitehall inn, Camden
9. Pentagoet Inn, Castine
10. Goose Cove Lodge, Deer Isle
11. Pilgrim's Inn, Deer Isle
12. Claremont Hotel and Cottages, Southwest
      Harbor
13. The Inn at Canoe Point, Hulls Point
14. Crocker House Country Inn, Hancock
      Point
15. Waterford Inne, East Waterford
16. Rangeley Inn, Rangeley
17. Country Club Inn, Rangeley

BLACK POINT INN

🛏	75 Rooms, $220/$330 MAP 5 Suites, $280/$360 MAP
💳	Visa, MC, Amex
🛁	All Private Baths
💡	Closed Nov. 1 to May 1
👧🐕	Appropriate for Children over 8; No Pets
R	Indoor/outdoor pool/ Jacuzzi, Putting green, Croquet, Golf, Tennis
☕	Breakfast, Lunch, Dinner; AP rates available Wine & Liquor Available
🚭	Non-Smoking Dining Room
⊢🪑🪑⊣	Conference Facilities
♿	

5 Quintessentially New England is this seaside resort inn, the favored retreat of generations of guests since the late 1800s. Easy, gracious hospitality and understated, genteel elegance, along with the vast ocean views, bracing salt air, hearty meals, beach-combing, sailing, and more, make this a world-class seaside resort-inn.

I-95 (N) to Exit 5 and U.S. Rte. l, 10 mi. (N) Turn R. on Rte. 207, 4.5 mi. to inn. Or, I-95 (S) to Exit 7, R. at Scarborough Old Orchard (Rte. l). L. at 3rd light onto Rte. 207 as above.

TEL. 207-883-4126
Reservations 800-258-0003
510 Black Point Rd.
Prouts Neck, ME 04074
Normand H. Dugas,
Innkeeper

CAPTAIN LORD MANSION

🛏	16 Rooms, $149/199 B&B
💳	Visa, MC, Discov
🛁	All Private Baths
💡	Open Year-round
👧🐕	Appropriate for Children over 6; No Pets
R	Antiquing, Shopping, Beaches, Sailing, Whale watching, Tennis, Golf, Fishing, Bicycling
☕	Full Breakfast BYOB
🚬	Smoking in Guest Rooms Only
⊢🪑🪑⊣	Conference Facilities (24)
♿	

3 The beautifully appointed, spacious rooms of this stately 1812 mansion, with its elliptical staircase and imposing cupola, feature period wallpapers, crystal chandeliers, fireplaces and many objects d'art. Superb comfort and gracious hospitality have been rewarded for many years with four diamonds by AAA. Many year-round activities are offered in this charming seacoast village.

ME Tpke., Exit 3. L. onto Rte. 35 for 5.5 mi. to Rte. 9 (E). Turn L., go over bridge. R. onto Ocean Ave.; after 3.10 mi., turn L. onto Green St.

TEL. 207-967-3141, 800-522-3141, FAX 207-967-3172

P.O. Box 800
Kennebunkport, ME 04046

Bev Davis & Rick
Litchfield, Innkeepers

CLAREMONT HOTEL & COTTAGES

 25 Rooms, $110/$170 MAP
4 Suites, $150/$190 MAP
14 Cotts., $75/$163 EP

 Mostly Private Baths

 Cottages Closed 10/24-5/22; Hotel 9/19-6/19

 Children Accepted; No Pets

 Tennis, Croquet, Rowboats, Bikes, Golf, Sailing, Swimming, Acadia Nat'l. Park

Breakfast and Dinner; Lunch mid-July and Aug. only. EP off-season ; Wine & Liquor Available

No Smoking in Guest Rooms

Conference Facilities (125)

Wheelchair Access (4 cottages)

ME Tpke., Exit 15 (Augusta), Rte. 3 (E) thru Ellsworth to Mt. Desert Is. Take Rte. 102 to SW Harbor, Follow signs.

TEL. 207-244-5036

Box 137,
**Southwest Harbor, ME
04679**

John Madeira, Jr., Manager

12 The dock and the Boathouse on Somes Sound are the center of much activity at this 105-year-old summer hotel, although croquet and the annual Claremont Classic run them a close second. On the National Register of Historic Places, the Claremont, with its panoramic views of mountains and ocean, offers serene and happy sojourns to its many returning guests.

COUNTRY CLUB INN

 19 Rooms $134/$154 MAP

Visa, MC, Amex

 All Private Baths

 Closed mid-Oct.–late Dec. late March – mid-May

Children &Pets accepted

 Pool, Golf, Hiking, Lake swimming, Boating, Lawn games, Skiing, XC Skiing, Snowmobiling, Canoeing, Antiquing.

Breakfast & Dinner; Box lunch available; Wine, Beer & Liquor available

 Smoking in designated area

 Conference facilities (25-100)

ME Tpke., Exit 12 to Rte. 4. I-91 in VT & NH to St. Johnsbury; (E) on Rte. 2 to Gorham & Rte. 16(N) to Rangeley.

TEL. 207-864-3831

P.O. Box 680
Rangeley, ME 04970

Sue Crory, Margie & Steve Jamison, Innkeepers

17 Few locations offer such beauty and grandeur in all seasons as Rangeley with its wide skies, vast mountain ranges, and sparkling lake. Magnificent scenery can be enjoyed from the guest rooms, dining room, and lounge of 2,000-foot-high Country Club Inn, in the heart of fishing, hiking, skiing and snowmobiling. Golf packages are available.

CROCKER HOUSE COUNTRY INN

🛏	11 Rooms, $75/$90 in season, B&B $60/$75 off season, B&B
💳	Visa, MC, Amex, Discov
🛁	All Private Baths
🛋	Closed Jan.1 — Apr. 20; Restaurant open Th., Fri., Sat., in Nov. & Dec.
🐕	Well mannered Children Accepted; Pets with prior permission
R	Spa, Croquet, Library, Clay Tennis courts, Antiquing, Golf, Acadia Nat'l Park region
🍽	Breakfast & Dinner; Sunday brunch Memorial-Labor Day
🚬	Smoking & Non-smoking Dining Rooms
🪑	Conference Facilities (36)
♿	

14 Sequestered on Hancock Point, this restored 109-year-old inn is a three minute walk from Frenchman Bay. The carriage house, converted in 1992, adds two spacious guestrooms, an additional common room and a spa. The restaurant, open to the public, continues to draw guests from distant places for its extraordinary cuisine and live jazz piano on Friday and Saturday nights.

From Ellsworth on U.S. Rt. 1 go 79 miles (N) to R. on Hancock Pt. Rd. Continue 5 mi. to inn on R. Mooring available with advance notification.

TEL. 207-422-6806

Hancock, ME 04640

Richard Malaby, Innkeeper

DOCKSIDE GUEST QUARTERS

🛏	16 Rooms, $57/$100 EP 6 Suites, $97/$132 EP Off season rates available
💳	Visa, MC, Personal Chks.
🛁	20 Private, 2 Shared Baths
🛋	Closed Oct. 23 - May 1 Winter apts. available
🐕	Children welcome No Pets
R	Boats, Bicycles, Fishing, Shuffleboard, Badminton, Croquet, Swimming, Golf Tennis, Outlet shopping, Historic sites
🍽	Breakfast, Lunch, Dinner; Lounge; Weddings, Group functions
🚬	Wine & Liquor available Non-smoking Rooms
🪑	Conference Facilities (30)
♿	

1 This small resort on a private peninsula in York Harbor offers views of ocean and harbor activities. The early Maine seacoast inn and multi-unit cottages contain attractive guest rooms with rambling porches where guests enjoy water views. Restaurant, wedding facilities, and marina on the premises. An ocean beach and the York Historic District are within walking distance.

From I-95 exit to U.S. 1 South. Rte. 1-A thru Old York to Rte. 103. Cross bridge & watch for signs to inn.

TEL. 207-363-2868

Harris Island Rd.
P.O. Box 205
York, ME 03909

The David Lusty Family, Innkeepers

GOOSE COVE LODGE

 10 Rooms, $140/$165 MAP
11 Cotts, $160/$200 MAP

 MC, Visa, Personal Checks

 All Private Baths

 Closed Mid-Oct. to April 30

 Children Accepted
Pets in off Season

 Nature Trails, Beach, Canoe, Golf, Sailing, Acadia Nat'l. Park

 Breakfast & Dinner, May-Oct.; B&B Option in Spring & Fall

No Smoking in Dining Room

Wheelchair Access (1 Room)

I-95 to Augusta, Rte. 3 to Belfast. Rte. 1 (N), 4 mi. past Bucksport. R. on Rte. 15, in town of Deer Isle R. on Sunset Rd., 3 mi. to inn sign & R. 1.5 mi. to inn.

TEL. 207-348- 2508

**Deer Isle,
Sunset, ME 04683**

Joanne & Dom Parisi, Innkeepers

10 This rustic and comfortable lodge is on a secluded peaceful cove where pine trees and rock ledges meet the ocean. Cottages have fireplaces, sundecks, and wonderful views. Pleasant day trips on land and water, evening entertainment, natural beauty, lobster cookouts and other excellent cuisine offer refreshment of body and spirit to guests of all ages.

HARTWELL HOUSE

 11 Rooms, $80/$135 B&B
3 Suites, $125/$175 B&B

 Visa, MC, Amex, Disc.

 All Private Baths

 Open Year-round

 Appropriate for Children over 14; No Pets

 Atlantic Ocean, Beach, Fishing, Swimming, Boating, Golf, Tennis, XC Skiing, Biking

 Breakfast

 Wine available

No Smoking

Conference facilities (10)

I-95 (N) & York/Ogunquit Exit. L. on Rte. 1 for 4.4 mi. to R. at Pine Hill Rd. L. at Shore Rd. for .2 mi. to inn.

**TEL. 207-646-7210
FAX 207-646-6032**

118 Shore Rd., P.O. Box 393
Oqunquit, ME 03907

Trish & Jim Hartwell, Renee & Alec Adams, Innkeepers

hartwell house

2 Sculpted flower gardens color the view from the balcony rooms overlooking the lawn sloping down to the river at this sophisticated inn. Early American and English antiques, stunning pastel fabrics, and fresh flowers add to the country house atmosphere. Within an easy walk is the wonderful Marginal Way and Perkins Cove.

THE INN AT CANOE POINT

🛏	3 Rooms, $75/$125 B&B 2 Suites, $110/$195 B&B
💳	Personal Checks accepted
🛁	All Private Baths
💡	Open Year-round
🐕	Not Appropriate for younger Children No Pets
R	Acadia Natl. Pk. adjacent, Hiking, Biking, Sailing, Mtn. Climbing, XC Skiing
🍽	Full Breakfast, Afternoon Refreshments; Port Wine in Rooms; BYOB
🚭	Non-Smokers Preferred
	Conference Facilities (20)
♿	

13 This secluded waterside inn among the pines is only moments away from lively Bar Harbor and next door to the unspoiled natural attractions of Acadia National Park. With views of Frenchman's Bay, mountains, trees, flowers, rocky coast and the ocean, guests will be tempted to laze by the fieldstone fireplace in the ocean room or out on the deck, listening to the rolling surf.

From Ellsworth, Rte. 3 (NE) approx. 15 mil. toward Bar Harbor, through Hulls Cove Village. Continue past Acadia Natl. Pk. entrance 1/4 mil to inn on L.

TEL. 207-288-9511

Box 216, Hulls Cove
(Bar Harbor), ME 04644

Don Johnson & Esther Cavagnaro, Innkeepers

THE NEWCASTLE INN

🛏	15 Rooms, $65/$130 B&B $140/$185 MAP
💳	Visa, MC
🛁	All Private Baths
💡	Open Year-around
🐕	Older, well behaved Children; No Pets
R	Walking trails, Beaches, Bicycling, Antiquing, Birding, Boating, Touring, XC Skiing
🍽	Breakfast – Guests only Dinner by Reservation Wine & Liquor available
🚭	No Smoking
	Conference Facilities (20)
♿	

7 Overlooking the harbor, boatyard and lovely flower gardens, the Newcastle Inn offers comfortably elegant guest rooms. In one of midcoast Maine's quintessential villages, with easy access to numerous attractions, the feeling of warmth, friendship and seclusion make this a retreat where guests may relax and unwind. Nationally acclaimed dining is a truly memorable experience.

Maine Tpke. to Exit 9; I-95 (N) to Brunswick Exit 22, Rte. 1(N); 6 mi.(N) of Wiscasset. Take R. on River Rd. Continue 1/2 mi. to inn on R.

TEL. 207-563-5685
800-832-8669

River Road
Newcastle, ME 04553

Ted and Chris Sprague, Innkeepers

OLD FORT INN

 16 Rooms $98/$230 B&B

 Visa, MC, Amex, Discov. Enroute

All Private Baths; 4 Jacuzzis

 Closed Dec. 10 — April

Appropriate for Children over 12; No Pets

Tennis Court, Pool, Bikes, Ocean, Golf, Walking, Jogging

Breakfast

Smoking Restricted

Conference Facilities (32)

I-95 Exit 3, turn L. on Rte. 35 for 5.5 mi. L. at light at Rte. 9 for 3.10 mi. to Ocean Ave. Go 9/10 mi. to Colony Hotel, then L. & follow signs 3/10 mi. to inn.

TEL. 207-967-5353;
800-828-3678
Old Fort Ave., P.O. Box M
Kennebunkport, ME 04046
Sheila & David Aldrich,
Innkeepers

4 A short walk from the ocean along a country road, this secluded inn in an old seaport town offers rooms with antiques, canopied and 4-poster beds, color TV and phones. Guests find new friends over a buffet breakfast of fresh fruit and homemade breads; a charming antiques shop, freshwater pool, and private tennis court provide pleasant diversion.

THE PENTAGOET INN

16 Rooms, $154/$174 MAP
1 Suite, $195 MAP

Visa, MC;
Personal checks preferred

All Private Baths

 Closed Nov. – April

 Appropriate for Children over 12 No Pets

 Boating, Hiking, Biking, Tennis, Golf

 Breakfast & Dinner; to the public by reservation

 Wine & Liquor available

No Smoking

I-95 to Augusta & Rte. 3 (E) to Belfast, turn L. (N) on Rte. 1 past Bucksport 3 mi. to R. (S) on Rte. 175. Turn (S) on Rte. 166 to Castine. Inn is on Main St.

TEL. 207-326-8616
800-845-1701
Main St., P.O. Box 4
Castine, ME 04421
Lindsey & Virginia Miller,
Innkeepers

9 Capacious porches, fresh flowers and nightly room freshening are just a few of the "perks" at this lovely old Victorian inn. With its feeling of a private country home, the Pentagoet offers excellent food and an extensive wine list. Tiny, historic Castine in Penobscot Bay provides fresh sea air, harbor activities in a tranquil setting.

PILGRIM'S INN

13 Rooms, $130/$170 MAP
1 Cottage, $180 MAP

No Credit Cards

Private & Shared Baths

Open mid-May to
mid-Oct.

Appropriate for Children
over 10
No Pets

Touring, Hiking,
Bicycling, Sailing, Golf,
Tennis

Breakfast & Dinner
Wine & Liquor available

Smoking in common
Rooms only

Conference Facilities (35)

11 Overlooking Northwest Harbor and a picturesque millpond, this 1793 Colonial home is surrounded by the unspoiled beauty of remote Deer Isle in Penobscot Bay. Glowing hearths, soft Colonial colors, pumpkin pine floors, antique furnishings, combined with warm hospitality and gourmet meals in the charming barn dining room, have pleased many happy and contented guests.

I-95 (N) to Augusta. Rte. 3 (N) to Belfast, thru Bucksport to Rte. 15 (S), thru Blue Hill. Over bridge to Deer Isle Village. Turn R., 1 block to inn on left.

TEL. 207-348-6615

Deer Isle, ME 04627

Dud & Jean Hendrick,
Innkeepers

RANGELEY INN

50 Rooms, $58/$100 EP
1 Suite, $85/$95 EP

Visa, MC, Amex

All Private Baths;
Several Whirlpools

Open Year-round

Children Accepted

Moose-watching, Touring, Antiques, Swimming, Boating, Hiking, Downhill & XC Skiing

Breakfast & Dinner; MAP optional; Dining Closed 4/15-5/15, early Dec.
Wine & Liquor Available

Limited Smoking in Dining Room

Conference Facilities (150)

Wheelchair Access (1 room)

16 The big blue clapboard building with the long veranda across the front has that grand old summer hotel look and the homelike, roomy lobby has a bit of an old-fashioned feeling. The elegant dining room is up to the minute with creative, interesting menus. Several acres of lawns and gardens border a bird sanctuary, and the area is a nature-lover's and sportsman's paradise.

On Rte. 4 past Farmington 40 mi. to Rangeley. From west take Rte. 16. Inn is on Main St.

TEL. 207-864-3341;
RES: 800-MOMENTS
(666-3687)
Box 398, Main St.,
Rangeley, ME 04970
Fay & Ed Carpenter,
Innkeepers

THE SQUIRE TARBOX INN

 11 Rooms, $120/$195 MAP
$65/$140 B&B

 Visa, MC, Amex, Discov

 All Private Baths

Closed late Oct. to
Mid-May

Appropriate for Children
over 14; No Pets

 Walking path, Rowboat on
premises, Beaches,
Harbors, Antiques nearby

 Breakfast for guests only;
Dinner to public by
reservation;
Wine & Liquor available

Smoking in limited area

I-95 to Brunswick, Exit 22, follow Rte.
1 (N) past Bath bridge 7 mi. to Rte. 144.
Continue 8.5 mi. on Westport Island.

TEL. 207-882-7693

R.R.2, Box 620, Route 144
Wiscasset, ME 04578

Bill & Karen Mitman,
Innkeepers

6 This handsome colonial farmhouse on a wooded hillside by a small inlet, is a respected full-service inn offering historical significance, a natural country setting, relaxed comfort and a diversity of Maine Coast interests. Quiet rural privacy is here for guests who seek moments of personal solitude. Known for its savory fireside dinners and goat cheese from its purebred dairy herd.

THE WATERFORD INNE

9 Rooms, $60/$90 EP
1 Suite, $90 EP

Amex

7 Private Baths
1 Shared Bath

Closed March, April,
Thanksgiving week

Children Accepted
Pets Accepted

Library, Parlor Games,
Down-hill & XC Skiing,
Swimming, Boating,
Hiking, Antiquing

Breakfast & Dinner
BYOB

Smoking Discouraged

 Conference Facilities (15)

I-95, Exit 11, to Rte. 26 (N) for 28 mi. to
Norway. L. fork on Rte. 118W for 9 mi.
L. on Rte. 37S for .6 mi. Turn R. past
store .5 mi. to inn.

TEL 207-583-4037
Box 149 Chadbourne Rd.
Waterford, ME 04088

Rosalie & Barbara
Vanderzanden, Innkeepers

15 Combining their considerable talents in hospitality and the domestic arts, Rosalie and Barbara Vanderzanden have made a very special inn out of the handsome farmhouse they have lovingly restored and furnished. Their attention to detail is apparent in beautifully decorated rooms and in the imaginative meals served on china from their 'round-the-world' collection.

WHITEHALL INN

🛏	50 Rooms, $125/$160 MAP Off Season $75/$105 B&B
	Visa, MC
	Private & Shared Baths
	Closed Oct. 15 to May 26
	Children Accepted No Pets
R	Tennis, Shuffleboard, Gardens, Library, Games, Rocking Chairs, Golf, State Park, Lakes, Sailing
	Breakfast & Dinner Wine & Liquor Available
	No Smoking in Dining Room
♿	

8 If ever an inn and a setting were made for each other, this is it. Tree-lined streets, comfortable old homes echo the feeling of old-fashioned friendliness and hospitality in this rambling, homey inn, originally built in 1834, and operating as an inn since 1901. The inn has been run by the Dewing family for 19 years.

Camden is 2 hrs. north of Portland on Rte. 1. Inn is .5 mi. north of village.

TEL. 207-236-3391

52 High St., P.O.Box 558,
Camden, ME 04843

The Dewing Family,
Innkeepers

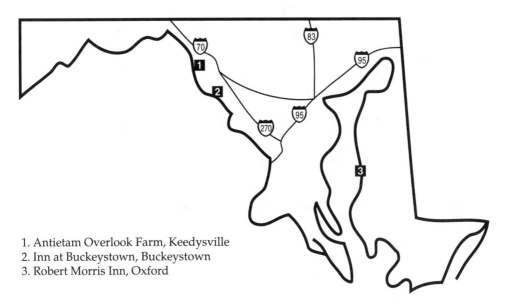

1. Antietam Overlook Farm, Keedysville
2. Inn at Buckeystown, Buckeystown
3. Robert Morris Inn, Oxford

ANTIETAM OVERLOOK FARM

6 Rooms, $103/$143 B&B

Visa, MC, Amex, Diners

All Private Baths

Open Year-around

Teenage Children Welcome: No Pets

Antietam National Battlefield, Hiking Trails, Game & Birdwatching, Antiquing in Quaint Villages

Memorable Country Breakfast, Comp. Wine, Soda, & After-dinner drinks; Wine available, BYOB

No Smoking

Call for directions and availability

TEL. (800) 878-4241

P.O. Box 30
4812 Porterstown Rd.
Keedysville, MD 21756

Barbara & John Dreisch,
Innkeepers

1 The 95-acre mountaintop farm over looking Antietam National Battlefield has extraordinary views of 4 states. The hand-hewn timber framing, rough sawn walls and stone fireplaces juxtaposed to the softly flowered furnishings and fine crystal create a warm comfortable atmosphere. Spacious suites include fireplaces, queen beds, old-fashioned bubble baths and private screened porches.

55

THE INN AT BUCKEYSTOWN

	3 Rooms, $167/$209 MAP 4 Suites, $188/$272 MAP
	Visa, MC, Amex
	All Private Baths
	Open Year-round By Reservation Only
	Appropriate for Children over 16 No Pets
	Lawn games on premises, Hiking, Antiquing, Civil War sites
	Breakfast & Dinner
	Complimentary Wine
	Smoking only in parlors
	Conference facilities (20)

2 Lovingly restored, this impressive 1897 mansion and 1884 church are in a nostalgic village, on the National Register of Historic Places. Rooms are luxuriously furnished with outstanding antiques and collectibles. A wraparound porch with rockers looks out on park-like grounds. Gourmet dining and the friendly ambiance bring guests back. "Best Inn of the Year Award" for 1990.

From I-70 or I-270, take Rte. 85(s) to Buckeystown. Inn is on left. (35 mi. from Dulles Airport.)

TEL. 301-874-5755
RES. 800-272-1190
3521 Buckeystown Pike,
Buckeystown, MD 21717
Daniel R. Pelz, Chase
Barnett, Rebecca Shipman-
Smith, Innkeepers

THE ROBERT MORRIS INN

	35 Rooms, $70/$180 EP
	Visa, MC
	All Private Baths
	Lodging Year-round B&B Dec.-Mid Mar. Rest. open Mid Mar.-Nov.
	Appropriate for Children over 10; No Pets
	Tennis, Biking, Golf, Antiquing, Sailing, Historic Car Ferry, Goose Hunting
	Full Service Wed.-Mon.; Cont. Bkfst. only Tues. Wine & Liquor available
	All Rooms Non-Smoking
	Executive Conference Facilities (10-20)
	Wheelchair Access, 2 rms.

3 Chesapeake Bay and the Tred Avon River play a big part in the life of this Eastern Shore country-romantic 1710 inn. Delicacies from the bay are featured in the nationally acclaimed seafood restaurant and the Tred Avon offers lovely views from many of the rooms and porches. Country furnishings add to the friendly feeling here in the historic waterside village of Oxford.

Hwy. 301 to Rte. 50 (E). Turn R. on Rte. 322 for 3.4 mi. Turn R. on Rte. 333 for 9.6 mi. to inn and ferry

TEL. 410-226-5111
312 No. Morris St.
P.O. Box 70
Oxford, MD 21654
Wendy & Ken Gibson,
Owners
Jay Gibson, Innkeeper

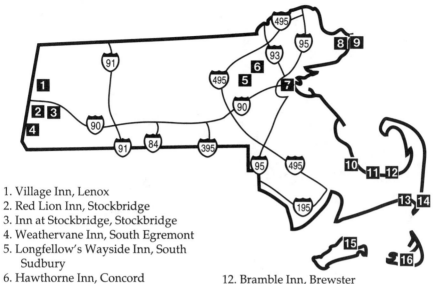

1. Village Inn, Lenox
2. Red Lion Inn, Stockbridge
3. Inn at Stockbridge, Stockbridge
4. Weathervane Inn, South Egremont
5. Longfellow's Wayside Inn, South Sudbury
6. Hawthorne Inn, Concord
7. Lenox Hotel, Boston
8. Yankee Clipper Inn, Rockport
9. Ralph Waldo Emerson, Rockport
10. Isaiah Jones Homestead, Sandwich
11. Charles Hinckley House, Barnstable
12. Bramble Inn, Brewster
13. Captain's House Inn, Chatham
14. Queen Anne Inn, Chatham
15. Charlotte Inn, Edgartown, Martha's Vineyard Island
16. Jared Coffin House, Nantucket Island

THE BRAMBLE INN AND RESTAURANT

12 Rooms, $75/$125 B&B
1 Suite, $115/$125 B&B

Visa, MC, Amex

All Private Baths

Closed Jan. 1 to April 15

Appropriate for Children over 8; No Pets

Tennis, Swimming, Fishing, Bicycling, Horseback, Riding, Whale-watching, Antiquing

Breakfast; Price-fix Dinner by reservation Wine & Liquor available

Smoking restricted

Wheelchair access (3 Rooms)

Rte. 6, Exit 10 & bear L. on Rte. 124 to R. on Rte. 6A for 1/8 mi. to inn on left.

TEL. 508-896-7644

2019 Main St.
Route 6A
Box 807
Brewster, MA 02631

Cliff & Ruth Manchester, Innkeepers

12 Dine superbly at one of Cape Cod's top three restaurants, where Ruth Manchester creates dishes sought after by *Bon Appetit* and *Gourmet*. Wide pine floors, antiques, and flowered wallpapers adorn the guest rooms in the three 18th and 19th century buildings of this family-owned and operated intimate inn on the historic north side of the Cape.

CAPTAIN'S HOUSE INN OF CHATHAM

🛏	15 Rooms, $100/$200 B&B 1 Suite, $150/$175 B&B
💳	Visa, MC, Amex
🛁	All Private Baths
💡🔥	Closed mid-Nov. to mid-Feb.
🐕👧	Doesn't meet needs of Children; No Pets
ⓡ	Beaches, Tennis, Golf, Boating, Theater, Fishing
◎🍽	Breakfast, Afternoon Tea BYOB
🚭	Non-Smoking Inn
⊢╫╫╫⊣	Conference Facilities (16)
♿	

13 A quiet getaway, without television, and cheerful, caring attention are here for guests who choose to stay at this historic, elegant 1839 inn set on two acres, a half-mile from Cape Cod's south shore beaches. The decor is reminiscent of Williamsburg with fine antiques, canopied beds, and fireplaces in warm, inviting guest rooms. This lovely inn has rated the AAA 4-diamond award.

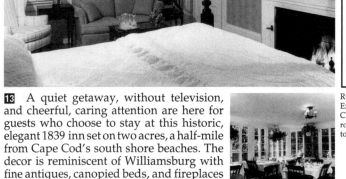

Rte. 6 (Mid-Cape Hwy.) to Rte. 137, Exit 11 (S) to Rte. 28; L. on Rte. 28 to Chatham Center. Continue around rotary on Rte. 28 toward Orleans .5 mi. to inn on L. **TEL. 508-945-0127**
369-377 Old Harbor Rd.
Chatham, Cape Cod, MA 02633
Cathy & David Eakin,
Innkeepers

CHARLES HINCKLEY HOUSE

🛏	2 rooms, $119/$139 B&B 2 suites, $149 B&B
💳	Personal Checks accepted
🛁	All Private Baths
💡🔥	Open Year-round
🐕👧	Appropriate for Children over 10; No Pets
ⓡ	Antiquing, Historic sites, Beaches, Golf, Tennis, Sailing, Fishing
◎🍽	Complimentary Breakfast; Dinner on weekends and holidays by reservation
🚭	No Smoking
⊢╫╫╫⊣	
♿	Wheelchair Access (1 room)

11 An architectural gem listed on the National Register of Historic Places on the Olde Kings Highway is this 1809 Colonial home of an early shipwright. The young innkeepers have lovingly restored and furnished it, polishing the wide pumpkin pine floors, refurbishing the fireplaces, and putting in 4-poster beds. The unspoiled natural beauty of Cape Cod Bay is just a stroll away.

Rte. 6 (mid-Cape Hwy.) Exit 6. Turn L. onto Rte. 132 for .5 mi. Turn R. onto Rte. 6A; continue 1.5 mi. to inn.
TEL. 508-362-9924
Olde Kings Hwy.,
(Rte. 6-A), P.O. Box 723
Barnstable, MA 02630
Les & Miya Patrick,
Innkeepers

THE CHARLOTTE INN

 21 Rooms, $95/$295 B&B
3 Suites, $175/$450 B&B

 Visa, MC, Amex

 All Private Baths

 Open Year-round

 Appropriate for Children over 14
No Pets

 Boating, Golfing, Tennis, Fishing, Swimming, Bicycling

 Comp. Continental Breakfast, Sunday Brunch, Dinner (weekends off-season). Wine & Liquor available

 Smoking discouraged

Woods Hole/Martha's Vineyard ferry (res. needed for car). In Edgartown, take first R. off Main St. to Summer St., continue 1/2 block to inn.

TEL. 508-627-4751

South Summer St.
Edgartown, MA 02539

Gery & Paula Conover, Innkeepers

15 Art, aesthetics, and exquisite attention to detail are the hallmarks of this beautifully restored inn, surrounded by lovely gardens and brick pathways. Original oils and watercolors and beautiful wallpapers adorn luxuriously furnished rooms, some with fireplaces. Cuisine at the French restaurant pleases the most sophisticated palates.

HAWTHORNE INN

 7 Rooms, $85/$160 B&B

 No Credit Cards

 All Private Baths

Open Year-round

Children Welcome
No Pets

Swimming (Walden Pond), Museums, Wooded trails for Hiking & XC Skiing, Canoeing on Concord River

Breakfast

No Smoking

Rte. 128-95, Exit 30-B (W) (Rte. 2A) for 2.8 mi. Bear R. at fork toward Concord for 1.2 mi. Inn across from Hawthorne's home.

TEL. 508-369-5610

462 Lexington Rd.
Concord, MA 01742

Gregory Burch & Marilyn Mudry, Innkeepers

6 On land where Emerson, Alcott, and Hawthorne lived, and among trees planted by these illustrious men, the Hawthorne Inn follows their lead in the cultivation of art and appreciation of the spiritual in life. Friendly, caring innkeepers and nature walks, where land, sky, and water refresh the senses, imbue this winsome, intimate inn with a very special feeling.

THE INN AT STOCKBRIDGE

	6 Rooms, $85/$205 B&B 2 Suites, $125/$225 B&B
	Visa, MC, Amex
	All Private Baths, 1 Whirlpool
	Open Year-round
	Appropriate for Children over 12 No Pets
	Swimming, Pool, Golf, Tennis, Hiking, Downhill & XC Skiing, Norman Rockwell Museum
	Breakfast, Dinners for groups can be arranged Complimentary Wine
	Smoking in Public areas
	Conference Facilities (20)

3 Consummate hospitality and outstanding breakfasts distinguish a visit at this turn-of-the-century Georgian Colonial estate on 12 secluded acres in the heart of the Berkshires. Close to Tanglewood, theaters, museums, and skiing, the inn has a gracious, English country house feeling, with two well-appointed living rooms, a formal dining room, and a baby grand piano.

Mass. Tpke. Exit 2 & (W) on Rte. 102 to Rte. 7 (N) 1.2 mi. to inn on R. From NYC, Taconic Pkwy. to Rte. 23 (E) & Rte. 7 (N) past Stockbridge 1.2 mi.

TEL 413-298-3337
FAX 413-298-3406
Rte. 7 (North), Box 618,
Stockbridge, MA 01262
Lee & Don Weitz,
Innkeepers

ISAIAH JONES HOMESTEAD

	5 Rooms, $70-$119 B&B
	Visa, MC, Amex, Discov.
	All Private Baths
	Open Year-round
	Children over 12 accepted; No Pets
	Museums, Antiques, Gift Shops, Beach, Fishing, Whale Watching, Tennis, Golf, Biking, Hist. Sites
	Breakfast & Afternoon Tea; Warm Cider by Fireside or Lemonade on Porch. Low Cholesterol Cooking featured No Smoking

10 This 1849 Italianate Victorian in the historic village of Sandwich, Cape Cod's oldest town, is within walking distance of most points of interest and fine restaurants. Beautifully furnished with antiques, oriental carpets, and fresh flowers, its quiet elegance harks back to a time when life was tranquil and travelers were pampered. Breakfast is served by candlelight.

Rte. 6 (mid-Cape-Hwy.) Exit 2, L on Rte. 130 and bear R. at fork for 2/10 mi. on L.

TEL. 508-888-9115
or 800-526-1625

165 Main Street
Sandwich, MA 02563

Shirley Jones Sutton,
Innkeeper

JARED COFFIN HOUSE

60 Rooms, $75/$175 B&B

Visa, MC, Amex, Diners, Discov

All Private Baths

Open Year-round

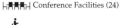
Children & Pets Accepted with prior approval

Beaches, Tennis, Sailing, Biking

All meals available on premises
Wine & Liquor available

No Pipes or Cigars in Restaurant

Conference Facilities (24)

Flights available from NYC, Boston, New Bedford, & Hyannis. Or take Hyannis ferry, leaving car in Hyannis — cars unnecessary on Nantucket.

TEL. 508-228-2400
Res: 800-248-2405 (M-F, 8-5);
FAX 508-228-8549
29 Broad St., P.O. Box 1580,
Nantucket, MA 02554-1580
Philip & Margaret Read,
Innkeepers

16 A collection of buildings from the mid-1800's tastefully restored to provide today's guest with the feeling of a gentler past. The inn is conveniently located in the Old Historic District near Main Street shops with easy access to island beaches and bike paths. The Tap Room and JARED's offer both casual and more formal dining featuring American cuisine.

THE LENOX HOTEL

219 Rooms, $99/$210 EP
3 Suites, $350 EP

All Private Baths

Open year-round

Children accepted
No Pets

New exercise room for guests, all Boston attractions, Health club, Racquet ball nearby; Jogging

Restaurant and Lounge
Room Service
Wine & Liquor available

Smoking in Common Rooms Only

Conference facilities (200)

Wheelchair access

Mass. Tpke., Exit 22, Copely Square ramp to L. on Dartmouth, 2 blocks to L. on Newbury St., 1 block to L. on Exeter, 1 block to hotel at corner of Exeter & Boylston.

TEL. 800-225-7676
IN MASS: 617-536-5300
710 Boylston St.,
Boston, MA 02116
The Saunders Family,
Innkeepers

7 This small hotel has been run by the same family for over 25 years. In the Back Bay area, next to Copley Square, the hotel offers several rooms with working fireplaces and many with country inn touches. Diamond Jim's Piano Bar and the Pub and Grill are popular attractions. New self-controlled heating and air conditioning has just been installed. Valet parking service.

MASSACHUSETTS

LONGFELLOW'S WAYSIDE INN

	10 Rooms, $85 B&B
	Amx, MC, Visa, DC, Disc.
	All Private Baths
	Closed Dec.. 24 & 25
	Children Accepted No Pets
	Historic sites, Famous Revolutionary War landmarks
	All Meals Wine & Liquor available
	Non-smoking Dining area
	Wheelchair Access to Dining Rooms

5 Immortalized in 1863 by Longfellow in his *Tales of a Wayside Inn*, the inn is located off U.S. Rt. 20 on Wayside Inn Road. Next to the inn is a working gristmill, (open April-November); the Red Stone School House of *Mary and Her Little Lamb* fame (open seasonal weather) and the Martha Mary Chapel for weddings. Reservations for lodging and for dining made well in advance.

Between Boston & Worcester off Rte. 20. 11 mi. (W) of Rte. 128 & 7 mi. (E) off Rte. 495. Sign on R., for Wayside Inn Rd.

TEL. 508-443-1776

Wayside Inn Rd. off Rte. 20
South Sudbury, MA 01776

Robert H. Purrington,
Innkeeper

THE QUEEN ANNE INN

	29 Rooms, $98/$215 B&B 1 Suite, $200 B&B
	Visa, MC, Amex, Diners
	All Private Baths; 2 Jacuzzis
	Closed Dec. 1-April 15
	Children Accepted Kennel nearby for Pets
	Indoor Spa, 3 Tennis Cts, Bikes, Boating, Scuba Diving, Fishing, Golf
	Continental Breakfast, Dinner, Dining room closed Tues.; 12/1- 5/17 Wine & Liquor Available
	Smoking discouraged
	Conference Facilities (30)

14 Spacious guest rooms, antiques, garden views, private balconies, working fireplaces, and private whirlpool baths are a few of the amenities that may be found here on Cape Cod's picturesque south shore. The intimate restaurant features superb cuisine, and pursuits to beguile quiet hours or to engage the energetic are all around.

Rte. 6 (E) to Exit 11, R. on Rte. 137 and L. on Rte. 28 for 3.5 mi. to light and R. fork to Queen Anne Rd. and up hill to inn.

TEL. 508-945-0394
RES.800-545-INNS

70 Queen Anne Rd.,
Chatham, MA 02633

Guenther Weinkopf,
Innkeeper

RALPH WALDO EMERSON INN

 34 Rooms, $85/$123 EP
2 suites, $96/$123

 Visa, MC, Discov.

 All Private Baths

 Closed Dec. 1-March 31

 Children Accepted
No Pets

 Saltwater Pool, Sauna,
Game Room, VCR, Golf,
Whale-Watching, Hiking,
Tennis

 Breakfast & Dinner, July-
Labor Day; Breakfast
Only April-July, Sept.-Nov.

 Smoking Accepted

 Conference Facilities (35)

Wheelchair Access (2
Rooms)

Rte. 128 (NO) to Rte. 127. At 1st light
(L) on Rte. 127 (N). Follow to Pigeon
Cove. Turn R. at inn sign on Phillips
Ave.

TEL. 508-546-6321

Phillips Ave., Box 2369
Rockport, MA 01966

Gary & Diane Wemyss,
Innkeepers

9 One of the last of the old summer hotels on Cape Ann, the Emerson's broad porches and Greek Revival architecture give it a classic majesty. Preserving the charm of yesteryear while keeping up with the times, the inn features a heated saltwater pool, a whirlpool and sauna, and a theater for movies. Popular seafood and shore specialties are always included on the menu.

THE RED LION INN

 95 Rooms, $65/$155 EP
10 Suites, $150/$250 EP

 Visa, MC, Amex, Diners,
Discov

 Private & Shared Baths

 Open Year-round

 Children Accepted
No Pets

Exercise room, Pool, Golf,
Tennis, Tanglewood, Jacobs
Pillow, Berkshire Theatre
Festival, Norman Rockwell
Museum, Chesterwood

 Breakfast, Lunch, Dinner;
MAP available for groups
Wine & Liquor available

 Non-smoking area in
dining room

 Conference Facilities (6-90)

Wheelchair Access (1 rm.)

I-90, Exit 2 at Lee, to Rte. 102 (W) to
Stockbridge.

TEL. 413-298-5545
FAX 413-298-5130

Main St.
Stockbridge, MA 01262

Jack & Jane Fitzpatrick,
Owners
Betsy Holtzinger, Innkeeper

2 This grand old inn in the Berkshire Hills is still the lively, delightful focus of village activity it has been since 1773. Its rambling porch, hung with summer pots of glowing fuchsias and festooned in winter with garlands and Christmas trees, welcomes travelers with cheerful cordiality, born of long tradition. Beautiful antiques and heirlooms abound. Massage therapist on premises.

THE VILLAGE INN

	32 Rooms, $40/$165 EP 1 Suite, $250/$375 EP
	Visa, MC, Amex, Diners, Discov, CB
	All Private Baths
	4 Jacuzzis Open Year-round
	Appropriate for Children over 6; No Pets
	Downhill & XC Skiing, Golf, Riding, Tennis, Swimming, Fishing
	Breakfast, English tea, Dinner exc. Mon. & Tues.
	Smoking Permitted only in common rooms
	Conference Facilities (50)
	Wheelchair Acces (6 rms)

1 In the center of the Berkshire village of Lenox, this Colonial inn, built in 1771, is near shops, galleries, parks, beautiful wooded trails, Tanglewood, summer dance and theater festivals, winter skiing, fall foliage, and spring flower excursions. Country antiques, some 4-posters, fireplaces, fine American regional cuisine, and afternoon English tea will brighten your stay in the Berkshires.

Mass. Tpke. (I-90), Exit 2, Rte. 20(W) to Rte. 183(S). Turn L. for 1 mi. to R. on Church St. & inn. From Rte. 7 to Rte. 7A & Church St. in Lenox.

TEL. 413-637-0020
800-253-0917
FAX 413-637-9756
16 Church St. P.O. Box 1810
Lenox, MA 01240
Clifford Rudisill and
Ray Wilson, Innkeepers

THE WEATHERVANE INN

	10 Rooms, $110/$160 MAP
	Visa, MC, Amex
	All Private Baths
	Open Year-round
	Appropriate for Children Over 7; No Pets
	Pool, Nature walks, Antiques, Museums, Tennis, Golf, Skiing, Tanglewood, Summer Theater
	Breakfast & Dinner B&B rates available Wine & Liquor available
	No Cigars or Pipes
	Conference Facilities (25)
	Wheelchair Access (2 rooms)

4 Renowned and caring Murphy family hospitality in an elegant farm & coach house with original 19th century architectural details and all of today's amenities, in a lovely little village. The charming Fireside Room and honor bar beckon guests seeking post-recreation recuperation before experiencing the Inn's superb cuisine. For 13 years guests have been returning as friends. (AAA★★★)

From NYC, Taconic Pkwy. to Rte. 23(E) 13 mi. to inn on R. From Mass. Tpke., Exit 2 & Rte. 102 to Rte. 7(S) to Rte. 23(W) to inn on L.

TEL. 413-528-9580;
FAX 413-528-1713
P.O. Box 388, Rte. 23
South Egremont, MA 01258
Murphy Family,
Innkeepers

YANKEE CLIPPER INN

27 rooms, $99/$198 B&B
13 Rooms w/ocean view

Visa, MC, Amex, Discov

All Private Baths

Closed Christmas Day

Appropriate for Children over 3
No Pets

Swimming pool, Tennis, Golf, Whale-watching, Deep Sea Fishing, Hiking, Biking

Breakfast & Dinner
BYOB

No Cigars or Pipes

Conference facilities (50)

Rte. 128 (N) to Cape Ann thru Gloucester. L. on Rte. 127 for 4 mi. to Rockport's 5 Corners & sharp L. & Pigeon Cove sign. Continue .5 mi. to inn.

TEL. 508-546-3407
800-545-3699
FAX 508-546-9730
96 Granite St.,P.O. Box 2399
Rockport, MA 01966
Bob & Barbara Ellis, Innkprs.

 Fresh ocean breezes and sweeping panoramic views have greeted guests here for over 40 years. The Inn and the 1840 Bulfinch House, both with antique furnishings, and the more contemporary Quarterdeck all offer country inn blandishments. There are historic sites in Boston, Salem, Concord and Lexington, and life can be lazy or exciting with Rockport's famous art colony close by.

WHAT MAKES COUNTRY INNS "DIFFERENT"?

There are various reasons why one country inn seems different from any other country inn. Here are some of the things, chosen at random, that make country inns special:

Gardens — formal English gardens with topiary bushes, "natural" gardens with wild flowers, vegetable and herb gardens, and everything in between . . .

Displays or use of local arts & crafts — paintings, sculpture, ceramics, baskets, handmade quilts and wallhangings . . .

Collections of artifacts & memorabilia - walking sticks, Revolutionary War firearms, antique pump organs, nickelodeons, ship models, African masks, Oriental tapestries, carved pipes, bells, and other objects from "the old country," farm tools . . .

Museum-quality collections - ancient documents and maps, antique china teapots, rare china, crystal, pewter, "Nanking Cargo" porcelain, Shaker pieces, clocks . . .

Historical references - pictures and books tracing the early history and development of a region, portraits on former owners, printed histories of the inns . . .

Amusing & interesting collections - antique dolls, shoes, & kaleidoscopes, folk art, samplers, hand-cut jigsaw puzzles, stuffed animals . . .

Community involvement - events such as 4th of July celebrations, blueberry or apple festivals, antique car meets, bike or foot races, pumpkin-carving contests, Easter egg hunts, and art shows . . .

Homage to poets - One inn has an Edna St. Vincent Millay Room, where the poet first recited one of her poems: another has many Scottish references, with poems, quotations, and portraits of Robert Burns and Walter Scott and other famous Scots . . .

Miscellaneous - Christmas festivities with huge, festooned trees and all sorts of entertainments and events sometimes including sleigh rides. A 1958 Bentley or a London taxicab for transporting guests to and from the airport . . . — **by Virginia Rowe**

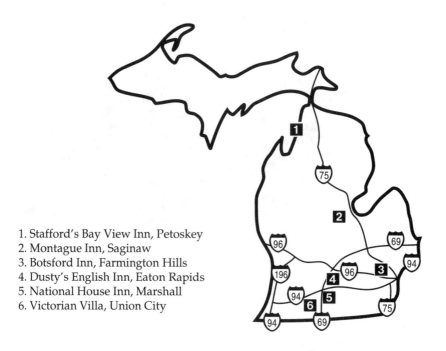

1. Stafford's Bay View Inn, Petoskey
2. Montague Inn, Saginaw
3. Botsford Inn, Farmington Hills
4. Dusty's English Inn, Eaton Rapids
5. National House Inn, Marshall
6. Victorian Villa, Union City

BOTSFORD INN

	65 Rooms, $45/$75 B&B 6 Suites, $100/$150 B&B
	Visa, MC, Amex, Diners,Discov
	All Private Baths
	Closed Dec. 25 & Jan. 1
	Children Welcome No Pets
R	Garden Courtyard, Tennis Courts, Kensington Park, YMCA, golf, XC & Downhill Skiing
	Breakfast Daily; Lunch & Dinner Served Tues.-Sun. Wine & Liquor available
	Non-smoking Dining areas
	Conference Facilities (125)
	Wheelchair Access (2 rooms)

3 Restored by Henry Ford in the 1920s, with many of his personal furnishings still intact, this inn was originally built in 1836 and later became a stagecoach stop. Spacious grounds, a rose garden, and towering trees invite the many birds seen through the floor-to-ceiling windows of the restaurant, where a hearty menu is offered. Victorian-style village shops are nearby.

I-94 (W) to I-275 (N). Exit M-102 &
continue to Grand River & 8-Mile Rd.
Inn is on L. with long picket fence.

TEL. 313-474-4800

**28000 Grand River Ave.,
Farmington Hills, MI
48336**

John Anhut, Innkeeper

DUSTY'S ENGLISH INN

 6 Rooms, $75/$125 B&B
1 Suite, $155/$195 B&B
1 Cottage, $125/$175 B&B

Visa, MC

All Private Baths

Open Year-round

2 Persons per room limit

No Pet facilities

Golf, Fishing, Canoeing, Hiking, Biking, XC-Skiing, Antiquing

Lunch, Dinner authentic English pub
Wine, Beer, Ales, Liquor

Smoke-free Inn

Conference Facilities (60)

Wheelchair Access (public rooms)

From I-96 in Lansing, take M-99 (S) 8 mi. From I-94, take M-99 (N) 22 mi.

TEL 517-663-2500
FAX 517-663-2639

728 S. Michigan Rd.
Eaton Rapids, MI 48827

Dusty Rhodes, Innkeeper

 A 1927 built Tudor-style riverside mansion on 15 acres. Rolling countryside with 2 miles of nature (xc-skiing in winter) trails along the Grand River and through woods. A 3 room suite and master bedroom are in the cottage complete with pool and fireplace sitting room. Six bedrooms in the inn find fireplaces, dining rooms, and walnut-paneled pub for pints of English ale or cocktails.

MONTAGUE INN

18 Rooms, $65/$150 B&B

Visa, MC, Amex

16 Private Baths
1 Shared Bath

Open Christmas Eve/Day, lodging only

Children Accepted
No Pets

Library, Lawn Games, Herb Garden, Formal Garden, Tennis, Antiquing

Breakfast; Lunch & Dinner Tues. to Sat.
Wine & Liquor available

No Smoking in guest rooms

Conference Facilities (40)

Wheelchiar Access (3 Rooms)

From I-75 exit on Holland Ave. (W) for 3.5 mi. Turn L. on Washington Ave., continue (S) 2 blocks to inn.

TEL. 517-752-3939

1581 S. Washington Ave.
Saginaw, MI 48601

Willy Schipper, Innkeeper

 This Georgian mansion, recently restored to its original splendor, is surrounded by eight acres of spacious lawns, flower gardens, and trees set beside a lake. The Montague Inn provides a peaceful and elegant oasis in the heart of the city. Fine cuisine is offered in the intimate dining room overlooking the beautiful grounds.

MICHIGAN

THE NATIONAL HOUSE INN

	16 Rooms, $67/$105 B&B 2 Suites, $112/$105 B&B
	Visa, MC, Amex
	All Private Baths
	Closed Dec. 25
	Children Welcome No Pets
R	Gift shop, Garden, Park, Tennis, Antiquing, XC Skiing
	Breakfast & Catered Dinners
	Area Smoking
	Conference facilities (36)

5 Marshall, a National Historic Landmark District and home of Win Schuler's restaurant, has many citations for its 850 structures of 19th-century architecture, including the National Register of Historic Places, on which this inn is also listed. Michigan's oldest operating inn, the first brick building in the county has been restored as a warm, hospitable inn, beautifully furnished, and lovely gardens.

I-94 to Exit 110; Rte. 27 (S) 2 mi. to Michigan Ave. Turn R. Marshall is halfway between Detroit & Chicago.

TEL. 616-781-7374

102 So. Parkview
Marshall, MI 49068

Barbara Bradley, Innkeeper

STAFFORD'S BAY VIEW INN

	34 Rooms, $71/132 B&B 6 Suites, $136/$180 B&B
	Visa, MC, Amex
	All Private Baths
	Open mid May-Oct. full time. Open Christmas Holiday Season & Jan.-March on weekends
	Children Welcome No Pets; Kennel nearby
R	Complimentary Croquet, Bikes. Hiking, XC Skiing, Beach, Golf, Tennis, Boating, Scenic Drives
	Breakfast, Lunch, Dinner, & Sun. Brunch in summer Sat. Dinner in winter
	Non Smoking Dining Rm. 16 Non-Smoking Rooms
	Conference Facilities (60)
	Wheelchair Access, most rooms

1 Judged one of the "Ten Best Inns" in the nation, the grande dame of classic Victorian architecture on Little Traverse Bay in the Historic Landmark Victorian cottage community of Bay View, sets the standard in fine dining and gracious service. Guests swim, sail the Great Lakes, rock on the front porch, cross-country ski out the front door, or enjoy the finest Alpine skiing in the Midwest.

From Detroit, I-75 (N) to Gaylord exit, Rte. 32 (W) to Rte. 131 (N) Petoskey. From Chicago, I-94 to Rte. I96 (N) to Rte. 131 (N) to Petoskey.

TEL. 616-347-2771

613 Woodland Ave.
P.O. Box 3
Petoskey, MI 49770

The Stafford Smith Family,
Innkeepers

THE VICTORIAN VILLA INN

 10 Rooms, $85/$125 B&B
MAP rates available

 Visa, MC, Discov, DC, Amex

 All Private Baths

 Open year-round

 Children Accepted
No Pets

 Antiquing, Hiking, Canoeing, Golf, Tandem Bicycles, Croquet, Fishing, Lawn Games

 Breakfast, Afternoon Tea, Dinner, Picnic baskets, Victorian theme Dinners

No Smoking

Conference Facilities (24)

Wheelchair Access (1 rm.)

From I-69, exit M-60 (Exit 25); 7 mi. (W) to Union City & left on Broadway St. (the Main St. of town). Continue to inn on No. Broadway.

TEL. 517-741-7383; 800-34-VILLA; FAX 517-741-4002
601 No. Broadway St.
Union City, MI 49094
Ron Gibson, Cynthia Coats, Emma Kimble, Innkeepers

6 A quiet and unhurried reflection of the 19th century in a quaint old river village, this romantic haven offers distinctively furnished rooms, delightful breakfasts, teas, picnic lunches, and special attention to guests. In addition to the many local attractions available, the inn features festive Victorian Xmas Weekends, Sherlock Holmes Mystery weekends and summer dinner theatre.

THE WONDERFUL WORLD OF COUNTRY INN COOKERY

Just as every country inn has its own individual style in furnishings and decoration, so, too, is its cuisine different and distinctive from every other inn. There are those who adhere to the principle that simple, wholesome, home-cooked, family-style meals, probably with a definite regional flavor, are the best. Others offer more sophisticated French, European, or even exotic ethnic cuisine choices. Nowhere will you find standardized hotel food.

The cook might be the innkeeper himself or herself, who also might be a graduate of the Cordon Bleu or the Culinary Institute of America—or just a naturally great cook. Some innkeepers are master chefs. Some inns hire well-known chefs, who give a special patina to their culinary presentations.

Dining rooms are usually arranged restaurant-style with small tables, but there are still a few places where meals are served family-style and guests sit together at a large table where everyone joins in the conversation. Sometimes meals are served on porches or terraces with lovely views, or in courtyards, patios, and gardens.

With the growing interest in wines, more inns are widening their selection and can boast extensive cellars of fine wines. Bed and breakfast inns often offer complimentary before-dinner wines and other refreshments, while some full-service inns follow the custom of having a get-acquainted cocktail hour before serving dinner.

Afternoon teas and Sunday brunches are opportunities to display all sorts of marvelous pastries and wonderful specialties and are usually served to the public as well as houseguests.

Vegetable and herb gardens are an integral part of a number of inns, which take great pride in the freshness and flavor of their produce. And nothing could be fresher for a guest than the fish he caught that afternoon and had cooked for his dinner that night - which is possible to do at a few inns.

(For a sampling of the kind of food you might find at a country inn, see page 73.)

— by Virginia Rowe

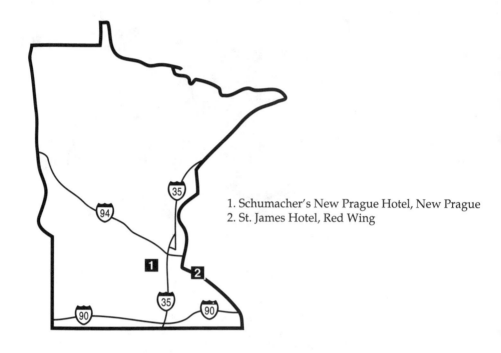

1. Schumacher's New Prague Hotel, New Prague
2. St. James Hotel, Red Wing

ST. JAMES HOTEL

60 rooms, $95/$145 EP

Visa, MC, Amex, Disc., Diners, Carte Blanche

All Private Baths, 6 Jacuzzis

Open year-round

Children accepted
No Pets

Shopping, Antiquing, Golf, Downhill & XC Skiing, River boat cruise

Breakfast, Lunch, Dinner; Sun. Brunch
Wine & Liquor available

19 Non-smoking Guest Rooms

Conference facilities (300)

Wheelchair access (100%)

2 Since 1875, a magnet for travelers to the scenic Mississippi River city of Red Wing. Nestled between limestone bluffs, this small, bustling hotel has been elegantly restored and outfitted. Impressive period furnishings, beautifully crafted quilts, genuine hospitality, and such special touches as complimentary champagne and turn-down service are a few of the pleasures you'll find.

From Minneapolis./St. Paul, take I-94E to US 61 S. To Red Wing.

TEl. 612-388-2846
800-252-1875

406 Main St.
Red Wing, MN 55066

Gene Foster,
General Manager

SCHUMACHER'S NEW PRAGUE HOTEL

 11 Rooms, $104/$150 EP

 Visa, MC, Amex, Discov

 All Private Baths
11 Whirlpool Tubs

 Closed Dec. 24 - 25

 No Pets

 18-hole Golf course, XC
Skiing, Biking, Fishing,
Casino

Breakfast, Lunch, Dinner
Wine, Beer & Liquor
available

No Pipes or Cigars

Conference Facilities (11)

From Mpls., 35W (S) to Exit 76 Elko, New Market (County Rd. 2), W, turn R for 10 mi. At Hwy 13, turn L, S, follow 13 2 mi., merges w/Hwy 19 W, follow 2 Hwys into New Prague. Hotel is on left hand side past center of New Prague.

TEL. 612-758-2133
FAX (612) 758-2400

212 W. Main St.
New Prague, MN 56071

Kathleen & John
Schumacher, Innkeepers

 Named one of the "Ten Best Inns" and "National Pork Restaurant" 1992, this charming Central European Inn is internationally known for its superb Czech and German cuisine by Chef/Proprietor John Schumacher. Bavarian folk painted furniture, eiderdown comforters, whirlpool tubs, gas fireplaces, Bavarian bar, and European gift shop add to the uniqueness of this inn.

Rates are quoted for 2 people for 1 night and do not necessarily include service charges and state taxes. An asterisk after the rates indicates a per-person rate for AP and MAP plans. For more detailed information, ask the inns for their brochures.

AP — American Plan (3 meals included in room rate)

MAP — Modified American Plan (breakfast & dinner included in room rate)

EP — European Plan (meals not included in room rate)

B&B — Bed & Breakfast (breakfast included in room rate)

 — Represents recreational facilities and diversions either on the premises of an inn or nearby

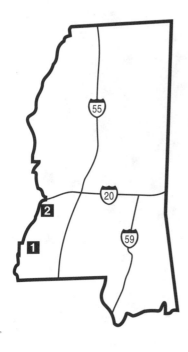

1. The Burn, Natchez
2. The Duff Green Mansion, Vicksburg

THE BURN

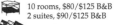 10 rooms, $80/$125 B&B
2 suites, $90/$125 B&B

 Visa, MC, Amex, Diners

All Private baths

Open Year-round

 School-age Children
No Pets

 Swimming pool, Golf and
Tennis nearby

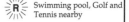 Plantation Breakfast;
special Dinners, Lunches,
Picnics for groups of 20+
Wine & Liquor available

 Conference Facilities (50)

 Wheelchair Access (2
rooms)

1 The Burn, built in 1834 by John Walworth, is the oldest documented, purely Greek Revivial residence in Natchez and is especially noted for its semi-spiral staircase, unique gardens and exquisite collection of priceless antiques. Southern hospitality reigns with a seated plantation breakfast and a private tour of the home.

From I-55 at McComb, MS, exit to Hwy. 98 (Natchez). Meadville to Hwy. 98/84 to end & Hwy. 61 at Washington. Turn L. (W) to Natchez. R. onto No. Union to inn on L.

Tel. 601-442-1344
800-654-8859
FAX 601-445-0606
712 No. Union St.
Natchez, MS 39120
Loveta Byrne, Innkeeper

THE DUFF GREEN MANSION

4 Rooms, $75/$100 B&B
3 Suites, $95/$150 B&B

8% Sales Tax

Visa, MC, Amex

Private Baths

Open Year-round

Children Welcome
Small Pets Accepted

Swimming pool on grounds; Golf, Tennis, Fishing, Hunting nearby; many Historic Sites within walking distance

Plantation Breakfast Refreshments, Cocktails Available

Smoking in designated areas

Conference Facilities (100)

Wheelchair Access (4 rms)

From I-20 Exit 4B to Clay St. Turn R. on Adams to First East St. Continue to inn.

TEL. 601-636-6968; 638-6662; 800-992-0037; FAX 601-634-1061
1114 First East St.,
Vicksburg, MS 39180
Harry & Alicia Sharp,
Innkeepers

2 One of the finest examples of Palladian architecture in the state (National Register of Historic Places), this 1856 mansion was pressed into service as a hospital for Confederate, and later Union, soldiers during the famous siege of Vicksburg. The 12,000-sq.-foot mansion in the historic Old Town was restored in 1985 and is luxuriously furnished in period antiques and reproductions.

Country Inn Food Sampler

Colonial corn and mussel chowder, cured salmon, rabbit in puff pastry, half duckling in apple and peppercorn sauce, baked grapefruit with a sautéed chicken liver, romaine soup, local fish baked in wine, leg of lamb with fresh rosemary, lobster pie, double-thick lamb chops, baked ham with peach glaze.

Homemade Georgia crackers with fresh fruit salad, Louisiana chicken with artichoke hearts and almonds, roast duckling with orange-cranberry sauce, sautéed mountain trout, vegetable strudel, steak and kidney pie, roast squab with fresh peaches, veal with pomegranate wine, crayfish fritters.

Carolina quail with savory cabbage, fillet of beef on fried eggplant, tomato cups with fresh corn, low country squash pie, local channel bass in puff pastry, smoked ham, grits, and cornbread, stuffed pork chops, Midwestern fish boils, cooked outside in huge iron cauldrons over a roaring fire and served with coleslaw, fresh-baked bread and cherry pie.

Desserts might be fudge walnut cake, pistachio cake, pecan pie, hot gingerbread with lemon sauce, triple mousse cake with whipped cream, deep dish apple pie, fruit cobbler, Indian pudding, sour cream apple pie, fresh figs filled with white chocolate mousse, homemade angel food cake with strawberries and whipped cream.

Some breakfast possibilities: Crepes Suzette, blueberry pancakes, herbed eggs with cheese and mushrooms, fresh fruit, sausage or ham biscuits, German apple pancakes, eggs Benedict, French toast with strawberries and whipped cream, cheddar egg bake with Dijon mustard and broccoli, fresh-baked muffins with quince jelly, poached pear in caramel sauce, kiwi with pureed raspberries. **— by Virginia Rowe**

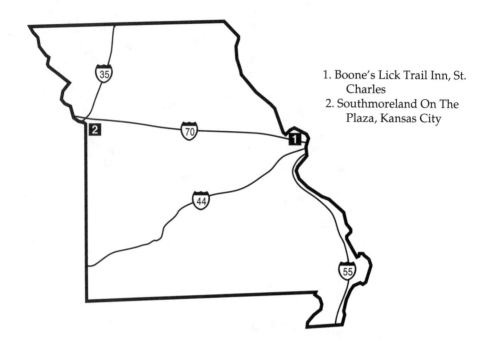

1. Boone's Lick Trail Inn, St. Charles
2. Southmoreland On The Plaza, Kansas City

BOONE'S LICK TRAIL INN

	4 Rooms, $65/$95 B&B 1 Suite, $85/$125 B&B
	Visa, MC, Amex, Discov, Diners (Govt.)
	All Private Baths
	Open Year-round
	Children Accepted; No Pets; Kennels nearby
R	Historic District, Antiquing, Dining, Goldernrod Showboat, Riverboat Casino, Biking/Hiking, State Park
	Full Breakfast; Lunches for Hikers/Bikers on request
	No Smoking
	Conference Facilities (10-16)
	Wheelchair Access Limited (2 Rooms)

1 It was THE highway west, predating the Santa Fe & Oregon Trails. They called it the Boone's Lick Trail. In the 1840's, a Federal style building, reflecting pioneer strength, rose at its side. Surrounded by roses, standing near "the wide Missouri," warmed by Midwestern hospitality. In the state's largest Historic District, guests sense trailblazers: Boone, Lewis, Clark, Pike, Sutter.

I-70 to exit 229 St. Charles Fifth St., (N) 3 blocks to Boonslick Rd. R. 4 blocks to Main St. Inn on SE corner of Main & Boonslick

TEL. (314) 947-7000
800-366-2427 (9-5 CST)

1000 South Main St.
St. Charles, MO 63301

V'Anne and Paul Mydler,
Innkeepers

SOUTHMORELAND ON THE PLAZA

12 Rooms $100/$135 B&B

Visa, MC, Amex

All Private Baths

Closed Christmas Eve & Christmas Day

Children over 13
No Pets

Nelson-Atkins Museum of Art, Country Club Plaza, Dining & Shopping, Theatre, Dinner Playhouse, Tennis, Swimming, Royals Baseball, Chiefs Football, Crown Center, Historic Westport & River Market

Breakfast, Wine & Hors d'oeuvres nightly

Smoking areas designated

Conference Facilities; A-V Equipment Available (14)

Wheelchair Accessible First Floor

From I-70, I-35, I-29 in downtown Kansas City, Missouri, take the Main Street exit S. several miles to E 46th St., turn E (L), go 1 1/2 blocks to the Inn on the left.

TEL. (816) 531-7979
FAX (816) 531-2407
116 E. 46th St.
Kansas City, MO 64112
Susan Moehl &
Penni Johnson, Innkeepers

2 Southmoreland's 1913 Colonial Revival styling brings New England to the heart of Kansas City's Historic, Arts, Entertainment and Shopping district — The Country Club Plaza. Business and leisure guests enjoy individually decorated rooms of this award winning Inn. Many offer decks, fireplaces or Jacuzzis. Sports and dining privileges are available at a nearby historic, private club.

A SHORT HISTORY OF THE AMERICAN COUNTRY INN

Often a hotbed of political activity, where plots were hatched and plans were made, American inns in Colonial days were more than simply hostelries providing bed and board. Along with the church and the New England town meeting, the American inn ranks as one of the oldest continuing institutions in our country. In the 17th century some communities were required by law to provide accommodations and provender for travelers. They were called variously taverns or inns or ordinaries. The center of village activity, those early inns sometimes served as churches, gaols, courtrooms, political campaign headquarters, theaters, runaway slave stations, smuggler's hideaways, and even bordellos and mortuaries. In the seaport cities of the South, Spanish Main pirates had their favorite tavern haunts with secret tunnels, through which unwilling sailors could be shanghaied onto waiting ships.

During the Revolution, inns served as way stations between military posts, storing arms and ammunition and passing along intelligence on the movements of British troops. General Washington's New York headquarters were in the now-famous Fraunces Tavern.

As roads began to thread the colonies, stagecoach stops sprang up, and with westward expansion, the tradition of finding food and refuge in ranches and cabins on the prairie and in the mountains later turned many a farm and ranch into an inn.

Railroads made the stagecoach obsolete and often the once-bustling towns and inns on the stagecoach routes became irrelevant and sank into oblivion. Other towns grew up beside the railroads, and "commercial travelers" patronized the new "commercial hotels." Trains carried families to the mountains, seashore, and mineral springs resorts for summer vacations. Tremendous hotels with huge staffs became a significant part of the American vacation scene and remained popular destinations for 75 years. Lodgings included 3 meals daily, hence the term "American Plan.' — **by Virginia Rowe**

1. Chesterfield Inn, West Chesterfield
2. Birchwood Inn, Temple
3. John Hancock Inn, Hancock
4. Inn at Crotched Mountain, Francestown
5. Dexter's Inn and Tennis Club, Sunapee
6. Moose Mountain Lodge, Etna
7. Lyme Inn, Lyme
8. Hickory Stick Farm, Belmont
9. Corner House Inn, Center Sandwich
10. Stafford's in the Field, Chocorua
11. Darby Field Inn, Conway
12. Christmas Farm Inn, Jackson
13. Philbrook Farm Inn, Shelburne

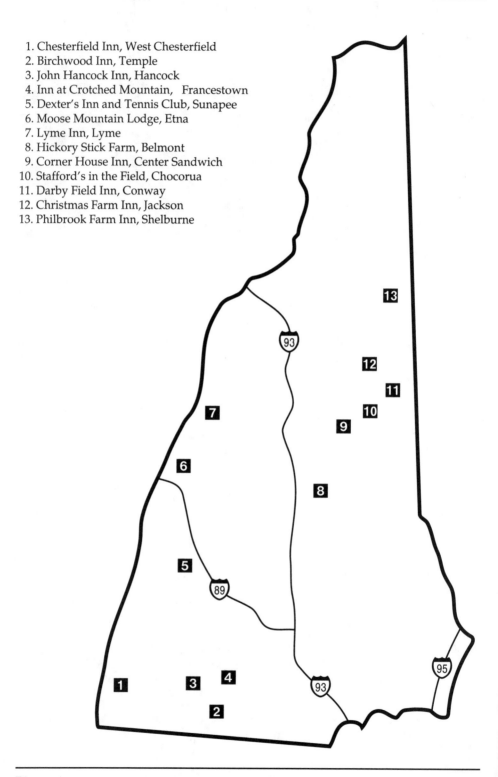

BIRCHWOOD INN

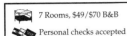

7 Rooms, $49/$70 B&B

Personal checks accepted

Private & shared Baths

Closed 2 wks. in April;
1 wk. in Nov.

Appropriate for
Children over 10
No Pets

Hiking, Antiquing,
Skiing, Golf, Swimming

Breakfast
Dinner Tues. - Sat.
BYOB

No Pipes or Cigars

Temple is on Rte. 45, 1.5 mi. (S) of Rte. 101, 10 min. (E) of Peterborough.

TEL. 603-878-3285

Route 45, Box 197
Temple, NH 03084

Judy & Bill Wolfe,
Innkeepers

2 Rufus Porter murals grace the small candlelit dining room of this family-run, original inn, resting by the common of a quiet Colonial town. On the National Register of Historic Places, the inn features guest and common rooms filled with interesting antiques and country dining with fresh foods prepared to order and carefully presented by the innkeepers.

CHESTERFIELD INN

11 Rooms, $99/$159 B&B
2 Suites, $159/$169 B&B
Visa, MC, Amex, Discov,
Diners
All Private Baths

Open Year-round

Children & Pets Welcome

Arts, Crafts, Music in
Keene & Brattleboro.
Swimming & Boating on
Spofford Lake

Breakfast; Dinner Tues.
thru Sat.; Foliage Season,
7 days; Wine & Liquor
available

Conference Facilities (20)

From I-91, take Exit 3 to Rte. 9 (E). Continue on Rte. 9 for 2 mi. to inn on L.

TEL. 800-365-5515

Route 9
West Chesterfield, NH 03466

Judy & Phil Hueber,
Innkeepers

1 Serving since 1787 as a tavern, a farm, and a museum, the inn's guest rooms today are spacious; some with fireplaces, or outdoor balconies, all with private baths, air conditioning, TV & telephone. Outside, the meadow overlooks Vermont's Green Mountains. Guests enjoy the cuisine of chef Carl Warner and enter the dining room through the kitchen to observe his magic in action.

CHRISTMAS FARM INN

🛏	20 rooms, $136/$150 MAP 10 suites, $170/$180 MAP
💳	Visa, MC, Amex
🛁	All Private Baths, 5 Jacuzzis
🕯	Open Year-round
🐕	Children Accepted No Pets
☀R	Swimming Pool, Putting Green, Game Room, Shuffleboard, XC & Down-hill Skiing, Golf, Tennis
🍽	Breakfast & Dinner Wine & Liquor available
🚭	Non-Smoking Main Dining Room
⊢🗤⊣	Conference Facilities (50)
♿	

12 In a setting of majestic mountains, crystal-clear rivers and leafy woods, the cluster of buildings that make up this rambling inn invite you to share the good life. Whether inside in cozily decorated rooms, outside at the garden swimming pool, or in the candlelit dining room feasting on delectable, fresh meals, guests enjoy the at-home feeling.

From Rte. 16 to Rte. 16A across covered bridge .5 mi. to schoolhouse. L. on Rte. 16B for .5 mi. to inn on R.

TEL. 603-383-4313
800-HI-ELVES

Box CC, Route 16B
Jackson, NH 03846

Will Zeliff, Innkeeper

CORNER HOUSE INN

🛏	4 rooms, $60/$70 B&B
💳	Visa, MC, Amex
🛁	1 Private, 1 Shared Bath
🕯	Closed Thanksgiving, Dec. 25
🐕	Children over 4 Well-behaved Pets allowed
☀R	Crafts & Antiques Shops, Museum, Art Gallery, Squam Lake, Tennis, Hiking, Skiing
🍽	Breakfast, Lunch, Dinner Wine & Liquor available
🚬	Smoking discouraged
⊢🗤⊣	Conference Facilities (70)
♿	

9 The picturesque village of Center Sandwich and the surrounding area, with "Golden Pond" (Squam Lake) and mountain trails, offer delightful diversions in any season. And a warm welcome awaits at the intimate 100-year-old Corner House, sparkling with country-Victorian antiques and beautiful crafts made by many local artisans and craftspeople. Food is special and fresh.

I-93, Exit 23 & Rt. 104 (E) to Meredith. R. at light on Rt. 25 (E) to Center Harbor. L. at 2nd light to Bean Rd. for 7 mi. to blinker. R. onto Main St. to inn.

TEL. 603-284-6219
800-832-STAY (7829)
Main St., P.O. Box 204
Ctr. Sandwich, NH 03227
Jane & Don Brown,
Innkeepers

THE DARBY FIELD INN

15 Rooms, $110/$180 MAP
1 Suite, $220/$280 MAP (4)

Visa, MC, Amex

14 Private, 1 Shared Bath

Open Year-round

Children Accepted
No Pets

Swimming pool, XC ski trails, Canoeing, Golf, Tennis, Hiking, Rock climbing

Breakfast & Dinner

Wine & Liquor available

Smoking Restricted

Rte. 16 (N) toward Conway. Turn L. .5 mi. before Conway at inn sign. 1 mi. to 2nd inn sign. Turn R. & continue 1 mi. to inn.

TEL. 800-426-4147
603-447-2181
P.O. Box D, Bald Hill
Conway, NH 03818
Marc & Maria Donaldson, Innkeepers

11 Beguiling guests with a spectacular view of distant mountains from its dining room, many guest rooms, and terrace swimming pool, this 1830 inn on the edge of the White Mountain National Forest is a favorite with outdoor enthusiasts. Well-groomed ski and hiking trails past rivers and waterfalls, a cozy pub, a massive stone fireplace, and hearty, delicious food are part of the picture.

DEXTER'S INN & TENNIS CLUB

17 Rooms, $130/$170 MAP
1 Cottage, $187.50 MAP

Visa, MC, Discover

All Private Baths

Closed Nov. 1 to May 1

Children Accepted
Pets Accepted

3 Tennis Courts, Pool, Lawn Games, Lake activities, Hiking, Golf

Breakfast, Dinner

Wine & Liquor available

Non-smoking Dining area

Conference Facilities (25)

I-89 (N), Exit 12 & Rte. 11 (W) for 5.5 mi. to L. on Winn Hill Rd. for 1.5 mi. From I-91 (N), Exit 8 & Rte. 11/103 (E) for 18 mi. to Newport & Rte. 103 for .1 mi. to L. on Young Hill Rd. for 1.2 mi.

TEL. 800-232-5571
603-763-5571
Box 703IIA, Stagecoach Rd.,
Sunapee, NH 03782
Michael Durfor & Holly Simpson-Durfor, Innkeepers

5 Tennis buffs love Dexter's, but so do all the guests who come for the breathtaking views, idyllic gardens, green lawns, bright guest rooms and excellent, bountiful food. The Simpson-Durfor family runs the inn like a well-appointed private home, offering friendly service and advice on the myriad diversions available in the area.

HICKORY STICK FARM

🛏	2 Rooms, $70 B&B
💳	Visa, MC, Amex, Discov.
🛁	All Private Baths
🏮	Closed Mon.; Restaurant winter hours restricted
👫	Appropriate for Children over 7; No Pets
R	Hiking, Nature trails, Birdwatching, Swimming, Boating, Skiing, Shaker Village
🍽	Breakfast (guests only) & Dinner by reservation Wine & Liquor available
🚭	Smoking Restricted
ⱵⱵⱵ	Conference Facilities (25)
♿	

8 Since 1950 the Roeder family has been serving thoughtful meals in the delightful Early American atmosphere of their converted Colonial farm buildings near Laconia. Two charming B&B guest rooms have been added as well as a screened gazebo with splendid mountain view. The trip over winding roads and quiet woods is part of the fun.

I-93, Exit 20 & Rte. 3 toward Laconia, approx. 5 mi. over Lake Winnisquam bridge .3 mi. to R. on Union Rd. for 1.5 mi. & L. on Bean Hill Rd. for .5 mi. to inn.

TEL. 603-524-3333

60 Bean Hill Road
Belmont, NH 03220

Scott & Linda Roeder,
Innkeepers

INN AT CROTCHED MOUNTAIN

🛏	13 Rooms, $100/$120 MAP
💳	No Credit Cards
🛁	Private & Shared Baths
🏮	Closed end of ski season to mid-May; late Oct. to Thanksgiving
🐕	Children Accepted Pets Accepted
R	Swimming pool, Tennis courts, XC and walking trails, Downhill Skiing, Ice Skating, Antique shops, Summer Theaters
🍽	Breakfast, Dinner Wine & Liquor available
🚬	Cigars or Pipes restricted
ⱵⱵⱵ	Conference Facilities (26)
♿	Wheelchair Access (4 Rooms)

4 An awe-inspiring setting and a spectacular view of Piscataquog Valley makes all the difference at this out-of-the-way Colonial inn. Walking and ski trails thread the woods; vegetable and flower gardens supply food and adornment for tables and rooms. Rose Perry's savory home cooking has the added zest of an occasional Indonesian dish.

From Manchester, Rte. 101 (W) to 114 (N) to Goffstown & 13 (S) to New Boston & 136 (W) to Francestown. R. at 47 (N) 2.5 mi. to L. on Mountain Rd. for 1 mi. to inn.

TEL. 603-588-6840
Mountain Rd.
Francestown, NH 03043

Rose & John Perry,
Innkeepers

THE JOHN HANCOCK INN

 11 rooms, $85/$105 B&B

 Visa, MC

 All Private Baths

 Open Year-round

 Appropriate for Children over 12
No Pets

 Historic Touring, Walking, Antiquing, Summer Theater, Year-round Sports

Breakfast, Dinner, Wine & Liquor available

No Smoking

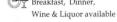 Conference Facilities (35)

Ramp for Access

From Keene, Rte. 9 (N) to Rte. 123 (E) to Hancock. From Peterborough, Rte. 202 (N) to L. on Rte. 123 to Hancock.

TEL. 603-525-3318
Outside N.H. **800-525-1789**
FAX 603-525-9301
Main Street
Hancock, NH 03449
Linda & Joe Johnston, Innkeepers

3 This is the oldest inn in continuous operation in New Hampshire, set in one of New England's most beautifully preserved villages. Dine on such regional specialties as Shaker Cranberry Pot Roast and Indian Pudding, walk the old drover's cow paths through tree lined streets to Norway Pond and sleep in four poster comfort while lulled to sleep by the Paul Revere church bell.

THE LYME INN

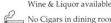 12 Rooms, $75/$105 B&B
2 Suites, $75/$105 B&B

 Visa, MC, Amex

 12 Private, 1 Shared Baths

 Closed Sun. after Thanksgiving to late Dec.; 2 wks. late Spring.

Appropriate for Children over 7, No Pets

Dartmouth College, Skiing, Swimming, Golf, Tennis, Canoeing

Breakfast & Dinner; Wine & Liquor available

No Cigars in dining room

I-91, Exit 14. Follow signs for Lyme. Inn is in center of town on the common.

TEL. 603-795-2222

On the Common
Lyme, NH 03768

Fred & Judy Siemons, Innkeepers

7 A treasure-trove of New England memorabilia and antiques, braided rugs, a collection of samplers and other folk art, and an engaging old-world atmosphere, the Lyme Inn is not far from Dartmouth College. Master chef Hans Wickert offers an interesting mix of continental & New England cuisine, and innkeepers Fred and Judy Siemons tender warm New England hospitality.

MOOSE MOUNTAIN LODGE

	12 rooms,$156/$166 MAP
	Visa, MC
	5 Shared Baths
	Closed Mar. 21-May 31; Oct. 20 to Dec. 26
	Appropriate for Children over 5; No Pets
R	Hiking & Skiing Trails, Swimming Pond, Large Porch, Appalachian Trail, Connecticut River
	Breakfast, Lunch & Dinner in winter; Breakfast & Dinner summer & fall
	No Smoking

6 Perched high on the side of Moose Mountain, with hiking and ski trails threading through 350 acres of woods and meadows, this big, old, comfortable lodge enjoys ever-changing views of the Connecticut River Valley. Meals are healthy, plentiful and delicious, beds are restful and the welcome is warm and friendly. Far from the sounds of civilization, peace and quiet reigns supreme.

I-89, Exit 18 (N) to Rte. 120 for 0.5 mi. to R. at Etna Rd. for 3.6 mi. to R. on Rudsboro Rd. for 2 mi. to L. on Dana Rd. for 0.4 mi. up mtn. to lodge.

TEL. 603-643-3529
Moose Mountain Rd.,
P.O.Box 272,
Etna, NH 03750
Peter & Kay Shumway,
Innkeepers

PHILBROOK FARM INN

	19 Rooms, $97/$126 MAP $100/130 MAP (beg. 7/93)
	4 Cottages $450/week No Credit Cards
	Private & Shared Baths
	Closed April 1 to May 1; Nov. 1 to Dec. 25
	Children Welcome Pets Accepted in Cottages
R	Swimming pool, Game room, Major Ski areas, Nat'l. forest Hiking, Golf
	Full Breakfast, Dining Room Lunches by Reservation, Trail Lunches to order, Dinner; B&B rates avail. BYOB
	Wheelchair Access (1 room)

13 The latchstring has been out at this venerable (National Register of Historic Places) inn since 1861 and 5 generations of the Philbrook family have been dispensing New England hospitality and wholesome, hearty, home-cooked New England meals ever since. As they say, "you will find simplicity rather than luxury, genuineness rather than pretension" at this peaceful retreat.

U.S. Rte. 2 (W—20 mi.) from Bethel, ME. or (E—6 mi.) from Gorham, NH. At inn sign turn on Meadow Rd. for 1 mi. to R. at North Rd. for .5 mi. to inn.

TEL. 603-466-3831

881 North Rd.
Shelburne, NH 03581

The Philbrook & Leger
Families, Innkeepers

STAFFORDS-IN-THE-FIELD

12 Rooms, $70/$140 B&B
4 Cotts, $100/$180 B&B

Visa, MC, Amex

9 Private, 3 Shared Baths

Open Year-round

Inquire Regarding Children
No Pets; Kennel Nearby

Walking Trails, Tennis, Croquet, XC Skiing, Golf, Swimming, Climbing, Antiques

breakfast & dinner
wine & liquor available

No Smoking in Dining Room

wheelchair access (2 rooms)

From Chocorua Village & Rte. 16, take Rte. 113 (W) 1 mi. to inn sign. From Rte. 93, Exit 23 to Rtes. 104 & 25 (E) to Rte. 16 (N) to village & Rte. 113 as above.

TEL. 603-323-7766
800-446-1112
Box 270
Chocorua, NH 03817
The Stafford Family,
Innkeepers

10 This circa 1778 Federalist country house has welcomed guests for nearly a century. Amidst rolling fields, surrounded by forests with trails. The inn's herb garden flavors the scrumptious gourmet meals served in the lantern-lit dining room. Rooms are furnished with country antiques and down quilts, and there is a wonderful porch for sitting and viewing the beauty of old New England.

WHO ARE THE INNKEEPERS?

Innkeepers who can lay claim to being the third or fourth generation of an innkeeping family are a rare breed, indeed. They have had the advantage of growing up in an inn and becoming thoroughly conversant and comfortable with the intricacies of innkeeping. There are only a very few of these younger innkeepers who are able to draw on a wealth of past experience.

Since the mid-1970s, more and more people have followed their dream of owning a lovely country inn, enjoying a slower-paced lifestyle and the opportunity to be creative and independent far away from urban pressures and the "fast track."

This dream has brought into the world of innkeeping such diverse types as advertising executives, bankers, school teachers, airline stewardesses, management consultants, engineers, interior decorators, social workers, architects, political speech writers, and many others who have left successful careers.

Some innkeepers came out of training in large hotel chains, many are graduates of hotel management schools and culinary institutes. A few are master chefs.

As is so often the case, the reality does not live up to the dream in all respects. Innkeeping is a hard taskmaster — the hours are long, the demands on time, energy, patience, perseverance, humor, and cash are great. However, the rewards, too, are great. There is the pride of accomplishment in creating an independent way of life, and in seeing the results of hard work, ingenuity, and creativity paying off.

Beyond the satisfaction of operating a successful inn is the sense of the personal pleasure in knowing that guests truly enjoy themselves and appreciate the atmosphere of the inn.

Innkeepers sometimes develop long-standing friendships with guests who return for visits over many years. In fact, just as there are a few third-and fourth-generation innkeepers, so there are a few third and fourth-generation guests. This is more likely to happen at resort-type inns, where families spend their vacations year after year.

Innkeepers or their assistants have many kinds of personal interactions with guests, sometimes sharing a recipe for a particularly favored dish, tracking down a baby sitter or the location of some esoteric antiques dealer, finding lost eyeglasses, mapping out a scenic drive, verifying a quotation in a book, recommending a doctor, a mechanic, a jeweler, or.....Making reservations at restaurants, reserving tickets for concerts and the theater, and calling taxis are among the more usual services in metropolitan areas.

This is just a glimpse at the kind of dedicated, intelligent and friendly people who are keepers of country inns. — **by Virginia Rowe**

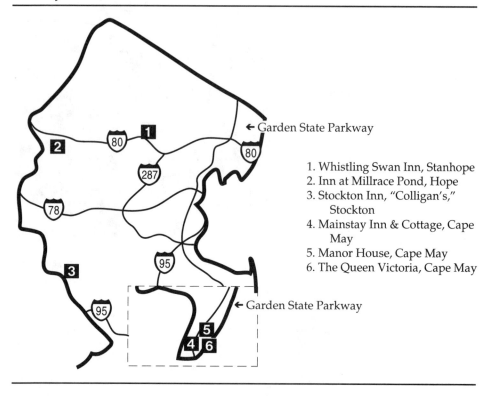

1. Whistling Swan Inn, Stanhope
2. Inn at Millrace Pond, Hope
3. Stockton Inn, "Colligan's," Stockton
4. Mainstay Inn & Cottage, Cape May
5. Manor House, Cape May
6. The Queen Victoria, Cape May

THE INN AT MILLRACE POND

	17 Rooms, $85/$130 B&B Corp. Rate Sun.– Thurs.
	Visa, MC, Amex
	All Private Baths
	Open Year-round Dining Room Closed for Dinner Christmas Day
	Children Accepted (limited); No Pets
	Tennis, Antiquing, Hiking, Fishing, Canoeing, Skiing, Golf, Bicycling, Winery tours, Waterloo Village.
	Breakfast; Dinner daily Sunday Lunch or Dinner served Noon- 8:00 p.m.. Wine & Liquor available
	Smoking in designated Rooms and areas
	Conference Facilities (30)
	Wheelchair Access (restaurant)

2 The 1769 gristmill in the historic village of Hope has been converted into a lovely inn, with additional rooms in the Millrace House and the stone Wheelwright's Cottage. In a green and peaceful setting along Beaver Brook, this authentically restored and furnished Colonial inn, offers a seasonal American menu and gracious service in the tradition of Colonial hospitality.

From I-80, Exit 12, take Rte. 521 (S) 1 mi. to 4-way stop., L. on Rte. 519 (N), .2 mi. to inn. From the south, Rte. 78 to Rte. 22 to Rte. 519 (N), travel 18 mi., take R. at blinker/4-way .2 mi. to inn.

TEL. 908-459-4884

Rte. 519, P.O. Box 359

Hope, NJ 07844

Dick Gooding & Gloria Carrigan, Innkeepers

MAINSTAY INN & COTTAGE

 9 rooms, $95/$165 B&B
3 suites, $105/$175 B&B

 No Credit Cards

 All Private Baths

 Closed mid-Dec. to mid-March

 Appropriate for children over 12; No Pets

 Croquet, Swimming, Tennis, Golf, Biking, Birdwatching, Historic attractions

 Breakfast, Afternoon Tea

No Smoking

 Conference facilities (24)

Take Garden State Pkwy. (S). In Cape May, Pkwy. becomes Lafayette St. Take L. at first light onto Madison Ave. Go 3 blocks, R. at Columbia Ave. Inn on R.

TEL. 609-884-8690

635 Columbia Ave.
Cape May, NJ 08204

Tom & Sue Carroll,
Innkeepers

 Once an exclusive gambling club, the Mainstay is now an elegant Victorian inn furnished in splendid antiques. Breakfast and afternoon tea are served each day either in the formal dining room or on the wide veranda. Located in Cape May's famous historic district, the inn is within walking distance of beaches, interesting shops and a vast selection of fine restaurants.

MANOR HOUSE

 8 Rooms, $65/$140 B&B
1 Suite, $95/$155 B&B

 Visa, MC

7 Private, 1 Shared Bath

 Closed Jan.

 Appropriate for Children over 12; Unable to Accommodate Pets

 Ocean swimming, Beach walking, Porch sitting, Birding, Golf, Historic Homes Tours

 Breakfast, Afternoon Tea

 Smoking on porch

Conference Facilities (12)

From zero-mi. mark on Garden State Pkwy. to Rte. 109 South becoming Lafayette St., turn L. on Franklin for 2 blks. to R. on Hughes for 1 1/2 blks. to inn on L.

TEL. 609-884-4710

612 Hughes St.
Cape May, NJ 08204-2318

Tom & Mary Snyder,
Innkeepers

 On a tree-lined residential street in the heart of the historic district, Manor House offers guests an exceptionally clean and unpretentiously comfortable starting point for relaxation, reading or roaming the beaches and streets of Cape May. Mary's made-from-scratch breakfasts and Tom's hospitality give the inn its reputation for fine food and its character.

85

THE QUEEN VICTORIA

🛏	17 Rooms, $85/$170 B&B 6 Suites, $125/210 B&B
💳	Visa, MC
🛁	All Private Baths
🏡	Open Year-round
🐕	Children Accepted No Pets
☀R	Ocean swimming, Historic tours, Birding, Shopping, Dining, Biking (free inn bikes), Tennis, Golf, Fishing
🍽	Full Breakfast, Afternoon Tea B.Y.O.B.
🚭	No Smoking Inside
Conference	Conference Facilities for 10-20
♿	Wheelchair Access (1 suite)

6 Three restored Victorian homes welcome you to The Queen Victoria. Fifty rocking chairs await you on porches, patios and sun decks. Colorful gardens in summer, and festive holiday decoration in winter add to your pleasure. Full buffet breakfast and afternoon tea will fortify you for a ride on the inn's bicycles, touring the historic district, nature walks or shopping nearby.

TEL. 609-884-8702

102 Ocean St.
Cape May, NJ 08204

Joan & Dane Wells,
Innkeepers

THE STOCKTON INN, "COLLIGAN'S"

🛏	3 rooms, $60/$85 B&B 8 suites, $90/$145 B&B
💳	Visa, MC, Amex, Discov
🛁	All Private Baths
🏡	Closed Dec. 25
🐕	Children limited No Pets
☀R	Canoeing, Rafting, Tubing, Ballooning, Fishing, Hiking, Riding, Antiquing
🍽	Lunch, Dinner, Sun. brunch
	Wine, Liquor & Beer available
Conference	Conference Facilities (60)
♿	

3 This inn, built in 1710 and serving travelers since 1796, has a colorful history and colorful guests, including Rodgers and Hart, who were inspired to write the song, "There's a Small Hotel With a Wishing Well." Complementing beautiful suites in the main inn and 3 outbuildings is the American-Continental cuisine, served in fireplace-warmed dining rooms or, in season, in the gardens.

N.J. Rte. 202 to N.J. Rte. 29 (River Rd.) 3 mi. (N) to Stockton. Inn is in center of town on Main St. (Across the river from New Hope, PA.)

TEL. 609-397-1250

Main St., P.O.Box C
Stockton, NJ 08559

Andrew McDermott,
Innkeeper

WHISTLING SWAN INN

9 Rooms, $75/$85 B&B
1 Suite, $95 B&B

Visa, MC, Amex, Discov

All Private Baths

Open Year-round

Children over 12 are
Welcome; No Pets Please

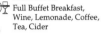

Near Waterloo Village,
Wineries, Antiquing, Winter Sports, State forests,
Shopping, Fairs, Shows,
Flea Markets

Full Buffet Breakfast,
Wine, Lemonade, Coffee,
Tea, Cider

No Smoking

Conference (10-12)

Bus & Train via N.J. Transit to
Netcong/Stahope. Exit 27 off I-80 via
route 183/206 one mile to Hess gasoline station. Turn on Main St. across
from Hess.

TEL 201-347-6369

110 Main St.
Stanhope, NJ 07878

Joe Mulay and Paula
Williams , Innkeepers

 Nestled in northwestern New Jersey's Skylands Tourism region only 45 miles west of New York City, this 1905 Victorian home has been converted to a B&B and renovated in two major segments of time. Each room has a private bath, queen size bed and period furnishings. Much of what is in the house is from Paula's grandmother's home in Oklahoma.

Matters Of Some Moment

Significant to the architectural heritage of our country, to communities, and to the public in general, is the reclamation of many historic and beautiful old buildings that have been brought back to life as country inns. Many of them are now listed on the National Register of Historic Places.

It was a slow process at first but, as interest in country inns grew, many wonderful things began to happen. For example, some of the inns of the 18th and 19th centuries that had been converted to other uses came back into their own. False ceilings were ripped away to find beautiful, heavy beams. Walls were removed to disclose handsome fireplaces. Layers of wallpaper were carefully peeled away to reveal beautiful 18th-century stenciling. Several inns in New England were discovered to have on their walls in remarkably preserved condition, the works of the famous itinerant artists, Rufus Porter and Moses Eaton. Porter was known for his murals and Eaton for his stencils.

Other valuable materials which have been (and are still being) saved and preserved are carved marble mantelpieces, beautiful glazed tiles, pressed tin ceilings, stained-glass windows, intricately carved moldings and balustrades, and various kinds of inlaid woods. Numerous previously lost or forgotten arts and crafts of construction and interior decoration have been recovered in the process.

Many buildings were saved from being torn down literally in the nick of time. In addition to the reclamation of former inns, buildings of all descriptions and former uses have been pressed into service. Former mansions and private residences are the most frequent beneficiaries of these conversions, but country inns may be found today in structures which were originally used as gristmills, barns, riding stables, log cabins, poorhouses, boarding houses, hospitals, schools, private clubs, and mountain lodges, to name a few.

Perhaps best of all, many American communities without village inns or small hotels since the late Victorian days find a new vigor and pride in their own restored inns and historic buildings, and the public is able to appreciate our architectural heritage and is enriched by having these beautiful old buildings available and accessible. — **by Virginia Rowe**

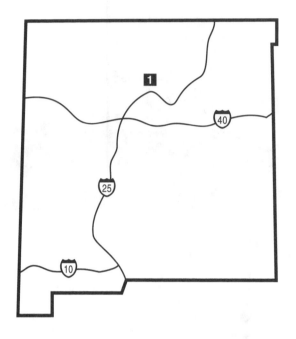

1. Grant Corner Inn, Santa Fe

GRANT CORNER INN

13 Rooms, $60/$135 B&B
Hacienda, $100/$115 B&B

Visa, MC

Private & Shared Baths

Open Year-round

Appropriate for Children over 6; No Pets

Skiing, Hiking, Fishing, Golf, Tennis, Swimming (fee)

Complimentary Breakfast; Picnic Lunches, Catered Dinners, Restaurant Serving Brunch to Public Sat. & Sun. Complimentary Wine

 Smoke-free inn

 Wheelchair Access (1 room)

Conference Facilities (20)

1 This elegant and delightful inn has an ideal location just two blocks from the historic plaza of downtown Santa Fe, among intriguing shops, galleries, and restaurants. Lush gardens, beautifully appointed guest rooms, fabulous gourmet breakfasts, and the gracious hospitality of the Walters family make this an experience not to be missed. Ample parking on the premises.

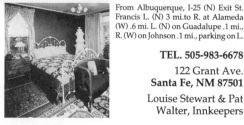

From Albuquerque, I-25 (N) Exit St. Francis L. (N) 3 mi.to R. at Alameda (W) .6 mi. L. (N) on Guadalupe .1 mi., R. (W) on Johnson .1 mi., parking on L.

TEL. 505-983-6678

122 Grant Ave.
Santa Fe, NM 87501

Louise Stewart & Pat Walter, Innkeepers

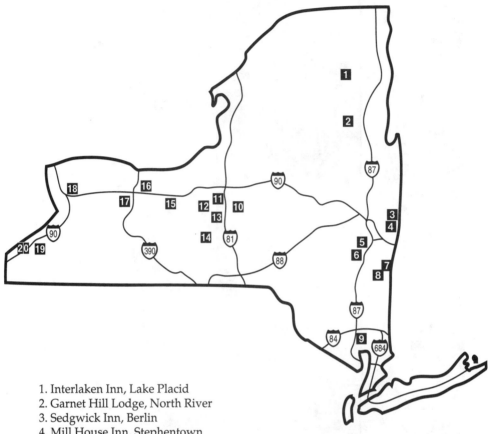

1. Interlaken Inn, Lake Placid
2. Garnet Hill Lodge, North River
3. Sedgwick Inn, Berlin
4. Mill House Inn, Stephentown
5. Greenville Arms, Greenville
6. Redcoat's Return, Tannersville
7. Simmon's Way Village Inn, Millerton
8. Beekman Arms, Rhinebeck
9. Bird and Bottle Inn, Garrison
10. Lincklaen House, Cazenovia
11. Sherwood Inn, Skaneateles
12. Springside Inn, Auburn
13. Ben Conger Inn, Groton
14. Rose Inn, Ithaca
15. Morgan-Samuels B&B Inn, Canandaigua
16. Oliver Loud's Inn, Pittsford
17. The Genesee Country Inn, Mumford
18. Asa Ransom House, Clarence
19. White Inn, Fredonia
20. William Seward Inn, Westfield

ASA RANSOM HOUSE

🛏	6 Rooms, $85/$125 B&B 3 Suites, $145 B&B
💳	Visa, MC, Discov
🛁	All Private Baths
🪑🏺	Closed Fri.; month of Jan.
🧑‍🦱🐕	Well-supervised Children welcome; No Pets
☀R☀	Niagara Falls, many Antique Shops within walking distance
☕🍷	Breakfast for Houseguests; Dinner Sun. thru Thurs. (Sat.-Houseguests only) Wine & Liquor available
🚭	No Smoking
⊢▪▪▪⊣	Conference Facilities (40)
♿	Wheelchair Access

18 On the site of the first gristmill built in Erie County (1803), this historic village inn offers country gourmet dining and fine New York State wines. Guests are romanced in the winter by the glowing fireplaces in the guest rooms, and enchanted in the summer by spacious grounds full of herbs and flowers. Clarence is known throughout the East for its antiques and treasures.

Traveling (E): I-90, Exit 49, L. on Rte. 78 for 1 mi. to R. on Rte. 5 for 5.3 mi. Traveling (W): I-90, Exit 48A & R. on Rte. 77 for 1 mi. to R. on Rte. 5 for 10 mi. to inn.

TEL. 716-759-2315
FAX 716-759-2791

10529 Main St. (Rte. 5),
Clarence, NY 14031-1684

Bob & Judy Lenz, Innkeepers

BEEKMAN ARMS

🛏	59 Rooms, $75/$99 EP 2 Suites, $125 EP
💳	Visa, Amex, Diners
🛁	All Private Baths
🪑🏺	Open Year-round
🧑‍🦱🐕	Children Accepted; No Pets in Delamater House
☀R☀	Hyde Park, Rhinebeck WW1 Aerdrome, Culinary Instit. of Amer., Golf,Tennis, XC Skiing
☕🍷	Breakfast, Lunch, Dinner Wine & Liquor available
🚭	4 rooms Non-smoking Non-smoking Dining area
⊢▪▪▪⊣	Conference Facilities (25)
♿	Wheelchair Access (2 rms)

8 The focus of activity in bustling, historic Rhinebeck, this inn has seen history being made since 1766 when its original section was built. Today its offers authentically furnished guest rooms, some with working fireplaces, a Colonial Tap Room and a beautiful greenhouse dining area where casual but elegant country fare is served.

NY Thruwy. (I-90) Rhinecliff Bridge Exit to Rte. 9 (S) 2 mi. to Rhinebeck Village. From Taconic Pkwy. take Rte. 199 (W) to L. on Rte. 308 to Rhinebeck Village.

TEL. 914-876-7077

4 Mill St., Route 9
Rhinebeck, NY 12572

Chuck LaForge, Innkeeper

BENN CONGER INN

 1 Room, $90/$110 B&B
3 Suites, $110/$220 B&B

 Visa, MC, Amex, Diners

 All Private Baths

 Open Year-round

 Children Welcome
No Pets – Kennel nearby

 Hiking, Biking, XC Skiing, Golf, Tennis, all Lake Sports, Antiques, Wineries

 Breakfast, Dinner
Wine & Liquor available

Smoking limited

Conference Facilities (60)

From I-81, Exit 12 (Homer) (S) on Rte. 281 for 2 mi. R. (W) on Rte. 222 for 9 mi. to Groton. Cross Rte. 38, making no turns. Inn is up hill on R.

TEL. 607-898-5817

206 W. Cortland St.
Groton, NY 13073

Alison & Peter Van der Meulen, Innkeepers

13 A revival mansion built for industrialist Benn Conger, it is best known as a hideaway for mobster Dutch Schultz. Its 18 pastoral acres, gracious public rooms including a library and conservatory, oversized suites, antiques, imported linens, amenities, Mediterranean-inspired cuisine and over 100 fine wines will please the most discriminating traveler. ("Wine Spectator" Award 1987-92).

THE BIRD & BOTTLE INN

2 Rooms, $195/$215 MAP
2 Suites, $215/$225 MAP

Visa, MC, Amex, Diners

All Private Baths

Closed Jan. 1 - 20

Not appropriate for Children
Pets not accepted

Hiking, Nature walks, Golf, XC Skiing, Boating

Breakfast, Dinner, Sun. brunch
Wine & Liquor available

Smoking accepted

Conference Facilities (50)

From Rte. I-84: Fishkill: (S) 8 mi. on Rte. 9. Inn on L. From NYC and Westchester: (N) on Rte. 9 A and 9, past Croton and Peekskill. Inn 8 mi. beyond Peekskill on Rte. 9 in Garrison area.

TEL. 914-424-3000

**Old Albany Post Rd. (Rte. 9)
Garrison, NY 10524**

Ira Boyar, Innkeeper

9 A famed landmark on the old Albany-New York Post Road since 1761, this inn continues to welcome travelers with traditional Hudson River Valley hospitality. An authentic old country inn, it is internationally renowned for its gourmet cuisine and comfortable, cozy rooms with woodburning fireplaces, 4-poster or canopied beds, and Colonial furnishings.

GARNET HILL LODGE

	23 Rooms, $120/$170 MAP
	No Credit Cards
	All private baths
	Closed Nov. 15 - 30
	Children Accepted No Pets
	Swimming, Tennis, Hiking, Boating, Fishing, XC Skiing, Museums, Downhill Skiing
	Breakfast, Lunch, Dinner Wine & Liquor Available
	Non-smoking Dining Area
	Conference Facilities (60)

2　The Log House of this rustic resort-inn was built in 1936, and the big fireplace in the living/dining room of varnished pine is a place where guests gather for conversation and fun. Nestled in the Adirondacks overlooking 13th Lake, amid spectacular scenery, the inn features hearty meals for hungry guests after a day of bracing outdoor activity.

From Albany on I-87 Exit 23 (Warrensburg). (N) on Rte. 9 to Rte. 28. (N) on Rte. 28, 22 mi. to North River. L. on 13th Lake Rd. 4.5 mi. to inn.

TEL. 518-251-2821

13th Lake Rd.
North River, NY 12856

George & Mary Heim,
Innkeepers

THE GENESEE COUNTRY INN

	9 Rooms, $80/$120 B&B 2 nite min (some wknds)
	Visa, MC, Diners
	All Private Baths
	Closed Dec. 24 & 25; Also Sun. Noon to Tues. Noon Nov.-Apr. exc. Holidays
	No Pets
	Trout fishing, Walking, Biking, Genesee Country Museum, Letchworth St. Pk., Rochester, Discount shopping, Gift Shop
	Breakfast houseguests; Luncheon for conferences; Tea, Cheese & Crackers; BYOB
	Conference Facilities (14)
	Wheelchair Access (1 rm)

17　This 1833 stone mill in beautiful Genesee country has been converted into a charming inn on 6 unique acres of woods, spring-fed millponds, and waterfalls. Guest rooms are charmingly decorated with authentic stenciling, some over-sized canopied beds, fireplaces, and wooded views. Breakfast served in common rooms overlooking water.

From NY Thrwy. (I-90) take Exit 47 and Rte. 19 S. to LeRoy. Go (E) on Rte. 5 to Caledonia, (N) on Rte. 36 to Mumford. L. on George St.

TEL. 716-538-2500
FAX 716-538-4565
948 George St.,
Mumford, NY 14511-0340
Glenda Barcklow, Proprietor,
Kim Rasmussen, Innkeeper

GREENVILLE ARMS

 14 Rooms, $88/$125 B&B

 Visa, MC

 All Private Baths

 Open May 1 – Dec. 1

 Well-supervised Children
No Pets

 Swimming pool, Tennis, Golf, Bicycling, Hiking, Hudson Valley & Catskill Sightseeing

 Breakfast for houseguests
Dinner by reservation
Wine & Beer available

Smoking restricted

 Conference Facilities (30)

From NYC: 2 hrs. (N) on I-87 to Exit 21 & Rte. 23(W) for 9 mi. Then (N) on Rte. 32 for 9 mi. to Greenville. Inn is on L., before traffic light.

TEL. 518-966-5219

Route 32, South St.
Greenville, NY 12083

Eliot & Letitia Dalton,
Innkeepers

5 Built in 1889 in the foothills of the northern Catskills, this lovely Queen Anne Victorian inn is set on 6 lush acres of shade trees, with gardens and swimming pool. Antiques, original artwork and Victorian details add to an atmosphere of warmth and relaxed comfort. Full country breakfasts and gourmet dinners are served in the brick-hearthed dining rooms.

INTERLAKEN INN

 11 Rooms, $100/$160 MAP
1 Suite, $160 MAP
1 Cottage, $125 B&B
Amex, MC, Visa, Encore

 All Private Baths

 Open Year-round

 Children accepted over 5
No Pets

 Olympic venues, Skiing, Golf, Tennis, Boating, Fishing, Hiking

 Full Breakfast, Dinner, Afternoon Tea
Sherry in each room

 Smoking limited to common rooms

 Conference Facilities (20)

TEL. 518-523-3180

800-428-4369

15 Interlaken Ave.
Lake Placid, NY 12946

Roy and Carol Johnson,
Innkeepers

1 In the heart of the Adirondack Mountains, site of the 1932 and 1980 winter Olympics, this 1906 Victorian Inn offers a wonderfully romantic setting with uniquely decorated, antique furnished rooms. Enjoy a peaceful setting and four seasons of outdoor activities. The Inn offers fine dining using the season's freshest bounty to provide guests with a unique dining experience.

LINCKLAEN HOUSE

 18 rooms, $70/$99 B&B
3 suites, $115/$130 B&B

 Visa, MC,

 All Private Baths

 Open Year-round

 Children accepted
Pets accepted

 Swimming, Golf, Tennis,
Downhill & XC Skiing

 Lunch, Dinner daily; Sun.
brunch buffet (seasonal)
Wine & Liquor available

 Smoking accepted

Conference facilities (50)
Banquet facilities (200)

10 Built in 1835 as a luxurious stopover for Colonial travelers, the Lincklaen House has long been a local landmark and has hosted such luminaries as President Grover Cleveland and John D. Rockefeller. The old-world atmosphere is now combined with modern comfort and gracious service, offering guests a return to an era of elegant hospitality.

From NY Thruwy. (I-90): Exit 34, take Rte. 13 (S) to Cazenovia. R. on Rte. 20, 1 block. From I-81: Exit 15 (La Fayette), E. on Rte. 20. 18 mi. to Cazenovia.

TEL. 315-655-3461

79 Albany St., Box 36
Cazenovia, NY 13035

Howard M. Kaler,
Innkeeper

MILL HOUSE INN

 7 Rooms, $80/$95 B&B
5 Suites, $105/$140 B&B

 Visa, MC, Amex

 All Private Baths

 Closed Mar. 15-May 15;
Dec. 1-Dec. 15

Children Accepted
(limited); No Pets

Swimming Pool on
grounds, Golf, Tennis,
Skiing, Hiking, Antiquing, Theater, Tanglewood

Complimentary Continental Breakfast, Afternoon Tea; Breakfast
menu available

No Smoking

Wheelchair Access (1
room)

4 "Once upon a time, a sawmill," now a country inn with Central European architecture and ambience, the inn's guest rooms all have an individual feeling, with fireplace suites for the romantic at heart. The rock gardens, shaded paths, and brook all have a peaceful and soothing effect. On the NY/MA border, within a short distance of all Berkshire attractions.

From NYC, Taconic Pkwy. (N), Exit Rte. 295, R. to Rte. 22. L. to Rte. 43, R. for 1.2 mi. to inn. From Boston, Mass. Tpke. (I-90), Exit B3, Rte. 22 (N) to Rte. 43. On NY/MA border.

TEL. 518-733-5606
(Mass.): 413-738-5348
Rte. 43
Stephentown, NY 12168
Frank & Ronnie Tallet,
Innkeepers

MORGAN-SAMUELS B&B INN

 6 Rooms, $99/$195 B&B

 Visa, MC, Amex, Discov

 All Private Baths

 Closed Thanksgiving, Christmas Eve & Day

 Pets outdoors only

 Tennis, Golf, Nearby Lake, Wineries, Outdoor Symphonies & Concerts, Sonnerberg Gardens, Horse drawn Sleigh Rides

 Breakfast, Dinner by Reservation; BYOB

 No Smoking

 Conference Facilities (15)

I-90 from E Exit 43 R. on 21 to 488-L. 1st R. to stop sign continue 3/4 mile to Inn on R.

TEL. (716) 394-9232
FAX (716) 394-9232

2920 Smith Rd.
Canandaigua, N.Y. 14424

Julie & John Sullivan, Innkeepers

15 As you travel the 2,000 ft. tree lined drive to the secluded 1810 English style mansion you sense a legendary atmosphere. Lawns and gardens canopied by noble trees, bordered by fields, give each room pastoral views. Quality antiques, oil paintings, fireplaces, tea room, library, commons room & French balconies. Candlelight gourmet breakfast with Mozart. Mobil ★★★ AAA◆◆◆

OLIVER LOUD'S INN

 8 Rooms, $135/$145 B&B
 Visa, MC, Amex, CB
Diners Club

 All Private Baths

 Open Year-round

 Children over 12 welcome
No Pets; kennel nearby

 Erie Canal towpath for hiking, Jogging, XC Skiing, Biking, Boating, Golf, Tennis, Museums, Sightseeing

 Cont. Breakfast hamper, Richardson's Canal House rest.; Wine & Liquor avail.

Smoking/non-smoking Rooms

Conference Facilities (20)

Wheelchair Access (1 room)

NY Thruwy. (I-90) Exit 45, to I-490 (W) for 3 mi. to Bushnell's Basin exit, turn R. & continue to Marsh Rd. signal & bear R. to inn.

TEL. 716-248-5200
FAX 716-248-9970

1474 Marsh Rd.
Pittsford, NY 14534

Vivienne Tellier, Innkeeper

16 Feeding ducks, building snowmen, visiting nearby shops, or rocking on the porch over-looking the Erie Canal, are some ways to relax at this circa 1810 stagecoach inn. Authentically furnished with antiques and period artwork, guests are pampered with V.I.P. welcome trays, as well as a breakfast hamper delivered to your room. King sized and canopy beds available.

THE REDCOAT'S RETURN

🛏	14 rooms, $75/$95 B&B
💳	Visa, MC, Amex
🛁	Private & Shared Baths
🛋	Open Year-round
🐕‍🦺	Inquire regarding Children; No Pets
R	Downhill & XC Skiing, Golf, Tennis, Swimming, Boating, Horseback Riding, Hiking, Antique Shopping
🍽	Breakfast; Dinner served Fri.-Mon. only Wine & Liquor available
🚭	Pipes & Cigars restricted
⌂ ♿	Conference Facilities (20-30)

6 Peg and Tom Wright's easy cordiality has been making guests comfortable for 19 years. Tom's English accent and his artistry in the kitchen (he was a chef on the Queen Mary) keeps them coming back for more. Whether it's snuggling up in front of a roaring fire, hiking, or enjoying spectacular views of the Catskills, it's always fun at this romantic, cozy inn.

NY Thruwy (N), Exit 20 (Saugerties). L. to Rte. 32 (N). Rte. 32 merges with Rte. 32A and at light, with 23A (W). At next light, L. onto County Rd. 16, 4.5 mi. to R. on Dale Lane. Inn on R.

TEL. 518-589-6379
Dale Lane
Elka Park, NY 12427
Tom & Peggy Wright,
Innkeepers

ROSE INN

🛏	11 Rooms, $100/$150 B&B 4 Suites, $175/$250 B&B
💳	Visa, MC
🛁	All Private Baths
🛋	Open Year-round
🐕‍🦺	Appropriate for Children over 10 No Pets; kennel next door
R	Lake Sports, Skiing, Tennis, Golf, Finger Lk. Wineries, Cornell University, Antiques, Cayuga Lake
🍽	Breakfast, Dinner prix fixe by reservation Wine available
🚭	No smoking
⌂ ♿	Conference Facilities (60)

14 Halfway between New York City and Niagara Falls, in the heart of the Finger Lakes, this 1851 Italianate inn is a gem of woodcraft, with a stunning circular staircase of Honduran mahogany. The high-ceilinged rooms are furnished with antiques from around the world. This is New York State's only Mobil **** and AAA ◆◆◆◆ inn.

From Ithaca, Rte. 13(N). Exit Rte. 34(N), 6 mi. to "T" (red flashing light). R. for .5 mi to fork, stay L. Inn is 3.5 mi. on R.

TEL. 607-533-7905
FAX 607-533-4202
Rte. 34 North, P.O. Box 6576
Ithaca, NY 14851-6576
Charles & Sherry Rosemann,
Innkeepers

THE SEDGWICK INN

 4 Rooms, $75/$85 B&B
1 Ste, $100 B&B; Annex $65

 Visa, MC, Amex, Diners

 All Private Baths

 Open Year-round

Children accepted in annex
Pets accepted in annex

Library, Gift & Gourmet shops, Downhill & XC Skiing, Swimming, Theatre, Tanglewood Music Festival, Art Museums

Breakfast, Light lunches, Gourmet Dinners

Wine & Liquor available

No Smoking in Inn guest rooms

 Conference Facilities (60)

Wheelchair Access in annex

From Albany: Rte. 787 (N) to Troy. Exit Rte. 7 (E) to Rte. 278. R. on 278 to Rte. 2, L. on Rte. 2 for approx. 15 mi. to Rte. 22. R. on 22 (S), 6 mi. to inn. From N.Y.C.: Taconic Pkwy (N), Exit Rte. 295 (E) to Rte. 22. L. on Rte. 22 (N) for 22 mi.

TEL. 518-658-2334
800-845-4886
Rte. 22, Box 250
Berlin, NY 12022
Edie Evans, Innkeeper

3 This historic country inn, once a stage-coach stop, sits on 12 acres in the Berkshire's beautiful Taconic Valley. Colonial, with Victorian overtones, the inn's rooms are handsomely furnished in antiques and interesting artifacts, including the original 1791 indentures. Gourmet dinners are served in the Coach Room Tavern. Rooms also available in motel annex.

THE SHERWOOD INN

 12 Rooms, $60/$75 B&B
5 Suites, $70/$125 B&B

Visa, MC, Amex, Diners, CB

All Private Baths

Open Year-round

Children Accepted
No Pets

Swimming, Boating, Golf, Downhill and XC Skiing, Fishing, Bicycling, Hiking

Breakfast, Lunch, Dinner; Dining room closed 12/24 & 25; Wine & Liquor available

Non-smoking dining area

 Conference Facilities (100)

From N. Y. Thruwy: Exit Weedsport, Rte. 34 (S) to Auburn. (E) on Rte. 20, 7 mi. to Skaneateles. From (S): Rte. 81 (N) to Cortland, Rte. 41 (N) to Skaneateles. L. on Rte. 20 for 1 mi.

TEL. 315-685-3405
26 West Genesee St.
Skaneateles, NY 13152
William Eberhardt,
Innkeeper

11 From the handsome lobby with its fireplace and piano to the pleasant guest rooms, many of which overlook beautiful Skaneateles Lake, gracious service and comfort are the keynotes here. American cuisine with a Continental touch, has been featured in *Bon Appetit*, and is served in the dining rooms and the friendly, casual tavern. The lovely village of Skaneateles offers many activities.

SIMMONS' WAY VILLAGE INN

🛏	9 Rooms, $115/$150 1 Suite, $265
💳	Visa, MC, Amex
🛁	All Private Baths
🛋	Open Year-round
🐕👧	Children Accepted No Pets
R	Skiing, Golf, Tennis, Swimming, Concerts, Summer Stock, Auto Racing, Antiquing, Historical sites
🍽	Breakfast, Brunch, Dinner; MAP available Wine & Liquor available
🚭	Smoking in restricted areas
⊢🏨⊣	Conference Facilities (25)
♿	Wheelchair Access

7 Graceful retreat in grand Victorian elegance and civility. Located near CT border in Berkshire foothills. Antiques, fireplaces, porches and historic, candlelit silver service highlight memorable accommodations and internationally acclaimed cuisine and wine selections. Selected by American Express/Hertz as "Quintessential Country Inn 1991" for a national ad campaign.

From N.Y.C. (90 mi.): Taconic Pkwy. to Rte. 44(E) or I-684 to Rte. 22 (N) to Rte. 44 (E) (Main St.). From Boston (160 mi.): Mass. Tpke., Exit 2, Rte. 102 (W) to Rte. 7 (S) to Rte. 44 (W). From Hartford: Rte. 44 (W) to Millerton.

TEL. 518-789-6235
33 Main St.
Millerton, NY 12546
Richard & Nancy Carter,
Innkeepers

SPRINGSIDE INN

🛏	8 Rooms, $60 B&B
💳	Visa, MC, Amex
🛁	Private and Shared Baths
🛋	Closed Memorial Day, July 4, Dec. 25
🐕👧	Children Accepted No Pets
R	Summer Dinner Theatre, Hiking, Swimming, Boating, Fishing, XC Skiing, Tennis, Winery Tours
🍽	Continental Breakfast, Dinner, Sun. Brunch Wine & Liquor Available
🚭	No Smoking in Guest Rooms
⊢🏨⊣	Conference Facilities (310)
♿	

12 Perhaps "inn of flowers" would be a good name for this 1830 red clapboard building, with its masses of flowers in gardens, tubs, baskets, and window boxes. On eight acres of lawns and trees, with a spring-fed pond and ducks, this homey, comfortable chef-owned inn offers delicious food along with summer dinner theater nearby.

From N. Y. Thruway: Exit 40, take Rte. 34 (S) thru Auburn to Rte. 38 (S) to traffic circle at lake. Take 2nd exit R. at (W) shore of Owasco Lake .25 mi. to inn.

TEL. 315-252-7247
41-43 West Lake Rd.
Auburn, NY 13021
The Dove Family,
Innkeepers

THE WHITE INN

 13 Rooms, $59/$149 B&B
10 Suites, $69/$169 B&B

 Visa, MC, Amex, DC, Discov.

 All Private Baths

 Open Year-round

 Children accepted
No Pets

 Bicycling, Wineries, Antiquing, XC/alpine Skiing, SUNY college activities, Chautauqua Institution, Golf, Boating, Fishing

Breakfast included exc. Sun.; Lunch, Dinner
Wine & Liquor available

Some Non-smoking rms. Non-smoking Dining area

Conference Facilities (60)

Wheelchair access (3 rooms)

NY Thruwy. Exit 59. At traffic light L. on Rte. 60 (S) to traffic light, R. on Rte. 20 (W), Main St. Inn on R.

TEL. 716-672-2103
FAX 716-672-2107

52 East Main St.
Fredonia, NY 14063

David Palmer & David Bryant, Innkeepers

19 An impressive ca. 1868 edifice with a pillared portico, beyond which are beautifully restored and decorated rooms. Superb cuisine has gained an enthusiastic following among guests and townsfolk. Nearby Chautauqua Institution offers varied cultural programs. Sailing on Lake Erie, antiquing, wineries, and summer band concerts await you.

WILLIAM SEWARD INN

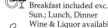 14 Rooms, $80/$135 B&B

Visa, MC, Discov.

All Private Baths

 Open Year-round

Children over 10 are welcome; No Pets, Boarding available nearby Chautauqua Institution, Lily Dale, Wineries, Antique & Speciality Shops, Skiing, Swimming, Boating, Tennis, Golf nearby.

Full Breakfast; Prix Fix Dinner available Thursday-Sunday by advance Reservation only; BYOB
No Smoking inside

Conference Facilities (15)

Wheelchair Access (2 Rooms)

4 mi. S. on Rte. 394 from I-90, Exit 60. 2.5 hrs. NE of Cleveland, OH; 2.5 hrs. N of Pittsburgh, PA; 1.5 hrs. SW of Buffalo, NY; 3 hrs. SW of Toronto, Canada

TEL. 716-326-4151

RR2, Box 14, S. Portage Rd.
Westfield, NY 14787

James L. and Debbie Dahlberg, Innkeepers

20 Although Chautauqua Institution is a major attraction, many travelers come specifically to stay at this 1821 antique-filled inn for rest and relaxation. The formal but comfortable ambience created with period antiques (mid-1800s-early 1900s) in the 1821-1880 portion of Inn as well as the period reproduction setting in the new carriage house lend well to total relaxation for guests.

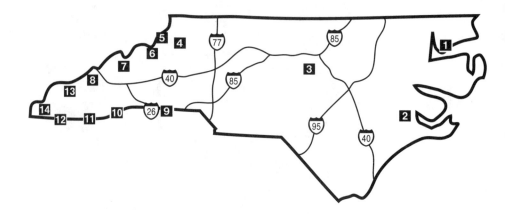

1. Lords Proprietor's Inn, Edenton
2. Harmony House Inn, New Bern
3. Fearrington House, Chapel Hill
4. Gideon Ridge Inn, Blowing Rock
5. Mast Farm Inn, Valle Crucis
6. Inn at Taylor House, Valle Crucis
7. Richmond Hill Inn, Asheville
8. Swag Country Inn, Waynesville
9. Pine Crest Inn, Tryon
10. Orchard Inn, Saluda
11. Waverly Inn, Hendersonville
12. The Greystone Inn, Lake Toxaway
13. Hemlock Inn, Bryson City
14. Snowbird Mountain Lodge, Robbinsville

THE FEARRINGTON HOUSE

14 Rooms, $150/$190 B&B 9 Suites, $190/$230 B&B
Visa, MC, Pers. Checks
All Private Baths
Closed Dec. 24-26
Children by special arrangement; No Pets
Swimming, Biking, Walking, Bird watching, Golf, Tennis, Sailing, Fishing
Breakfast, Lunch, Dinner Outstanding Wine list; BYOB
Smoking limited
Conference facilities (40)
Wheelchair Access (1 room)

3 In a cluster of low, attractive buildings grouped around a courtyard and surrounded by gardens and rolling countryside, this elegant inn offers luxurious quarters in a country setting. A member of Relais et Chateaux, the restaurant's sophisticated regional cuisine, prepared in the classical techniques, has received national acclaim, including AAA's 4–diamond award.

Chapel Hill, U.S. 15-501 (S) 8 mi. to Fearrington Village.

TEL. 919-542-2121
FAX 919-542-4202
2000 Fearrington
Village Center
Pittsboro, NC 27312
Jenny & R.B. Fitch, Owners;
Valerie Komives,
Innkeeper

GIDEON RIDGE INN

 9 Rooms, $100/$130 B&B

 Visa, MC, Amex

 All Private Baths

 Open Year-round

 Appropriate for Children over 12
No Pets

 Hiking, Horseback Riding, Golf, Tennis, Village & Crafts shops, Blue Ridge Pkwy. Grandfather Mtn.

 Full Breakfast, Dinners & Lunches for groups by prior request; BYOB

 Smoking limited

Conference Facilities (12-16)

U.S. 321, 1.5 mi. (S) of village of Blowing Rock, turn (W) on Rock Rd., L. on Gideon Ridge Rd. at fork. Go to top of the ridge.

TEL. 704-295-3644

6148 Gideon Ridge Rd.
P.O. Box 1929
Blowing Rock, NC 28605
Cobb & Jane Milner,
Innkeepers

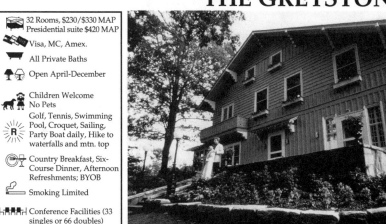

4 Surrounded by six stone terraces on top of Gideon's Ridge, the inn overlooks the Blue Ridge Mountains. This sturdy 1930 stone house, offers rooms decorated with antiques and family heirlooms. While at the inn, guests may relax in the library with its massive stone fireplace, enjoy an exceptional breakfast in the dining room and stroll through woods and gardens.

THE GREYSTONE INN

32 Rooms, $230/$330 MAP
Presidential suite $420 MAP

Visa, MC, Amex.

All Private Baths

Open April-December

Children Welcome
No Pets

Golf, Tennis, Swimming Pool, Croquet, Sailing, Party Boat daily, Hike to waterfalls and mtn. top

Country Breakfast, Six-Course Dinner, Afternoon Refreshments; BYOB

Smoking Limited

Conference Facilities (33 singles or 66 doubles)

Ramp to one Guest Room

From Asheville: I-26 E. 9 mi. to Rt. 280 to Brevard, US 64 west 17 mi to Lake Toxaway. From Atlanta I-85 N. to Rt. 11 (1st exit in S.C.) after 33 mi. L on Rt 130 (becomes N.C. Rt. 281) to US 64; R for 1.2 mi. to Lk. Toxaway on left.

TEL. 704-966-4700
800-824-5766
Greystone Lane
Lake Toxaway, NC 28747
Tim/Boo Boo Lovelace, Inkps.

12 This romantic, historic inn is located on a beautiful mountain lake. Unique is the intimate, tranquil setting combined with complete resort amenities only steps away. Our daily tariff includes luxurious, lakeside accommodations (many with fireplaces, balconies and Jacuzzi tubs), exceptional cuisine, watersports equipment, boats, tennis and hiking trails. Championship golf is on site.

HARMONY HOUSE INN

	9 Rooms, $80 B&B
	Visa, MC, Amex
	All Private Baths
	Open Year-round
	Children accepted No Pets
R	Historic district, Tryon Palace, 2 rivers, Croatan Forest, Golf, Tennis, Boats
	Full Breakfast BYOB
	No Smoking
	Conference facilities (10-12)

2 As the Ellis family grew, so did their ca. 1850 home, with additions ca. 1860 and ca. 1880. In 1900, the home was sawn in half and widened, with a second front door, hallway, and staircase, plus a wonderful front porch. Comfortable elegance is evident throughout this unusually spacious Greek Revival inn, decorated with local and family furniture and memorabilia of the period.

I-95, Exit 70 (E) to 4th New Bern exit to E. Front St., then L. on Pollock St. Hwy. 17 runs 1 blk. (N) of Pollock St.

TEL. 919-636-3810
800-392-6231

215 Pollock St.
New Bern, NC 28560

A.E. & Diane Hansen,
Innkeepers

HEMLOCK INN

	23 rooms, $113/$128 MAP 3 cotts., $137/$155 MAP
	No Credit Cards
	All Private Baths
	Open mid-April-Oct.; Weekends only Nov.-mid-Dec.
	Children welcome No Pets
R	Hiking, Ping-pong, Shuffle-board, Skittles, Smoky Mtn. Natl. Park, Tubing, Cherokee Indian Res.
	Breakfast at 8:30 A.M., Dinner at 6 P.M., Mon. to Sat. & 12:30 P.M. Sun.
	Non-smoking dining room
	Wheelchair access (8 rooms)

13 High, cool, quiet, and restful, this inn is beautifully situated on top of a small mountain on the edge of the Great Smoky Mountains National Park. There's a friendly informality in the family atmosphere and authentic country furniture. Honest-to-goodness home cooking and farm-fresh vegetables are served bountifully from Lazy Susan tables.

Hwy. 74, Hyatt Creek Rd.- Ela exit & bear R. to L. turn on Hwy. 19 for approx. 1 mi. to R. turn at inn sign. Take country road 1 mi. to L. turn at next inn sign.

TEL. 704-488-2885

Galbreath Creek Rd.
P.O. Drawer EE,
Bryson City, NC 28713

Morris & Elaine White; Ella Jo & John Shell, Innkeepers

THE INN AT THE TAYLOR HOUSE

5 Rooms, $95 B&B
2 Suites, $135 B&B

Visa, MC

All Private Baths

Closed Dec. 15 – April 15

Children by prior arrangement; No Pets

Hiking, Fishing, Horseback riding, Canoeing, Championship Golf, Skiing, Grandfather Mtn., Blue Ridge Parkway, Shops & Restaurants

Breakfast; Arrangements for private parties, weddings & family reunions

Smoking on porch only

Boone/Banner/Elk accessible from any direction. NC Hwy. 105(N) for 2.8 mi. to Valle Crucis. L. on Hwy. 194 for 8/10 mi. to inn.

TEL. 704-963-5581

Highway 194, P.O.Box 713
Valle Crucis, NC 28691

Chip & Roland Schwab,
Innkeepers

6 A bit of Europe in the peaceful, rural heart of the Blue Ridge Mountains, this charming farmhouse is decorated with fine antiques, oriental rugs, artwork, and European goose-down comforters on all the beds. Bright fabrics, wicker furniture and flowering plants invite guests to rock on the wide wraparound porch, while the friendly hospitality and memorable breakfasts add to their pleasure.

THE LORDS PROPRIETORS' INN

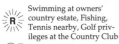

20 Rooms, $80/$120 B&B
MAP Rate Available

Personal checks accepted

All Private Baths

Open Year-round
Exc. Dec. 24 & 25

Children Welcome
No Pets

Swimming at owners' country estate, Fishing, Tennis nearby, Golf privileges at the Country Club

Breakfast, Dinner
Wine available with dinner

Smoking in parlors and on porches

Conference Facilities (30)

Wheelchair Access (1 Room)

From N.C. 32 and U.S. 17 continue on Broad St. to the inn.

TEL 1-800-348-8933

300 No. Broad St.
Edenton, NC 27932

Arch, Jane & Martha
Edwards, Innkeepers

1 In the Historic District of Edenton, called "the South's prettiest town," this inn comprises three restored homes on over an acre of grounds, with large and finely appointed guest rooms, three spacious parlors, and large porches with rockers. Among dogwood trees in the center of the complex is the beautiful separate dining room, where breakfasts and dinners are served.

MAST FARM INN

	9 Rooms, $80/$130 MAP 3 Cabin Suites, $130/$155
	Visa, MC
	10 Private, 1 Shared Baths
	Closed Mar. 7 to April 21; Nov. 7 to Dec. 26
	Appropriate for Children over 12; No Pets
	Fishing, Hiking, Skiing, Golf, Canoeing
	Breakfast, houseguests only; Dinner, Tues. - Sat.; Sun. Lunch; BYOB
	No Smoking
	Wheelchair Access (1 room)

5   Relax before a cheery fire or rock on the wraparound front porch and enjoy the view of the mountain valley. Life at this restored, antique-filled inn (National Register of Historic Places) is pleasant and peaceful. Rooms are clean and cozy. Lodging in the main house, blacksmith shop, woodwork shop, and loom house are simple, and the food is country cooking with a gourmet touch.

Boone/Banner/Elk area accessible from any direction. Watch for Valle Crucis sign on NC 105. Mast Farm Inn is 2.6 mi. from NC105 on SR1112.

TEL. 704-963-5857
FAX 704-963-6934
P.O.Box 704
Valle Crucis, NC 28691
Sibyl & Francis Pressly,
Innkeepers

THE ORCHARD INN

	9 Rooms, $95/$110 B&B 3 Cottages $105/$125 B&B
	MC, Visa; Pers. Checks
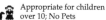	All Private Baths
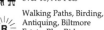	Open Year-round
	Appropriate for children over 10; No Pets
	Walking Paths, Birding, Antiquing, Biltmore Estate, Blue Ridge Parkway, Golf
	Breakfast included; Dinner by reservation; Picnics on request; BYOB
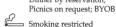	Smoking restricted
	Conference Facilities (20)

10   Guests enjoy a truly memorable dining experience to the strains of Mozart and Schumann on the glassed-in, wraparound porch with a breathtaking view of the southern Blue Ridge Mountains. This turn-of-the-century country house has a touch of plantation elegance, with a large fireplace, many antiques, folk art, and masses of books and magazines to beguile guests.

I-26, NC Exit 28 & turn toward Saluda for 2 mi. to L. on Hwy. 176 for .5 mi. to inn on R.

TEL. 704-749-5471
P.O. Box 725
Saluda, NC 28773
Ann & Ken Hough,
Innkeepers

PINE CREST INN

22 Rooms, $95/$130 B&B
8 suites, $130/$140 B&B

Visa, MC

All Private Baths

Open Year-round

Pets not accepted
Golf, Tennis, Swimming, Hiking, Horseback riding, Biltmore House & Gardens, Blue Ridge Pkwy., Chimney Rock., Fence Equestrian & Nature Ctr.
Full Breakfast, Dinner Box Lunches
Liquor & Wine available
Smoking Permitted

Conference Facilities (15 – 60)

From I-26, Exit 36 to Tryon. Follow Rte. 108/176 to town of Tryon. Turn on New Market Rd. Follow signs to inn.

TEL. 800-633-3001;
704-859-9135
200 Pine Crest Lane
Tryon, NC 28782
Jeremy & Jennifer
Wainwright, Innkeepers

9 Famed hunt country and foothills of the Blue Ridge Mountains are the setting for this classic inn. On the National Register, the inn features fireplaces, verandas, crisp mountain air, exceptional dining and gracious service. Fresh grilled trout, crab cakes, rack of lamb, & roast duck are specialties. The four-diamond inn has an extensive library, intimate bar, elegant rooms & manicured grounds.

RICHMOND HILL INN

19 Rooms, $125/$215 B&B
2 Suites, $215/$300 B&B

Visa, MC, Amex
All Private Baths

Open Year-round

Children Accepted; Pets Not Permitted

Croquet Lawn on site, Biltmore Estate tours, Blue Ridge Pkwy., Antiques & Crafts Shopping
Breakfast, Dinner; Sun. Brunch; Wine & Liquor Available
Non-Smoking Guest Rooms
Conference Facilities (60)

Wheelchair Access (1 Room)

From I-240, Exit 19/23, L. at bottom of Ramp; L. onto Riverside Dr., R. on Pearson Bridge Rd., R. on Richmond Hill Dr.
TEL. 704-252-7313
800-545-9238

87 Richmond Hill Dr.
Asheville, NC 28806

Susan Michel-Robertson, Innkeeper

7 This 1889 Queen Anne mansion was one of the most elegant and innovative structures of its time. Now on the National Register, the inn's rich oak paneling, handcarved fireplaces, and high ceilings provide an unusually luxurious setting in the Blue Ridge Mountains. Canopy and 4-poster beds, a highly-acclaimed gourmet restaurant, fresh mountain air are just a few of the attractions.

SNOWBIRD MOUNTAIN LODGE

🛏	21 Rooms, $112/$130 AP
💳	Visa, MC, Discov
🛁	All Private Baths
🕯🏮	Open mid-April-early Nov.
🐕	Appropriate for children over 11; No Pets
☀R☀	Hiking, Rafting & Horseback riding nearby, Fishing, Boating, Cherokee Indian sites, Horseshoes, Billiards, Ping-pong, Shuffleboard
◉🍽	Breakfast, Lunch, Dinner BYOB
🚬	Smoking in restricted areas
⊢▪▪▪⊣	
♿	Wheelchair Access (4 Rooms)

14 High up in Santeetlah Gap, not far from the giant hardwood trees of the Joyce Kilmer virgin forest, is this secluded, rustic and picturesque mountain lodge, built of chestnut logs and native stone. Huge fireplaces, comfortable beds in pleasant rooms, a spectacular view and plentiful, delicious meals make this an exceptional vacation retreat.

Robbinsville, at Hardees, Rte. 129)N) for 1.5 mi. to L. on NC Rte. 1116 for 3.3 mi. to R. at stop sign (Rte. 1127) for 6.7 mi. to lodge.

TEL 704-479-3433

275 Santeetlah Rd., Robbinsville, NC 28771

Jim & Eleanor Burbank, Innkeepers

THE SWAG COUNTRY INN

🛏	14 rooms, $150/$275 AP 2 suites, $250/$275 AP
💳	Visa, MC
🛁	All Private Baths
🕯🏮	Open late May through October
🐕	Children over 7 No Pets
☀R☀	Marked nature trails, Hiking, Racquetball, Sauna, Croquet, Badminton, Pond Fishing, Horseback riding nearby
◉🍽	All 3 Meals, hors d' oeuvres; Coffee beans & grinders in rooms; BYOB
🚬	No inside Smoking
⊢▪▪▪⊣	Conference Facilities (30)
♿	Wheelchair Access (3 rooms)

8 This mountain hideaway is built of hand-hewn logs and is situated on 250 acres of secluded and unspoiled land. The Swag Country Inn is perched at 5,000 feet, with a private entrance into The Great Smoky Mountains National Park. Guests enjoy 50-mile breathtaking views. It offers countless amenities, such as a fine library, fireplaces, Jacuzzis, and exceptional cuisine.

NC I-40, Exit 20 to Hwy. 276 for 2.8 mi. to Swag sign. Just after sign, turn R. 4 mi. up blacktopped road to Swag gate. L. on gravel driveway 2.5 mi. to inn.

TEL. 704-926-0430; 926-3119; FAX 704-926-2036 212-570-9756 Off Season

Hemphill Rd.,Rte. 2, Box 280A **Waynesville, NC 28786**

Deener Matthews, Innk.

THE WAVERLY INN

15 Rooms, $75/$95 B&B
1 Suite, $145 B&B

Visa, MC, Amex, Discov.

All Private Baths

Open Year-round

Children Welcome;
No Pets

Biltmore Estate, Flat Rock
Playhouse, Antiquing, Golf,
Blue Ridge Pkwy., Hiking,
Horseback Riding, Fishing

Full Breakfast; Refreshments; Evening Social
Hour; Arrangements for
Private Parties, BYOB

Smoking Limited

From I-26, NC Exit 18B, US-64 (W); Continue 2 mi. into Hendersonville. Bear R. onto Rte. 25(N) for 800 yards. Inn is on L. at corner of 8th Ave. & N. Main.

TEL. 800-537-8195
704-693-9193
783 N. Main St.
Hendersonville, NC 28792
Darla Olmstead, John &
Diane Sheiry, Innkeepers

11 In an area rich with history and natural scenery, this National Register inn is the oldest surviving inn in Hendersonville's historic district. Walking distance to fine restaurants, exceptional shopping and antiquing. Polished wood, turn-of-the-century fittings, 4-poster beds, wide porches and rocking chairs are only part of the picture that brings guests back to this comfortable, friendly place.

The IIA Gift Certificate
A Lovely Gift for Someone Special

The gift of an overnight stay or a weekend at a country inn can be one of the most thoughtful and appreciated gifts you can give your parents or children, dear friends, or valued employees for Christmas, a birthday, an anniversary, or any special occasion. Innkeepers and other employers are discovering this is an excellent way of rewarding their employees, while at the same time giving them some much needed rest and relaxation.

An IIA gift certificate means that you can give the gift of a stay at any one of over 250 member inns from Kennebunkport, Maine to Southern California; from Quebec, Canada to Key West, Florida: from Martha's Vineyard, Massachusetts to Seaview, Washington. We have inns in the Blue Ridge Mountains, on ranches in the western desert, near state parks and forests and nature preserves, in restored villages in historic districts, on lakes and by the sea. Choose your pleasure.

An IIA gift certificate is good for two years, and may be purchased through the IIA office by personal check or Mastercard or Visa. With each gift certificate, we send along a brand new copy of the *Innkeepers Register*. For further information call **800-344-5244.**

A five dollar ($5) postage and handling fee will be added to all gift certificate purchases.

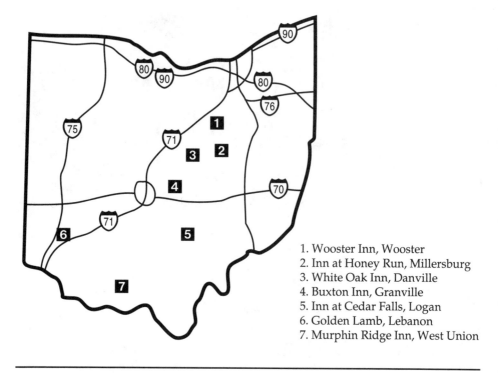

1. Wooster Inn, Wooster
2. Inn at Honey Run, Millersburg
3. White Oak Inn, Danville
4. Buxton Inn, Granville
5. Inn at Cedar Falls, Logan
6. Golden Lamb, Lebanon
7. Murphin Ridge Inn, West Union

THE BUXTON INN

	12 Rooms, $65/$70 B&B 7 Suites, $70/$85 B&B
	Visa, MC, Amex
	All Private Baths
	Closed Dec. 25, Jan. 1
	Children Accepted; No Pets
	Golf, Tennis, Swimming, Bicycling
	Breakfast, Lunch, Dinner, Sat & Sun. Brunch; Wine & Liquor Available
	Smoking Accepted
	Conference Facilities (60)
	Wheelchair Access (2 Rooms)

4 Looking very much like a typical New England village, this college town bears the imprint of the pioneers who settled here in 1805. A short 7 years later the Buxton Inn began dispensing hospitality and sustenance and hasn't stopped yet. Noted nationally for its gourmet kitchens, with an intriguing mixture of antique furnishings and modern amenities, it continues its proud tradition.

From I-70; take Rte. 37 exit. (N) for 8 mi. on Rte. 37 into Granville. From Columbus; take Rte. 16 (E) for 25 mi. into Granville.

TEL. 614-587-0001

313 E. Broadway
Granville, OH 43023

Orville & Audrey Orr,
Innkeepers

THE GOLDEN LAMB

17 Rooms, $58/$90 B&B
1 Suite, $110

Visa, MC, Amex, DC, Discov, CB

All Private Baths

Dining Room closed Dec. 25

Children Accepted
No Pets

Golf, Tennis nearby

Lunch & Dinner, Mon.-Sat.; Sun. — Dinner only
Wine & Liquor available

Non-smoking Dining area

Conference Facilities (80)

From I-75 Exit at Rte. 63. Take Rte. 63 (E) 7 mi. to Lebanon. From I-71 Rte. 48 (N) 3 mi. to Lebanon. Inn at corner of Main (Rtes. 48 & 63) and Broadway.

TEL. 513-932-5065

27 S. Broadway
Lebanon, OH 45036

Jackson Reynolds,
Innkeeper

6 This illustrious inn (National Register of Historic Places) in America's heartland, the oldest in Ohio, has been in continuous operation since 1803. It has hosted 10 U.S. Presidents, Mark Twain, Charles Dickens, and Henry Clay. Antique-laden guest rooms boast the names of famous visitors, and everywhere are reminders of a lively and fascinating history. Exceptional American foods.

THE INN AT CEDAR FALLS

10 Rooms, $65/$90 B&B
Cabins $90/$125 B&B

Visa, MC

All Private Baths

Open Year-round
Closed Dec. 25

Children's accommodations limited;
No Pets

Hiking, Hammocks, Swimming, Canoeing, Riding

Breakfast; Dinner by reservation; Lunch for special occasions; BYOB

Specified Smoking areas

Conference Facilities (20)

Wheelchair Access (1 Room)

From Columbus: Rte. 33 (S) to Logan exit, R. on Rte. 664, 9.5 mi. L. on Rte. 374. Inn is 1 mi. on L.

TEL. 614-385-7489

21190 State Route 374
Logan, OH 43138

Ellen Grinsfelder, Innkeeper

5 The deceptively rustic 1840 Log House is an open kitchen-dining room, serving the most refined of gourmet dishes, prepared from home-grown produce. Guest rooms in the barn-shaped inn building combine antique beds, private baths, and sweeping views of meadows, woods, and wildlife. The rugged and beautiful Hocking Hills State Park flanks the inn on three sides.

THE INN AT HONEY RUN

	36 rooms, $79/$150 B&B 1 suite, $99/$125 B&B
	Visa, MC, Amex
	All Private Baths
	Closed Dec. 19-26, Jan. 2-9
	Children accepted No pets
R	Birdwatching, Nat. trails, Game room, Amish Ctry, Cheese Factories, Craft Shops, Golf, Tennis
	Breakfast, Lunch, Dinner BYOB for guest rooms only
	Some Non-smoking guest rooms, No smoking in dining room
	Conference Facilities (72)

2 In Ohio's Amish country on 60 scenic acres of woods and pasture, this prize winning, contemporary inn provides a serene retreat from daily pressures. Feast on fresh trout, country chicken, fresh fruits and vegetables. Marvel at the earth-sheltered honeycomb rooms with private patios, whirlpool tubs, fireplaces. Visit Holmes County Quilt, Furniture, Craft and Cheese shops.

From Millersburg: Rtes. 62/39 (E) for 2 blocks. L. on Rte. 241 (N) for 1.9 mi. R. (E) on County Rd. 203 for 1.5 mi.

TEL. 216-674-0011
FAX. 216-674-2623

6920 County Road 203
Millersburg, OH 44654

Marjorie Stock, Innkeeper

MURPHIN RIDGE INN

	10 Rooms, $75 B&B
	No Credit Cards
	All Private Baths
	Closed Jan. 1st-Feb. 12, and every Mon. & Tues.
	Children Welcome; No Pets
R	Swimming, Tennis, Hiking, Basketball, Shuffle Board, Amish Shops, Serpent Mound, Appalachia Preserve, Herbs
	Lunch & Dinner Wed. thru Sun.; BYOB
	No Smoking
	Conference Facilities (25-30)
	Wheelchair Access (6 rms.)

7 A tranquil 19th Century farm setting offers a step back in time. The brick farmhouse (1810) with dining rooms & original fireplaces, serves unique folk cuisine. The custom-furnished contemporary guest house provides modern comforts. Nearby Amish shops and Nature Conservancy's Edge of Appalachia preserve. Restaurant open to the public. Reservations suggested.

Rte 32 E. Rte. 41 S. To Dunkinsville 6 mi, R. on Wheatridge 1 1/2 mi. R. on Murphin Ridge 1/2 mi.

TEL. (513) 544-2263

750 Murphin Ridge Rd.
West Union, OH 45693

Mary & Robert Crosset Jr.,
Innkeepers

WHITE OAK INN

 10 Rooms, $60/$140 B&B
(3 Rms. with Fireplaces)

 Visa, MC

All Private Baths

Closed Christmas

 Appropriate for Children
over 12; No Pets

 Lawn games, Bicycling,
Amish country touring,
Antiquing, Golf, Fishing,
Canoeing, Hiking

Breakfast; Dinner by
reservation; Comp. Sherry
BYOB

No Smoking

Conference facilities (25)

From I-71: Rte 36 (E) or Rtes. 95 (E) and 13 (S) to Mt. Vernon. Then U.S. Rte 36 (E) 13 mi. to Rte 715. From I-77: Rte. 36 (W) 43 mi. to Rte 715. Take Rte. 715 (E) 3 mi. to inn.

TEL. 614-599-6107
29683 Walhonding (S.R. 715)
Danville, OH 43014
Ian & Yvonne Martin,
Innkeepers

 Turn-of-the-century farmhouse in a quiet, wooded country setting. Antiques and period decor, large fireplace in the common room, front porch with swings and rockers, a screen house and elegant meals make your stay a memorable occasion. Experience simple country pleasures and personal attention found only at a small inn. AAA rated ◆◆◆, Mobil Travel Guide rated ★★★.

THE WOOSTER INN

 15 Rooms, $73/$80 B&B
2 Suites, $95/$115 B&B

Visa, MC, Amex, Diners,
Discov.

All Private Baths

Closed Dec. 25

Well Supervised Children
accepted; Pets Accepted

 Golf, Tennis, Amish
settlements, Football Hall
of Fame in Canton, Wooster College activities

Breakfast, Lunch, Dinner,
Wine & Beer available

Non-Smoking Dining
Room

Conference Facilities (40)

Wheelchair Access

I-71 (S) to Burbank. L. on Rte. 83 (S), 18 mi. Wooster Exit, R. at Rte. 585 (S) for 200 ft. R. at Wayne Ave. Inn .7 mi. on L. I-71 (N) to US-30 E., 24 mi to Wooster Exit at Madison R. Follow to Beaver to Wayne Ave. 2 mi. Turn R, 2 blks. to inn.

TEL. 216-264-2341
FAX 216-264-9951 (24 hr.)
801 E. Wayne Ave.
Wooster, OH 44691
Andrea Lazar, Innkeeper

The
Wooster
Inn
Breakfast, Lunch, & Dinner
Open to the public

 The spacious campus of the College of Wooster is the setting for this pleasant inn, which overlooks the college golf course, where inn guests may play. Tastefully decorated rooms offer modern comfort and quiet, and cuisine in the attractive dining room is excellent and fresh. The Ohio Light Opera and college events provide cultural and recreational diversions.

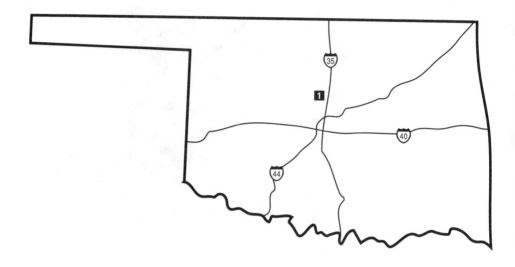

1. Harrison House, Guthrie

HARRISON HOUSE

	34 Rooms, $57/$107 B&B
	Visa, MC, Amex, Discov, Diners
	All Private Baths
	Open Year-round
	Children Accepted Pets w/prior permission
R	Historic sites, Museums, Rodeo, Theater, Golf, Horseback riding, Fishing
	Breakfast Wine Available
	Smoking accepted
	Conference facilities (425)
	Wheelchair Accessible (2 Rooms)

1 A gem of Victoriana in a handsome red brick building in the center of historic Guthrie, which celebrated its centennial in 1989. Transformed from an impressive 1902 bank building into a charmingly decorated, invitingly warm country inn, it perfectly expresses the pioneering spirit and character that typifies a gentler, bygone era. (National Register of Historic Places.)

From I-35: Exit 157 from (N); Exit 153 from (S). From (N): (W) 1.6 mi. on Noble to Division, L. 3 blocks to Harrison. R. 1 block. From (S): 4.3 mi. on Division to Harrison. L. 1 block.

TEL. 405-282-1000
800-375-1001
124 W. Harrison
Guthrie, OK 73044
Jane & Claude Thomas,
Owners

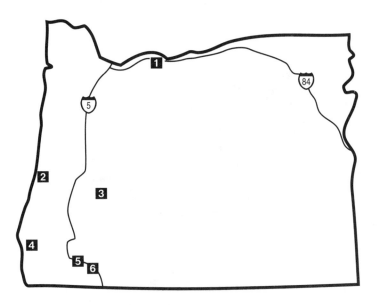

1. Columbia Gorge Hotel, Hood River
2. The Johnson House, Florence
3. Steamboat Inn, Steamboat
4. Tu Tu' Tun Lodge, Gold Beach
5. Jacksonville Inn, Jacksonville
6. Winchester Inn, Ashland

COLUMBIA GORGE HOTEL

42 Rooms, $175/$225 B&B

Visa, MC, Amex, Diners, Discov

All Private Baths

Open Year-round

Pets Allowed

Golf, Downhill & XC Skiing, Windsurfing, Fishing, Rock Climbing, Rafting, Mountain Biking

"Farm" Breakfast, Lunch & Dinner Liquor & Wine available

Non-smoking Dining Room

Conference Facilities (200)

Wheelchair Access (all rooms)

From Portland, OR, take I-84 (E) to Exit 62.

TEL. 503-386-5566
RES. 800-345-1921
FAX. 503-386-3359

4000 Westcliff Dr.
Hood River, OR 97031

Patrick J. Halloran
Innkeeper

1 A spectacular setting high above the Columbia River, in the heart of the National Scenic Area, with sweeping vistas of the gorge & Mt. Hood, this circa 1921 hostelry (National Register) has preserved the 1920s feeling in its furnishings. River Ct. dining offers superb Northwest cuisine and "world famous farm breakfast." Acres of gardens with 206-foot falls cascading at its back.

JACKSONVILLE INN

8 rooms, $80/$125 B&B
1 Suite, $175 B&B

Visa, MC, Discov, Amex, Diners

All Private Baths

Open Year-round

Children Accepted
No Pets

Museum, Antiques, Hiking, Wineries, Swimming, White Riv. Rafting, Shopping, Shakespeare Fest., Britt Music Festival

Restaurant, Bistro
Sun. Brunch, Lounge
Wine & Liquor available

Non-smoking Rooms

Conference Facilities (80)

5 Housed in one of Jacksonville's early (1861) permanent structures, built during the gold rush, the inn has locally quarried sandstone walls flecked with bits of gold in the dining room and lounge. In addition to guest rooms furnished with restored antiques, the inn boasts one of Oregon's most award-winning restaurants, with superb dining and a connoisseur's wine cellar.

I-5(N), Ex. 30, R. Crater Lk. Hwy (Hwy. 62) to Medford. R. on McAndrews, L. on Ross Lane, R. on W. Main (238), R. on Calif. St. I-5(S), Exit 27, L. on Barnett, R. on Riverside; L. on Main St. R. on Calif.

TEL. 503-899-1900; 800-321-9344; FAX 503-899-1373

175 E. California St.
Jacksonville, OR 97530
Jerry & Linda Evans,
Innkeepers

THE JOHNSON HOUSE

6 rooms, $75/$105 B&B

Visa, MC

Private Baths

Open Year-round

Appropriate for Children over 12; No Pets

Ocean Beaches, Dunes, Woods, Lakes, River, Whale-watching, Horseback Riding, Hiking, Fishing

Full Breakfast;
Complimentary Wine

BYOB

Smoking on porches

2 This is like "grandmother's house," with treasured heirlooms, amusing photographs and curios, where you are welcomed with a cup of tea. The 1892 Victorian inn is in the center of Old Town, a waterfront community on Oregon's scenic central coast. Blue and ivory guest rooms feature lace curtains, down comforters, and many books. Breakfasts are lavish and imaginative.

1 block (N) of Siuslaw River; 2 blocks (E) of Coast Hwy. 101; corner First & Maple in Old Town.

TEL. 503-997-8000

216 Maple St.
Florence, OR 97439
Ronald & Jayne Fraese,
Innkeepers

STEAMBOAT INN

 8 Cabins, $85 EP
7 Cotts./suites, $125/$195

 Visa, MC

 All Private Baths

 Limited services in winter

 Children Accepted
No Pets

 Fishing for steelhead, 35 mi. of public water, Backpacking, Hiking

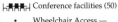 Breakfast, Lunch, Dinner by reservation
Wine & Beer Available

No Smoking

Conference facilities (50)

Wheelchair Access — inquire

I-5 to Roseburg. Steamboat Inn is 38 mi. (E) on Rte. 138. Inn is 70 mi. (W) of Crater Lake and 40 mi. (W) of Diamond Lake, on Rte. 138.

TEL. 503-496-3495 or 498-2411; FAX 498-2411 (2 rings +*2)
Steamboat, OR 97447-9703
Sharon & Jim Van Loan, Innkeepers
Patricia Lee, Manager

3 Imagine being lulled to sleep by sounds of the North Umpqua River! Nestled among towering firs, this inn's comfortable, cozy streamside cabins and hideaway cottages provide luxurious privacy. Gourmet meals served in a convivial atmosphere, Umpqua National Forest with its hiking trails, waterfalls, and the river — a steelhead fisherman's dream — are just a taste of the delights here.

TU TU' TUN LODGE

 16 rooms, $85/$123 EP
2 Suites, $85/$165 EP

 Visa, MC

All Private Baths

Closed Oct. 27-April 27; Year-round River Suites

 Sept.-June Children Very Welcome; Pets Welcome

Heated Pool, Player Piano, 4-Hole Pitch & Putt, Horseshoes, Pool Table, Salmon, Steelhead Fishing, Hiking, White-water Jet Boat Trips

 Breakfast, Lunch, Dinner, MAP available; Wine & Liquor Available

 No Smoking in Dining Room

Conference Facilities (40)

Wheelchair Access (8 Rooms)

Gold Beach, Hwy. 101 (E) 7 mi. along north side of Rogue River to Lodge.

TEL. 503-247-6664

96550 North Bank Rogue
Gold Beach, OR 97444

Dirk & Laurie Van Zante, Innkeepers

4 Casual elegance in the wilderness is the key at this lodge, nestled between the forest and the Rogue River, not far from the rugged Oregon coast. Guests enjoy hors d'oeuvres around the large stone fireplace, congenial gourmet dining, and madrone wood fires on the terrace at dusk. Exciting boat trips, Chinook salmon fishing, or relaxing in solitude are options here. Mobil ★★★★ AAA ◆◆◆◆.

OREGON
THE WINCHESTER COUNTRY INN

	7 Rooms, $88/$125 B&B
	Visa, MC
	All Private Baths
	Open Year-round
	Children Accepted No Pets
R	White water rafting, Hiking, XC & Downhill Skiing, Shakespeare Festival, Boating, Sailing, Music
	Breakfast, Sunday brunch, Dinner Wine & Liquor available
	Smoke-free Inn
	Conference facilities (35)

6 A true country inn in the heart of the city, this handsomely restored, century-old Victorian home (National Register) invites you to enjoy an atmosphere of sophisticated country living. Beautiful tiered gardens and gazebo welcome guests each morning for breakfast. Guest rooms offer antiques, balconies and patios. Gourmet dinners and champagne Sunday brunch are served.

From I-5 (N), 1st Ashland exit. R. on Valley View, L. on Hwy. 99 for 3 mi. to Ashland. R. on 2nd St. From I-5 (S), 1st Ashland exit, for 4 mi. to Ashland. L. on 2nd St.

TEl. 503-488-1113 or 488-1115; 800-972-4991
35 So. Second St.
Ashland, OR 97520
Michael and Laurie Gibbs, Innkeepers

Rates are quoted for 2 people for 1 night and do not necessarily include service charges and state taxes. An asterisk after the rates indicates a per-person rate for AP and MAP plans. For more detailed information, ask the inns for their brochures.

AP — American Plan (3 meals included in room rate)

MAP — Modified American Plan (breakfast & dinner included in room rate)

EP — European Plan (meals not included in room rate)

B&B — Bed & Breakfast (breakfast included in room rate)

R — Represents recreational facilities and diversions either on the premises of an inn or nearby

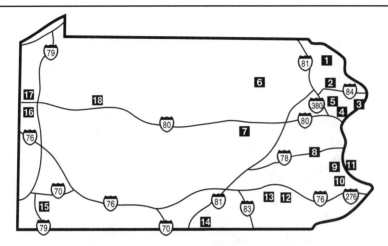

1. Inn at Starlight Lake, Starlight
2. The Settler Inn, Hawley
3. Cliff Park, Milford
4. Sterling Inn, South Sterling
5. The French Manor, South Sterling
6. Crestmont, Eagles Mere
7. Pine Barn Inn, Danville
8. Glasbern, Fogelsville
9. 1740 House, Lumberville
10. Barley Sheaf Farm, Holicong (Lahaska on maps)
11. Whitehall Inn, New Hope
12. Smithton Inn, Ephrata
13. Cameron Estate Inn, Mount Joy
14. Hickory Bridge Farm, Orrtanna
15. Century Inn, Scenery Hill
16. The Tavern, New Wilmington
17. Tara, Clark
18. Gateway Lodge, Cooksburg

BARLEY SHEAF FARM

8 Rooms, $110/$175 B&B
2 Suites, $116/$145 B&B

Amex, MC, Visa

All Private Baths

Closed Christmas week

Appropriate for Children over 8; No Pets

Pool, Historic touring, Shopping, Antiquing

Breakfast

Smoking allowed

Conference Facilities (20)

On Rte. 202, .5 mi. (W) of Lahaska. From N.J. take Rte. 202. From Rte. 276 and south, take Rte. 263 (N) to Buckingham and Rte. 202 to inn.

TEL. 215-794-5104

Route 202, Box 10
Holicong, PA 18928

Ann & Don Mills,
Innkeepers

10 Barley Sheaf is an early Bucks County farm comfortably situated at the end of a long tree-lined drive. Once owned by playwright George S. Kaufman, Barley Sheaf fulfills everyone's expectations of what a romantic country inn should be. The hospitality is likewise everything one might hope for. Exceptional guest rooms, gracious common rooms and an outstanding breakfast.

CAMERON ESTATE INN

	18 Rooms, $65/$110 B&B
	Visa, MC, Amex, Diners, Discov
	16 Private, 2 Shared Baths
	Closed Christmas Eve & Day
	Appropriate for Children over 12; No Pets
	Library, TV, Lawn Games, Golf, Swimming & Tennis nearby
	Breakfast, Dinner, Sun. Brunch Wine & Liquor available
	Smoking Accepted
	Conference Facilities (60)

13 The Inn & Restaurant occupy the rural Lancaster County estate of Simon Cameron, Abraham Lincoln's first Secretary of War. Rooms at Cameron are furnished in grand style and are individually decorated; 7 have fireplaces. The restaurant offers a fine selection of American and French food as well as the appropriate wines. Groff's Farm Restaurant, the county's finest, is also nearby.

Rte. 283 to Rte. 772(S) to 1st light in Mt. Joy and R. on Main to L. at next light (Angle St.) to R. on Donegal Springs Rd. for 4 mi. to the inn.

TEL. 717-653-1773
Fax 717-653-9432
R.D. 1, Box 305,
1895 Donegal Springs Rd.
Mount Joy, PA 17552
Stephanie Seitz, Larry
Hershey, & Mindy
Goodyear, Innkeepers

CENTURY INN

	5 Rooms, $78/$90 EP 4 Rooms, $100/$130 EP
	No Credit Cards
	All Private Baths
	Closed Dec. 23-Feb. 13
	Children Accepted No Pets
	Tennis, Croquet, Many Small Shops in Scenery Hill
	Breakfast, Houseguests only; Lunch, Dinner Wine & Liquor Available
	Smoking accepted
	Conference Facilities (175)

15 It's not hard to believe this is the oldest operating inn (1794) on the National Pike (U. S. 40) when you see the hand-forged crane in the original kitchen and the vast array of rare antiques adorning this intriguing inn. Called one of the dining super stars in the Pittsburgh area, the inn is a favorite destination for both country inn buffs and gourmands.

From I-70, Bentleyville Exit. Rte. 917(S) to Rte. 40. 1 mi.(E) to the inn.

TEL. 412-945-6600
Scenery Hill, PA 15360
Megin Harrington,
Innkeeper

CLIFF PARK INN & GOLF COURSE

 18 rooms, $100/$145 B&B

 Visa, MC, Amex, Diners

 All Private Baths

Closed Dec. 24 – 25

Children Accepted with Parents; No Pets

 9-hole Golf Course, Hiking Trails, Delaware River for Swimming, Fishing, Rafting, Canoeing, XC Skiing

 Breakfast, Lunch & Dinner; MAP rates available Wine & Liquor Available

Smoking Permitted

Conference Facitlities (20)

 Wheelchair access (5 rms.)

I-80 to Ex. 34B; Rte. 15N becomes 206N, into Milford, PA. Thru traffic light, 2 blks. L. onto 7th & go 1.5 mi. to inn. From I-84, Ex. 10, Milford, (E) on Rte. 6 for 2 mi. R. on 7th St. for 1.5 mi. to inn.

TEL. 717-296-6491
800-225-6535 (outside PA)
RR4, Box 7200
Milford, PA 18337-9707
Harry W. Buchanan III,
Innkeeper

3 Surrounded by one of America's oldest golf courses (1913) and 600 secluded acres of wood and fields, this historic inn offers old-fashioned hospitality, heirlooms reflecting the life and times of the Buchanan family. Antiques and lace grace the guest rooms and the maple-shaded veranda overlooks the golf course. Their master chef specializes in American, French and Cajun cuisine.

CRESTMONT INN

 16 Rooms, $125/$140 MAP 4 Suites, $155/$170 MAP

Personal Checks Accepted

All Private Baths

Open May 1 - Nov. 1; late fall & winter weekends

Appropriate for Children over 6; No Pets

Swimming pool, 6 Har-Tru Tennis courts, Golf, Lake activities, Hiking trails, Ice Skating, XC Skiing, Tobogganing, Cultural activities, summer months

Country Breakfast & Dinner; to the public by res. Wine & Liquor available

Smoking Accepted

Conference Facilities (20)

 Wheelchair Access (9 rooms)

From I-80, Exit 34 to 42 (N) for 33 mi. to Eagles Mere village. Continue thru town & follow Crestmont signs.

TEL. 717-525-3519

Crestmont Dr.
Eagles Mere, PA 17731

Robert & Kathleen Oliver,
Innkeepers

6 A warm, welcome awaits you at this familiar landmark in a lovely turn-of-the-century village. Enjoy spacious grounds, waterfall, gardens, resident musicians, lake activities, a cozy cocktail lounge and gourmet dining. Guest rooms withVictorian porches make for enjoyable relaxation. As Norman Simpson said, "Eagles Mere is one of the last unspoiled resorts in the East."

THE FRENCH MANOR

🛏	6 Rooms, $120/$150 B&B 3 suites, $160/$200 B&B
💳	Visa, MC, Amex, Discov
🛁	All Private Baths
💡🔥	Open Year-round
🐕👧	Not suitable for Children No Pets
ⓇⅢ	Hiking, Croquet, Beautiful scenery, Swimming, Tennis, XC Skiing, Ice Skating nearby
◎🍽	French restaurant MAP rates available Wine & Liquor available
🚭	Non-smoking Dining
⊢▦⊣	Conference Facilities (15)

5 Built by art connoisseur Joseph Hirschorn, modeled after his Provence, France manor, this stone chateau atop Huckleberry Mtn. overlooks 45 acres of the beautiful northern Poconos. In 1932, using native woods & fieldstone, 165 artisans & craftsmen created this elegant inn and French restaurant, built to beguile the most discerning guest. New in '93, Carriage House suite, with Jacuzzi.

From NYC: I-80(W), PA Exit 52 to Rte. 447(N) to Rte. 191(N) to S. Sterling. Turn L. on Huckleberry Rd. From Phila: NE extension of PA Tpke. to Pocono Exit 35. Follow Rtes. 940(E), 423(N) to 191(N) 2.5 mi. to Huckleberry Rd.

TEL. 717-676-3244
RES. 800-523-8200
Box 39, Huckleberry Rd.
South Sterling, PA 18460
Ron & Mary Kay Logan,
Innkeepers

GATEWAY LODGE

🛏	8 Rooms, $85/$164 EP 8 Cottages, $80/$120 EP w/Fireplaces
💳	Visa, MC, Amex, Discov Private and Shared Baths
💡🔥	Closed Wed. & Thurs. Thanksgiving week; Dec. 24-25
🐕	Children (inquire) No Pets
ⓇⅢ	Indoor pool & Sauna for main inn guests only, XC Skiing, Bicycling, Fishing, Summer Theater, Hiking
◎🍽	Breakfast daily; Dinner except Mon. Aftnoon. tea. Full Bar Service. EP, MAP, B&B available.
🚭	Smoking restricted
⊢▦⊣	Conference Facilities (75)
♿	

18 Amid some of the most magnificent forest scenery east of the Rocky Mountains, this rustic log cabin inn has been called one of the ten best country inns in the U.S. Guests gather around the large stone fireplace in the living room and savor wonderful home-cooked meals by kerosene light. Main inn guests may enjoy the indoor swimming pool.

From east: I-80, Exit 13 to Rte. 36 (N) to Cook Forest. Inn is on Rte. 36, 1/4 mi. (S) of Cooksburg Br. From west: off I-80, Exit 8 (Shippenville) to Rte. 66 to Leeper (13 mi.) to Rte. 36 (S) (7 mi.). Inn is on Rte. 36 1/4 mi. (S) of Cooksburg Br.

814-744-8017
(PA: 800-843-6862)
Route 36, Box 125,
Cooksburg, PA 16217
The Burney Family

GLASBERN

	10 Rooms, $95/$145 B&B 13 Suites, $110/$200 B&B
	Visa, MC, Amex
	All Private Baths, 16 Whirlpools
	Open Year-round
	Children Accepted No Pets
	Swimming pool, Trails thru 100 acres, Bicycling, Hot air ballooning, Fishing
	Breakfast; Dinner Tues.- Sat. Wine & Liquor Available
	Smoking Allowed
	Conference Facilities (16)

From I-78 take Rte. 100(N) for .2 mi. to L. at light (W) for .3 mi. to R. on Church St. (N) for .6 mi. to R. on Pack House Rd. for .8 mi. to the inn.

TEL. 215-285-4723
Pack House Rd., R.D. 1,
Box 250
Fogelsville, PA 18051-9743
Beth & Al Granger,
Innkeepers

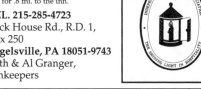

8 An ingeniously contemporized Pennsylvania farm with exposed timber, cathedral ceilings, and many windows. The Carriage House rooms have skylights, fireplaces, and whirlpools. With views of the valley and a swimming pool, Glasbern offers deep-country tranquility in a warm and luxurious atmosphere. AAA & Mobil 3 stars, AB & B 4 crowns.

HICKORY BRIDGE FARM

	7 Rooms, $75/$89 B&B
	Visa, MC
	All Private Baths
	Closed Christmas week
	Children Accepted No Pets
	Gettysburg touring, Fishing, Swimming, Hiking, Bicycling, Golf, Skiing
	Breakfast, Houseguests, Dinner, Fri., Sat., Sun.
	No Smoking
	Conference facilities
	Wheelchair Access

Gettysburg, Rte. 116(W) to Fairfield and R. 3 mi.(N) to Orrtanna. Or Rte. 977 to Rte. 30(E) for 9 mi. Turn (S) at Cashtown for 3 mi. to inn.

TEL. 717-642-5261
96 Hickory Bridge Rd.
Orrtanna, PA 17353
Robert & Mary Lynn
Martin, Dr. & Mrs. James
Hammett,Innkeepers

14 A quaint country inn and restaurant located just outside of Gettysburg on a family operated farm. Fine country dining Friday, Saturday and Sunday in a restored Pennsylvania barn. The inn is open seven days a week, B&B. A quiet setting with a restaurant, a museum, a gift shop, rooms and cottages. A wonderful "country place."

THE INN AT STARLIGHT LAKE

	26 Rooms, $82/$154 MAP 1 Suite, $130/$200 MAP
	Visa, MC
	Private and Shared Baths
	Open Year-round
	Children Accepted No Pets
R	Swimming, Boating, Tennis, Ice Skating, XC Skiing, Lawn Sports, Fishing, Golf
	Breakfast, Lunch, Dinner, Sunday Brunch Wine & Liquor available
	No Smoking in Dining Room
	Conference facilities (60)

1 Since 1909, guests have been drawn to this classic country inn on a beautiful, clear lake in the northeastern Pennsylvania highlands. The atmosphere is warm, congenial, and informal. There are activities for all seasons; swimming, x-country skiing. Lakeside dining offers outstanding American and continental cuisine which changes with the seasons, home baked goods and pastas.

From N.Y. Rte. 17, Exit 87 (Hancock). On Rte. 191 (S) 1 mi. to Rte. 370 (W), turn R. 3 mi. to sign on R. take R. 1 mi. to inn. From I-81, Exit 62, local roads; map sent on request.

TEL. 717-798-2519
800-248-2519
Starlight, PA 18461
Judy & Jack McMahon,
Innkeepers

THE PINE BARN INN

	75 Rooms, $46/$68 EP
	Visa, Amex, CB, Disc, MC, Diners
	All Private Baths
	Open Year-round
	Children Accepted; Pets (ltd. accommodations)
R	Golf, Tennis, Swimming, Horseback riding, Racquetball nearby
	Breakfast, Lunch, Dinner Wine & Liquor available
	Non-smoking dining area
	Conference Facilities (50)
	Wheelchair Access (1 Room)

7 A part of the history and tradition of Danville for over 100 years, this inn began life first as a barn and then as a riding stable. Today, the restaurant and original rooms still occupy the original barn, with many additional rooms in more   recently completed buildings. The restaurant has been renowned for decades for its fresh seafood and homemade pies and pastries.

From I-80, Exit 33, Rte. 54 (E) 2 mi. to Danville. L. 1st traffic light, signs to Medical Ctr. Inn at entrance to Geisinger Med. Ctr.

TEL. 717-275-2071; 800-627-2276; FAX 717-275-3248
#1 Pine Barn Place
Danville, PA 17821
Martin & Barbara Walzer,
Innkeepers

1740 HOUSE

 23 Rooms, $70/$100 B&B
1 Suite, $70/$100 B&B

 Personal Checks Accepted

All Private Baths

 Open Year-round

 No Children
No Pets

 Pool at inn, Canoeing,
Riding, Golf, Individual
A/C

 Breakfast, Daily to houseguests; Dinner, Tues. thru
Sat., by res.; BYOB

 Non-smoking Dining
Room

 Conference facilities (22)

Wheelchair Access (3
Rooms)

From NY & NJ use 202 (S) to Rte. 32.
From I-95 use New Hope/Yardley exit
(N) to New Hope. Lumberville is 7 mi.
(N) of New Hope on Rte. 32.

TEL. 215-297-5661

River Rd. (Hwy. 32)
Lumberville, PA 18933

Harry Nessler & Robert
John Vris, Innkeepers

9 An intimate view of the river from a lovely room with a private terrace or balcony is only one of the pleasures at this 18th-century, restored farmhouse on the the banks of the Delaware River. *Newsweek, McCall's, Glamour, & Harper's Bazaar* have all listed The 1740 House as one of their 10 favorite inns. The excellent restaurant is open to the public.

THE SETTLERS INN

16 Rooms, $75/$95 B&B
3 Suites, $110/$125 B&B

Visa, MC, Amex

All Private Baths

Open Year-round

Appropriate for Children
No Pets

Lake Wallenpaupack,
Upper Delaware River,
Promised Land State Park,
Golf, Skiing, Horseback,
Canoeing, Fishing, Glass
Museum, Antique Shops

Breakfast, Lunch, Dinner
Wine & Liquor available

Smoking designated areas

Conference Facilities (100)

Wheelchair Access -
Dining Room only

TEL. 717-226-2993
800-833-8527

Four Main Avenue
Hawley, PA 18428

Jeanne & Grant Genzlinger,
Innkeepers

2 Reminiscent of a small European hotel, this Tudor Manor is in the Victorian village of Hawley. Chestnut wood beams, bluestone fireplace, leaded windows, outdoor patio & herb gardens add to the ambiance. Regional cuisine and friendly personal service. Lake Wallenpaupack, the upper Delaware River, & many recreational activities are nearby. Antique shops and summer theatre in town.

SMITHTON INN

	8 Rooms, $65/$115 B&B 1 Suite, $140/$170 B&B
	Visa, MC, Amex
	Private Baths, some Whirlpools
	Open Year-round
	Children and Pets by prior arrangement
	Library, Gardens, Croquet, Touring, Antiques, Epharta Cloister
	Breakfast
	No Smoking
	Wheelchair Access (1 Room)

12 A romantic 1763 stone inn located in Lancaster County among the Pennsylvania Dutch. Rooms are large, bright and cheerful with working fireplaces, canopy beds, desks, leather upholstered furniture, Penn. Dutch quilts, candles, chamber music, refrigeration, feather beds (by prior arrangement), books, and reading lamps. Common rooms are warm and inviting with fireplaces.

From North, PA Tpke. Exit 21 & Rte. 222 (S). From South, Hwy. 30 to Rte. 222 (N). From North or South, Exit Rte. 222 at Rte. 322 (W) for 2.5 mi. to inn.

TEL. 717-733-6094

900 W. Main St.
Ephrata, PA 17522
Dorothy Graybill,
Innkeeper

THE STERLING INN

	40 Rooms, $130/$160 MAP 16 Suites, $170/200 MAP
	Visa, MC, Amex, Discov All Private Baths
	Open Year-round
	Children Accepted No Pets
	Indoor Pool, Lake, Tennis, Hiking, Horseback Riding, Golf, XC Skiing, Sleigh Rides, Antiquing
	Breakfast, Lunch, Dinner. B&B rates on request Wine & Liquor available
	No Smoking in Dining area
	Conference facilities (125)
	Wheelchair Access (3 rm.)

4 The country inn you've always looked for, but never thought you'd find. A friendly, romantic atmosphere with beautiful gardens, crystal clear streams, a waterfall, Victorian suites with fireplaces, & horse-drawn sleigh rides. Attractive rooms, indoor pool & spa, & outstanding meals make this family operated, 130-year-old inn everything you thought a country inn should be.

I-84, Exit 6, Rte. 507 (S), 3 mi. to Rte. 191 (S), 3 mi. to inn. I-80 (W) Exit 50, Rte. 191 (N) 25 mi. to inn. I-80 (E) Rte. 380 to Rte. 423 (N), to 191 (N), .5 mi. to inn.

TEL. 717-676-3311
RES: 800-523-8200
Rte. 191
South Sterling, PA 18460
Ron & Mary Kay Logan,
Innkeepers

TARA — A COUNTRY INN

 25 Rooms $158/$278 MAP
2 Suites $318 MAP

 Visa, MC, Discov

All private Baths

 Open Year-round

Not appropriate for Children
Kennels nearby for Pets

 Bocci, Croquet, Boating, Golf, Biking, Pool Table, Antiquing, XC Skiing, Swim Pools, Sauna, Steam

 Breakfast, Lunch, Dinner, B&B rates available
Wine & Liquor available

Smoking in designated areas

Conference Facilities (80)

From I-80, exit 1N, Rte. 18 (N) for 8 mi. Inn is located on (E) side overlooking Lake Shenango

TEL. 412-962-3535
800-782-2803

3665 Valley View, Box 475
Clark, PA 16113

Jim & Donna Winner, Innkeepers

17 If you loved the movie *Gone With the Wind*, you will love Tara. Built in 1854, this magnificent mansion reflects the golden days of the antebellum South, with rooms charmingly decorated to recall the grace and grandeur of yesteryear. Delightfully different cuisine, from gourmet to family-style, is served in the three totally different restaurants. (A 4-diamond inn.)

THE TAVERN AND LODGE

5 Rooms, $49/$75, B&B

Tavern—No Credit Cards
Lodge — Visa, MC

All Private Baths

Tavern Closed July 4, Dec. 25, Thanksgiving & Tues.

Children Accepted
Pets Accepted

 Golf, XC Skiing, Fishing

Continental Breakfast, Houseguests; Lunch, Dinner

Smoking Accepted

Conference Facilities (50)

I-80 E; Exit 1S onto Rte. 60 (S), to Rte. 18 (S). (E) on Rte. 208, 1 mi. to inn. I-80 W; Exit 2, (N) to Mercer. (S) on Rte. 158, 9 mi. to inn. I-79; Exit Rte. 208 (W), 14 mi. to inn.

TEL. 412-946-2020
Lodge: 412-946-2091
101 N. Market St.
New Wilmington, PA 16142
Mary Ellen Durrast, Innkeeper

16 This delightfully old fashioned restaurant in the fascinating Amish country of northwestern Pennsylvania has won followers for over sixty years with bounteous home style cooking. With the legendary sticky rolls, creamed chicken on a biscuit, and wonderful baked ham, plus over 25 other selections, guests enjoy delightful dining in charming surroundings. Guest rooms across the street.

THE WHITEHALL INN

6 Rooms, $130/$170 B&B

Visa, MC, Amex, CB, Diners, Discov.

4 Private, 1 Shared Bath

Open Year-round

Appropriate for Children over 12; No Pets

Swimming Pool, Horseback Riding, XC Skiing, Public & Private Golfing, Tennis, Hiking, Delaware River Water Sports

4-Course Breakfast, Afternoon Tea; Wine Available

No Smoking on Property

Conference Facilities (15)

11 Experience the 4-course candlelight breakfast and afternoon high tea called "sumptuous" by *Bon Appetit*. Classical music is everywhere, fireplaces add a romantic touch, and family antiques provide a hint of home. Enjoy the rose garden and pool in the warmer months. Feed the dressage horses a carrot. Relax and do nothing. Mike and Suella extend a special welcome to their guests.

Hwy. 202 (S) from New Hope to Lahaska. L. on to Street Rd. to 2nd intersection, bear R. on Pineville Rd. Continue 1.5 mi. to inn on R.

TEL. 215-598-7945

RD2, Box 250
1370 Pineville Rd.
New Hope, PA 18938

Mike and Suella Wass, Innkeepers

A SHORT HISTORY OF THE AMERICAN COUNTRY INN

Often a hotbed of political activity, where plots were hatched and plans were made, American inns in Colonial days were more than simply hostelries providing bed and board. Along with the church and the New England town meeting, the American inn ranks as one of the oldest continuing institutions in our country. In the 17th century some communities were required by law to provide accommodations and provender for travelers. They were called variously taverns or inns or ordinaries. The center of village activity, those early inns sometimes served as churches, gaols, courtrooms, political campaign headquarters, theaters, runaway slave stations, smuggler's hideaways, and even bordellos and mortuaries. In the seaport cities of the South, Spanish Main pirates had their favorite tavern haunts with secret tunnels, through which unwilling sailors could be shanghaied onto waiting ships.

During the Revolution, inns served as way stations between military posts, storing arms and ammunition and passing along intelligence on the movements of British troops. General Washington's New York headquarters were in the now-famous Fraunces Tavern.

As roads began to thread the colonies, stagecoach stops sprang up, and with westward expansion, the tradition of finding food and refuge in ranches and cabins on the prairie and in the mountains later turned many a farm and ranch into an inn.

Railroads made the stagecoach obsolete and often the once-bustling towns and inns on the stagecoach routes became irrelevant and sank into oblivion. Other towns grew up beside the railroads, and "commercial travelers" patronized the new "commercial hotels." Trains carried families to the mountains, seashore, and mineral springs resorts for summer vacations. Tremendous hotels with huge staffs became a significant part of the American vacation scene and remained popular destinations for 75 years. Lodgings included 3 meals daily, hence the term "American Plan." — **by Virginia Rowe**

1. Inn at Castle Hill, Newport
2. The Inntowne, Newport
3. Larchwood Inn, Wakefield
4. Hotel Manisses, Block Island
5. 1661 Inn, Block Island

HOTEL MANISSES

17 Rooms, $75/$300 B&B

Visa, MC, Amex

All private baths; 4 Jacuzzi

Open year-round; Dining Room open daily mid-May–Nov. 3; Wkends only Nov.–mid-May

Appropriate for Children over 10; No Pets

Swimming, Boating, Fishing

Buffet Breakfast Complimentary Wine & Nibble hour; Dinner Wine & Liquor available

Smoking accepted

Conference Facilities (80)

Wheelchair Access (3 Rooms)

By ferry: Providence, Pt. Judith, Newport, RI & New London, CT. By air: Newport, Westerly, Providence, RI & New London, Waterford, CT. Contact inn for schedules.

TEL. 401-466-2421

Spring St.
Block Island, RI 02807

The Abrams Family, Innkeepers

4 This elegant, restored Victorian hotel is listed on the National Register of Historic Places. Guest rooms offer antique furnishings, private baths and some Jacuzzis. The grounds abound with gardens and fountains. The award-winning dining room serves dinner every evening. After-dinner drinks and flaming coffees are served in the parlors.

INN AT CASTLE HILL

 15 Rooms, $50/$180 B&B
1 Suite, $130/$225 B&B

 Visa, MC, Amex

Private and Shared Baths

 Lodging closed Dec. 24;
Dining room closed Nov.
-late Apr.

 Appropriate for Children
over 12; No Pets

 Beaches, Walking Paths,
Golf, Tennis, Bicycling

 Lunch, Tues.-Sat.; Sun
Brunch; Dinner, Mon.-
Sat.; Wine & Liquor
Available

 Non-smoking Dining
area

1 Echoes of Newport's Gilded Age are everywhere in this spacious mansion, built in 1874 on 32 acres of secluded shoreline on the edge of Narragansett Bay. Roomy and distinctive guest rooms and baths, with many original furnishings and fittings, breathtaking views of harbor and ocean, and fresh sea breezes beguile guests who enjoy the fine European cuisine and friendly service.

I-95 to Rte. 138 (E) exit downtown Newport to Farewell St., R. to America's Cup Ave. straight to Memorial Blvd., R. on Bellevue Ave., L. on Ocean Ave. 5 mi. (S) of downtown.

TEL. 401-849-3800
Ocean Drive
Newport, RI 02840
Jens Thillemann, Manager,
Paul McEnroe, Innkeeper

THE INNTOWNE

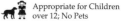 21 Rooms, $110/$200 B&B
5 Suites, $195/$250 B&B

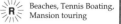 Visa, MC, Amex

 All Private Baths

 Open Year-round

 Appropriate for Children
over 12; No Pets

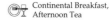 Beaches, Tennis Boating,
Mansion touring

 Continental Breakfast,
Afternoon Tea

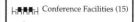 Smoking Accepted

Conference Facilities (15)

2 This in-town Colonial mansion with a garrison roof is right in the center of bustling Newport, just a block from the water. Rooms are bright and gay with elegant antiques, good reproductions, and paintings. A few steps from the door are beautiful sunsets, towering sailboat masts, quaint and fashionable shops, and many restaurants.

Cross Newport bridge, R. at 1st exit sign. R. at bottom of ramp, straight to Thames St. Inn is on corner of Thames and Mary Sts. across from Brick Marketplace.

TEL. 401-846-9200; 800-457-
7803; FAX 401-846-1534
6 Mary St.
Newport, RI 02840
Carmella Gardner, Innkeeper

LARCHWOOD INN

 19 Rooms, $40/$90 EP

 Visa, MC, Amex, D.C., Discov, C.B.

Private and Shared Baths

 Open Year-round

 Children Accepted
Pets Allowed

 Ocean Swimming, Fishing, Golf, Tennis, Historic Touring, Bicycling, Boating

Breakfast, Lunch, Dinner
Wine and Liquor available

Non-smoking dining area

Conference Facilities (125)

From NYC and South; I-95 (N) to Exit 3A(Rte. 138E) to Kingston, Rte. 108 to Wakefield - Rt. on Main St., follow to inn on Rt. From Boston and points North; I-95(S) to Exit 9(Rte. 4) which becomes Rte.1. Exit at first sign for Wakefield, follow Main St. to inn on R.

TEL. 401-783-5454
FAX 401-783-1800
521 Main St.
Wakefield, RI 02879
Francis & Diann Browning, Innkeepers

3 Watching over the main street of this quaint New England town for 160 years, this grand old house, surrounded by lawns and shaded by stately trees, dispenses hospitality along with good food and spirits from early morning to late night. Historic Newport, picturesque Mystic Seaport, and salty Block Island are a short ride away.

THE 1661 INN

 19 Rooms, $50/$300 B&B

 Visa, MC, Amex

 14 Private Baths; 5 Jacuzzis

 Open Year-round

 Children Accepted
No Pets

 Swimming, Boating, Fishing, Bicycling, Lawn Games

Breakfast
Comp. Wine & Nibble hr.
Wine & Liquor Available

Smoking Accepted

Conference Facilities (80)

By Ferry: Providence, Pt. Judith, Newport, RI, and New London, CT. By air: Newport, Westerly, Providence, RI and New London, Waterford, CT. Contact inn for schedules

TEL.401-466-2421;466-2063
Spring Street
Block Island, RI 02807
The Abrams Family
Innkeepers

5 This gracious inn overlooks the Atlantic Ocean. Some rooms offer ocean views, private sun decks, Jacuzzis and fireplaces. The ocean view dining room serves a bountiful buffet breakfast every morning. During July and August lunch is served daily. Guests can dine at the Hotel Manisses every evening.

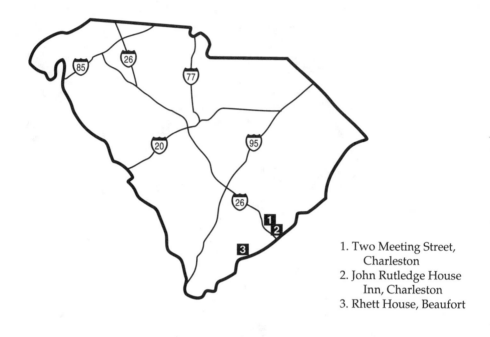

1. Two Meeting Street, Charleston
2. John Rutledge House Inn, Charleston
3. Rhett House, Beaufort

JOHN RUTLEDGE HOUSE INN

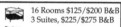 16 Rooms $125/$200 B&B
3 Suites, $225/$275 B&B

 Amex, MC, Visa

 All Private Baths

 Open Year-round

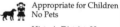 Appropriate for Children
No Pets

Historic District, Homes,
& Garden Tours, Market
area within walking
distance

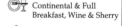 Continental & Full
Breakfast, Wine & Sherry

 Conference Facilities (20)

2 Built in 1763 by John Rutledge, a signer of the United States Constitution, this elegant home is now a bed and breakfast inn. All guests receive wine and sherry in the ballroom, evening turndown with chocolate at bedside and continental breakfast and newspaper delivered to the room each morning. Free on-site parking. AAA Four Diamond. Historic Hotels of America.

Call for directions.

TEL. 803-723-7999
800-476-9741

116 Broad St.
Charleston, SC 29401

Richard Widman
Innkeeper

THE RHETT HOUSE

 10 Rooms, $95/$175 B&B

 Visa, MC, Personal Checks

 All Private Baths

 Open Year-round

 Appropriate for Children over 5; No Pets

 Antiques, Historic Homes, Biking, Golf, Beach, Tennis, Pool, Carriage Rides, Gardens

 Breakfast, Afternoon tea; Picnic Lunch & Gourmet Dinners, Wine & Liquor

 Smoking on Verandas

Conference Facilities (20)

Wheelchair Access (3 Rm)

I-95, Exit 32 & follow signs, to Beaufort, R. on Craven St. for 4 blks. to Newcastle St. & inn.

TEL 803-524-9030

1009 Craven St.
Beaufort, SC 29902

Steve & Marianne
Harrison, Innkeepers

3 Near the waterfront in this historic town, Rhett House is a restored antebellum (1820) mansion, furnished with antiques, homespun quilts, pretty fabrics, fresh cut flowers, fireplaces & wicker on a spacious veranda. Candlelit dinners in front of the fireplace, and classical music, are truly memorable. History-laden Beaufort, Charleston, Savannah and Hilton Head offer rich exploring.

TWO MEETING STREET INN

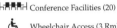 9 Rooms $95/$155 B&B

No Credit Cards

All Private Baths

Closed Christmas (3 days)

Appropriate for Children over 8 years; No Pets

Easy access to Shopping, Antiquing, Golfing, Fine Dining, Plantations, Beaches, Museums

Continental Breakfast Afternoon Tea and Sherry,

No Smoking

From 26E, exit Meeting Street. Travel south - Located on corner of Meeting and South Battery at White Point Garden.

TEL. 803-723-7322

2 Meeting Street
Charleston, SC 29401

Pete and Jean Spell
Innkeepers

1 "The Belle of Charleston's B&Bs," this Queen Anne mansion ca. 1890 in Charleston's Historic District, overlooks White Pt. Gardens at The Battery. Guests are charmed with Tiffany stained glass windows, four poster canopy beds, oriental carpets & English antiques. Continental breakfast enjoyed in the garden/courtyard or formal dining room & evening sherry is served on the front Piazza.

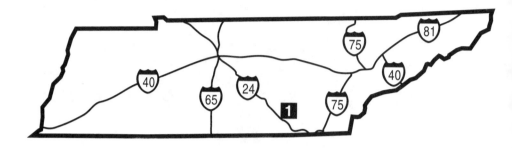

1. Adams Edgeworth Inn, Monteagle

ADAMS EDGEWORTH INN

	12 Rooms $55/$95 B&B 2 Suites, $125/$150 B&B
	Visa, MC,
	All Private Baths
	Open Year-round
	Children welcome by prior arrangement; No Pets, kennel nearby
R	TN Aquarium, Sewanne University, Sauna, Music, Theatre, Hike, Tennis, Swim, Bike, Chautauqua
	Breakfast, picnics on request, Candlelight Dinners by reservation; BYOB Smoking Restricted
	Conference Facilities (22)
	Wheelchair Access (1 Room)

1 This 1896 National Register Inn features English decor, antiques, fine art, collector quilts, fireplaces, hand made mattresses on beautiful beds. It is one of 170 Victorian homes in the Monteagle Assembly. Nestled in a wilderness atop the Cumberland Mtns, the Assembly is an 1880 "Camelot" in a forest garden of brooks & tall trestle bridges. Musical & cultural events.

I-24, exit 134, R 1/2 mi., L under archway to stone gate, call Inn for access (#0230)

TEL. (615) 924-2669
FAX (615) 924-3236

Monteagle Assembly
Monteagle, TN 37356

Wendy & David Adams,
Innkeepers

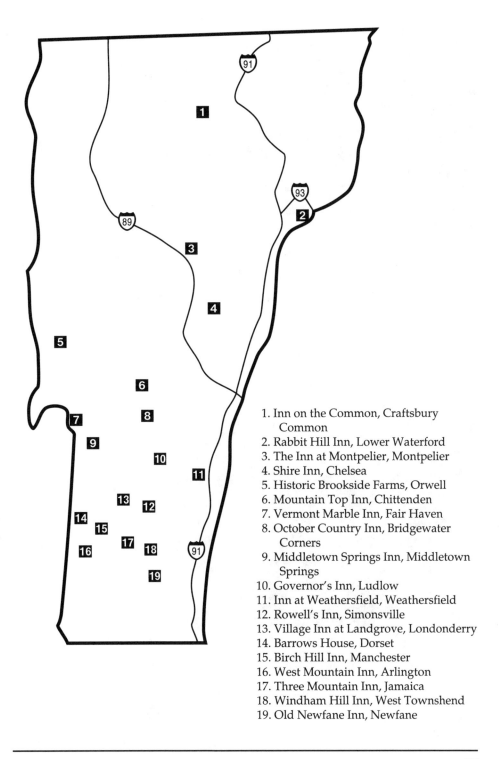

1. Inn on the Common, Craftsbury Common
2. Rabbit Hill Inn, Lower Waterford
3. The Inn at Montpelier, Montpelier
4. Shire Inn, Chelsea
5. Historic Brookside Farms, Orwell
6. Mountain Top Inn, Chittenden
7. Vermont Marble Inn, Fair Haven
8. October Country Inn, Bridgewater Corners
9. Middletown Springs Inn, Middletown Springs
10. Governor's Inn, Ludlow
11. Inn at Weathersfield, Weathersfield
12. Rowell's Inn, Simonsville
13. Village Inn at Landgrove, Londonderry
14. Barrows House, Dorset
15. Birch Hill Inn, Manchester
16. West Mountain Inn, Arlington
17. Three Mountain Inn, Jamaica
18. Windham Hill Inn, West Townshend
19. Old Newfane Inn, Newfane

BARROWS HOUSE

🛏	21 Rooms, $160/$180 MAP 7 Suites, $185/$210 MAP
💳	Visa, MC
🛁	All Private Baths
🛋	Open Year-round
🐕👫	Children Welcome Pets in 2 Cottages only
ⓇＲ	Heated Pool, Sauna, Tennis Courts, Bike, Skiing, Hiking, Historic & Fine Arts centers, Shopping
◉Ｙ	Breakfast, Dinner, Brown bag Lunch on request; B&B available, Liquor & Wine available
🚬	Smoking permitted with restrictions
⊢🪑🪑⊣	Conference Facilities (22)
♿	Wheelchair Access Ltd.

14 The Barrows House is a collection of white clapboard buildings situated on 11 acres in the heart of a small picturebook Vermont town. Guests have a choice of 28 accommodations in eight different buildings, all with a history & style of their own. Best of all, dining at the Barrows House is an informal & delicious adventure in American regional cuisine.

Manchester, Rte. 30 (N) 6 mi. to inn on R. Accessible from Vt. Rtes. 7, 4, 11, 30 and I-91 & 87.

TEL. 802-867-4455

Route 30
Dorset, VT 05251

Linda & Jim McGinnis,
Innkeepers

BIRCH HILL INN

🛏	5 Rooms, $100/$120 B&B 1 Cottage, $110 B&B
💳	Visa, MC, Amex
🛁	All Private Baths
🛋	Closed Nov. 1 - Dec. 26 Apr. 10 - May 30
🐕👫	Appropriate for Children over 6; No Pets
ⓇＲ	Pool, Trout Pond, Walking & XC Ski Trails, Antiquing, Summer Theatre
◉Ｙ	Breakfast & Tea; Dinner for house guests Fri. & Sat.; BYOB
🚬	Smoking accepted in living room
⊢🪑🪑⊣	
♿	

15 This inn has a spectacular location. On a back road away from busy village streets, among fabulous white birches, the inn has the feeling of a gracious home and quiet, peaceful retreat. Each cheerfully decorated room has views of surrounding mountains, farm and gardens. Hearty breakfasts and fine country dinners are among the pleasures to be found here.

In Manchester Center, Junction of Rtes. 7A & 30, take Rte. 30 (N) for 2.7 mi. to Manchester West Rd. go L. (S) for 3/4 of mi.

TEL. 802-362-2761

West Road, P.O. Box 346
Manchester, VT 05254

Pat & Jim Lee, Innkeepers

THE GOVENOR'S INN

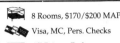

- 8 Rooms, $170/$200 MAP
- Visa, MC, Pers. Checks
- All Private Baths
- Open Year-round
- Not appropriate for young Children; No Pets
- XC & Downhill Skiing, Antiquing, Golf, Boating, Fishing, Hiking, Winery, Summer Theater
- Full Breakfast, Dinner, Afternoon Tea, Picnics, Wine & Liquor available
- No Smoking

Ludlow is located at junction of Rtes. 100 & 103. Inn is (S) on Rte. 103, just off village green.

TEL. 802-228-8830; 800-GOVERNOR (468-3766)

86 Main Street
Ludlow, VT 05149

Charlie & Deedy Marble, Innkeepers

10 This may be the ultimate experience at an elegant Victorian country inn. From pot-pourri scented air to the soft strains of classical music to the beautifully kept heirlooms, attention is given to every detail of pleasure and comfort. National recognition & awards for excellence and cuisine only add to the warm hospitality. Judged one of the nation's "10 Best Inns" for a 3rd year. (Mobil ★★★★)

HISTORIC BROOKSIDE FARMS

- 5 Rooms, $85/$150 B&B
  1 Suite, $150/$185 B&B
- No Credit Cards
- Private & Shared Baths
- Open Year-round
- Appropriate for Children
  No Pets
- Hiking, XC Skiing, Boating, Fishing, Golf, Tennis, Horseback riding
- Breakfast, Dinner for houseguests; Lunch by request; Wine available with Dinner
- Smoking Restricted
- Conference Facilities (50)
- Wheelchair Access 1 Rm.

From I-87 (N), exit 20 (Glen Falls). L. on Rte. 9 to Rte. 149 (E) to Rte. 4 (E) to Rte. 22A (N) on 22A for 13 mi. From I-89 (N) exit White River Junction, Rte. 4 (W) to 22A (N).

TEL. 802-948-2727

Route 22A
Orwell, VT 05760

Joan & Murray Korda
Innkeepers

5 This magnificent 200-year-old Greek Revival mansion is an architect's dream, where antique furnishings, paintings, & music abound. Skiers have only to step out the door to enjoy 300 acres of trails and meadow skiing. The farm provides wholesome food for the table, with beef, lamb & vegetable gardens. 3 generations of innkeepers welcome guests to this homey setting.

THE INN AT MONTPELIER

🛏	19 Rooms, $93/$143 B&B
💳	Visa, MC, Amex, Diners
🛁	All Private Baths
💡	Open Year-round
👧🐕	Children Welcome; No Pets
☀R	Downhill Skiing, 25 miles. State Capitol, Shops, & 100 acre park a short walk.
🍽🍷	Breakfast; Dinner daily; Restaurant closed Monday eves. Wine & Liquor available
🚬	Smoking Accepted
⊦▉▉⊣	Conference Facilities (16)
♿	Wheelchair Access (Restaurant only)

3   An elegant, comfortable historic inn where fine dining and caring service are our specialties. Enjoy fireside dining or relax on Vermont's grandest porch. Each guest room is uniquely decorated with antiques, reproductions, fine art and many have fireplaces. Guest pantries offer at-home convenience and warmth with refreshments at any time. TV, telephone and air-conditioning.

I-89 to exit 8 Montpelier. Go to 4th light, turn L onto Main St. Inn approximately 3 blocks on right.

TEL. (802) 223-2727; FAX (802) 223-0722

147 Main St. **Montpelier, VT 05602**

Maureen & Bill Russell, Innkeepers

THE INN AT WEATHERSFIELD

🛏	9 Rooms, $175/$200 MAP 3 Suites, $200/$210 MAP
💳	Visa, MC, Amex, Discov, CB, Diners
🛁	All Private Baths
💡	Open Year-round
🐕	Appropriate for children over 8; Pets Accepted with prior notice
☀R	Tennis, Fishing, Swimming, Golf, Skating, Carriage & Sleigh Rides, Sauna & Fitness rooms.
🍽🍷	Breakfast & Dinner; High Tea; Wine & Liquor Available
🚬	Smoking Restricted
⊦▉▉⊣	Conference Facilities (50)
♿	Wheelchair Access (3 Rooms)

11   Congeniality and caring make this 18th-century stagecoach stop special. With its working beehive oven, 12 fireplaces, nooks for quiet conversation, fitness center and sauna, and many guest rooms with working fireplaces, this beautiful inn satisfies many interests. A gourmet kitchen, horse-drawn sleigh and carriage, a pond, and lawn sports are a few of the attractions. (1992 Mobil★★★★)

From I-91 (N), Exit 7 (Springfield), Rte. 11 (W) to Rte. 106 (N). Inn 5 mi. on left. From I-91 (S), Exit 8, Rte. 131 (W) to Rte. 106 (S). Inn is 4 mi. on right.

TEL. 802-263-9217; 800-477-4828; FAX 802-263-9219
Route 106, Box 165, **Weathersfield, VT 05151**
Mary Louise & Ron Thorburn, Innkeepers

INN ON THE COMMON

 16 Rooms, $190/$260
MAP

 Visa, MC

 All Private Baths

 Open Year-round

Children Accepted
Pets Accepted

 Pool, Tennis Court,
Gardens, XC Skiing, Golf,
Lake, Trails

 Breakfast & Dinner
Wine & Liquor available

No Smoking in Dining
Room

 Conference Facilities (20)

From I-91 (N), Exit 21, Rte. 2 (W) to Rte.
15 (W),. In Hardwick, Rte. 14 (N) 7 mi.
turn R., 3 mi. to inn. From I-91 (S) Exit
26, Rte. 58 (W). Rte. 14 (S) 12 mi. to
marked L. turn.

**TEL. 802-586-9619; RES. 800
521-2233; FAX 802-586-2249**
Main Street, **Craftsbury
Common, VT 05827**
Michael & Penny Schmitt,
Innkeepers

1 With the ambiance of a sophisticated
country house hotel, this inn offers outstanding cuisine and an award-winning wine cellar. With beautiful gardens and wonderful
views, the lovely and comfortable guest
rooms are elegantly decorated with antiques
and artworks, some with fireplaces, are
spread among a compound of 3 meticu-
lously restored Federal houses. (AAA◆◆◆◆)

MIDDLETOWN SPRINGS INN

 10 Rooms, $112/$182 MAP
$65/$135 B&B

Visa, MC

8 Private, 1 Shared Bath

 Open Year-round

Appropriate for Children
over 6; No Pets

XC Skiing, Golf Swim-
ming, Antiquing, Boating,
Horseback Riding, Biking,
Hiking, Shopping

Breakfast & Dinner
Wine & Beer available

Smoking Restricted

 Conference Facilities (10)

From Rte. 4, Exit 6 to Rte. 4A (W) .1 mi.
to Rte. 133 (S) 11.5mi. to inn. From Rte.
7, take Rte. 30 (N) (Manchester Center)
to Pawlet, Rte. 133 (N) 12mi. to inn.

TEL 802-235-2198
On the Green, Box 1068
**Middletown Springs,
VT 05757**
Eugene & Jayne Ashley,
Innkeepers

9 Relax and enjoy the gracious elegance of
an 1879 Victorian mansion overlooking the
village green in this historic spa town convenient to Rutland, Manchester, Dorset, and
the Lake Region. You are welcome for bed
and breakfast only, or enjoy a candlelight
dinner in our formal dining room (by prior
arrangement please).

VERMONT
MOUNTAIN TOP INN AND RESORT

🛏	35 Rooms $150/$394 MAP 22 Chalets $216/$384 MAP
🛁	Visa, MC, Amex
	All Private Baths
🏠	Open Year-round
👨‍👩 🐕	Children Welcome No Pets—Kennels nearby
Ⓡ	Full resort — XC Skiing, Skating, Horseback& Sleigh Rides, Swimming, Sailing, Golf, Tennis
🍽	Breakfast, Lunch, Dinner Wine & Liquor available
🚭	No Smoking in dining room
⊢▪▪▪⊣	Conference Facilities (180)
♿	

6 Commanding a spectacular lake & mountain view on a 1,000-acre estate, this inn offers a complete resort experience. Included in the rates are tennis, heated pool, pitch 'n' putt golf, ice skating and skates. Sailing, fishing, horseback riding, xc skiing and equipment, horse-drawn sleigh rides, & much more are available. Attractive, congenial surroundings, and fine dining complete the picture.

Chittenden is 10 mi. (NE) of Rutland. (N) on Rte. 7 or (E) on Rte. 4 from Rutland. Follow state signs to "Mountain Top Inn."

TEL 802-483-2311
or 800-445-2100
Mountain Top Rd.
Chittenden, VT 05737
William Wolfe, Innkeeper

OCTOBER COUNTRY INN

🛏	10 Rooms, $115/$140 MAP
🛁	MC, Visa
	Private and Shared Baths
🏠	Closed early Nov., Re-opening for Thanks-giving, Closed April
🐕	Children Accepted No Pets
Ⓡ	Skiing, Tennis, Golf, Summer Theater, Cool-idge Homestead, Swim-ming Pool, Games, Books
🍽	Full Breakfasts; Family-style Dinners; Wine & Liquor Available
🚭	Non-smoking Inn
⊢▪▪▪⊣	
♿	

8 Casual and comfortable, swim in our pool, ski, bicycle, antique, sightsee, or enjoy the cozy living room of our 19th century farmhouse as the aromas of fresh herbs, baking breads, and homemade desserts fill the air. Mornings include a big cooked breakfast with homemade granola and warm muffins. Away from the crowds, and close to Killington, Woodstock, and Dartmouth.

TEL. 802-672-3412;
800-648-8421

Upper Road, P.O. Box 66
Bridgewater Corners
VT 05035
Richard Sims & Patrick

OLD NEWFANE INN

 6 Rooms, $95/$110 B&B
2 Suites, $125/$150 B&B

 Personal Checks Accepted
All Private Baths

 Closed Apr. & Nov.

 Appropriate for Children over 12; No Pets

 Downhill & XC Skiing, Hiking, Swimming, Golf

 Continental Breakfast, Dinner, Wine & Liquor available

Smoking Permitted

 Conference Facilities (16)

I-91 (N), Exit 2 (Brattleboro). Follow signs to Manchester on Rte. 30 (N). Inn is on Rte. 30 in Newfane, across the village green.

TEL. 802-365-4427

Court Street, P.O. Box 101
Newfane, VT 05345

Eric & Gundy Weindl
Innkeepers

19 Creating new attention for this 200-year-old hostelry, chef-owner Eric Weindl's French-Swiss cuisine has earned kudos from many food critics and delighted guests. He prides himself on the freshness and quality of his provisions. The low-ceilinged candlelit dining room offers the perfect dining experience. Pleasant guest rooms evoke a feeling of yesteryear.

RABBIT HILL INN

 16 Rooms $149/$219 MAP
4 Suites $189/$219 MAP

 Visa, MC

 All Private Baths

 Closed Nov. 1-15 & April

 Appropriate for Children over 12; No Pets

 Downhill & XC Skiing, Hiking, Swimming, Golf

 Breakfast & Dinner Wine & Liquor available

 No Smoking

 Conference Facilities (20)

From I-91 (N or S), Exit 19 to I-93 (S). Exit 1 R. on Rte. 18 (S), 7 mi. to inn. From I-93 (N), Exit 44, L. on Rte. 18 (N), 2 mi. to inn.

TEL. 802-748-5168; 800-762-8669; FAX 802-748-8342
Route 18
Lower Waterford, VT 05848
John & Maureen Magee,
Innkeepers

2 Full of whimsical and charming surprises, this 1795 Federal-period inn has been lavished with love and attention. Many rooms with fireplaces and lacy canopied beds, soft music, candlelit gourmet meals, and turndown service make this an enchanting hideaway in a restored village overlooking the mountains. One of the nation's "10 Best Inns" 3 years in a row – 4-diamond dining.

ROWELL'S INN

5 Rooms, $140/$160 MAP

Visa, MC, Personal Checks preferred

All Private Baths

Closed Apr. & 1st 2 weeks of Nov.

Appropriate for Children over 12; No Pets

Skiing, Golf, Tennis, Fshing, Bicycling, Hiking

Breakfast & Dinner for houseguests only; Wine & Beer available

Smoking Accepted with some restrictions

12 This 1820 stagecoach stop (National Register of Historic Places) continues to welcome weary travelers with a brand of hospitality those early guests never enjoyed. With antiques & memorabilia, cozy fireplaces, an English-style pub, & a kitchen overflowing with enticing aromas, this inn offers guests hearty, scrumptious dishes, & casual, homey comfort in authentic period surroundings.

The inn is on Rte. 11 (an east/west rte.) connecting Rtes. 7 & I-91. The inn is 7 mi. (W) of Chester and 7 mi. (E) of Londonderry.

TEL. 802-875-3658

RR #1, Box 267-D,
Simonsville, VT 05143
Beth & Lee Davis
Innkeepers

SHIRE INN

6 Rooms, $80/$95 B&B
$144/$168 MAP

Visa, MC

All Private Baths

Open Year-round

Appropriate for Children over 6; No Pets

XC & downhill Skiing, Skating, Sleigh Rides, Bicycling, Swimming, Canoeing, Antiquing

Breakfast & Dinner Wine & Beer available

No Smoking

4 This inn overlooks a river with a wooden bridge in a pristine Vermont village (National Register of Historic Places). One of the most attractive historic homes is this 1832 Federal brick building, with its fanlight and black shutters. with five working fireplaces, spiral staircase, high ceilings, canopied beds, and many books, this inn offers elegant hospitality, along with exceptional meals.

I-89, Vt. Exit 2 (Sharon) L. for 300 yds., R. on Rte. 14 (N). R. onto Rte. 110 (N). 13 mi. to Chelsea. From I-91 Exit 14, L. onto Rte. 113 (N/W) to Chelsea.

TEL. 802-685-3031
800-441-6908
Main Street, Box 37
Chelsea, VT 05038
James & Mary Lee Papa,
Innkeepers

THREE MOUNTAIN INN

 14 Rooms $150/$190 MAP
1 Suite, $200/$230 MAP

 Amex, Visa, MC, Discov

 All Private Baths

 Closed April 1 — Mid May

 Children over 8 welcome No Pets

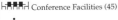 Swimming pool, Hiking, Bicycling, Tennis, Golf, Horseback riding, XC and Downhill Skiing nearby.

Breakfast & Dinner Wine & Liquor available

Smoking restricted

Conference Facilities (45)

Jamaica is located on Rte. 30, 1/2 hr. (E) of Manchester (Rte. 7) and 1/2 hr. (W) of Brattleboro, (I-91, Exit 2).

TEL. 802-874-4140

P.O. Box 180R
Jamaica, VT 05343
Charles & Elaine Murray,
Innkeepers

17 Capture the feeling of Vermont's past in this authentic 1790's inn where the innkeepers make the guests feel welcome, comfortable, and at ease. Relax, surrounded by mountain views. Rooms with canopied beds and fireplaces. Featured in *Gourmet*. Fireplaces in two romantic dining rooms with choices of menu. Hiking in Jamaica State Park. Backroads maps available.

VERMONT MARBLE INN

 8 Rooms, $145/$185 MAP
4 Suites, $195/$210 MAP

 Visa, MC, Amex

 All Private Baths

 Open Year-round

 Children over 12 No Pets

 Water sports, Skiing, Golf, Bicycling, Horseback riding

Breakfast, Dinner, Afternoon Tea Wine & Liquor available

 Smoking accepted

Conference Facilities (30)

I-87, Edit 20. Rte. 149 (W) to Rte. 4 (N). Edit 2 in Vt., follow sign to Fair Haven. Straight down street to town green.

TEL. 802-265-8383
800-535-2814

On the Town Green
Fair Haven, VT 05743

Bea & Richard Taube,
Shirley Stein, Innkeepers

7 This totally restored Victorian marble mansion with its hand-carved, working fireplaces and high ceilings offers an elegant and romantic intimacy. The candlelit breakfast is truly a banquet, and the award-winning cuisine has earned rave reviews. The warm hospitality of the innkeepers is legend. Judged one of the nation's "10 Best Inns." AAA◆◆◆◆

141

THE VILLAGE INN AT LANDGROVE

	18 Rooms, $65/$105 B&B
	Visa, MC, Amex, Discov
	Private and Shared Baths
	Closed Apr. 1-Jun. 1 Nov. 1-Dec. 1
	Children Welcome No Pets
	Tennis Courts, Heated Pool, Platform Tennis, Hay & Sleigh Rides, Golf, XC & Downhill Skiing
	Breakfast & Dinner Wine & Liquor available
	No Smoking in Dining or Sleeping Rooms
	Conference Facilities (40)

13 The principle of "Vermont continous architecture" extended this original 1840 farmhouse into the rambling inn it is today. It is in a true country inn setting, tucked into a valley in the mountains, with gravel roads and a town population of 200. There's candlelit, fireside dining, and a mix of activities and fun for all ages at this informal, engaging country inn.

I-91 (N), Exit 2 (Brattleboro). Rte. 30 (N), R. onto Rte. 11. L. at signs for Village Inn, bear L. in village of Peru. From Rte. 7 (N), (E) in Manchester on Rte. 11. Continue as above.

TEL. 802-824-6673
800-669-8466
R.D. 1, Box 215, Landgrove
Londonderry, VT 05148
Jay & Kathy Snyder
Innkeepers

WEST MOUNTAIN INN

	12 Rooms $142/$158MAP 3 Suites, $179 MAP
	Visa, MC, Amex, Discov
	All Private Baths
	Open Year-round
	Children Welcome No Pets
	Hiking, Swimming, Tubing, Fishing, Canoeing, XC & Downhill Skiing, Tennis, Theatre, Museums
	Breakfast & Dinner Wine & Liquor available
	Smoking Restricted
	Conference Facilities (50)
	Wheelchair Access 2 Rms.

16 Llamas and African violets are only two of the delightful surprises at this happy, relaxed country inn, high on a hill above the Battenkill River. In addition to Wes Carlson's herd of treking llamas and the custom of presenting guests with a lovely African violet, there are cheerful rooms, exceptional New England country cuisine, and a spirit of genuine warmth and hospitality.

Rt. 7 (N), Exit 3. Take access road to end, R. on Rte. 7A into Arlington. L. on Rte. 313 for .5 mi. L. on River Rd. to inn.

TEL. 802-375-6516

Box 481
Rte. 313 & River Rd.
Arlington, VT 05250
Mary Ann & Wes Carlson,
Innkeepers

WINDHAM HILL INN

- 15 Rooms, $160/$190 MAP
- Visa, MC, Amex
- All Private Baths
- Closed Apr. to mid-May, early Nov.
- Appropriate for Children over 12; No Pets
- XC Ski Learning Center, floodlit Skating pond, Downhill Skiing, Summer Concerts, Hiking
- Breakfast & Dinner
- Non-smoking Inn
- Conference Facilities (30)

I-91 (N). Exit 2 (Brattleboro Rte. 30 (N) for 21.5 mi. R. on Windham Rd. 1.5 mi. to inn.

TEL. 802-874-4080

R.R. 1, Box 44
West Townshend, VT
05359
Ken & Linda Busteed
Innkeepers

On 160 acres, threaded by rock walls & magnificent views across the hills. The friendly, unobtrusive innkeepers welcome guests to this peaceful, secluded retreat, with its antique shoe collection, sparkling rooms, memorable meals, award winning amenities, & closeness to nature. Designated an "Inn of Distinction" having been judged one of the nation's 10 best inns for the third year.

What Makes Country Inns "Different"?

There are various reasons why one country inn seems different from any other country inn. Here are some of the things, chosen at random, that make country inns special:

Gardens — formal English gardens with topiary bushes, "natural" gardens with wild flowers, vegetable and herb gardens, and everything in between . . .

Displays or use of local arts & crafts — paintings, sculpture, ceramics, baskets, handmade quilts and wallhangings . . .

Collections of artifacts & memorabilia - walking sticks, Revolutionary War firearms, antique pump organs, nickelodeons, ship models, African masks, Oriental tapestries, carved pipes, bells, and other objects from "the old country," farm tools . . .

Museum-quality collections - ancient documents and maps, antique china teapots, rare china, crystal, pewter, "Nanking Cargo" porcelain, Shaker pieces, clocks . . .

Historical references - pictures and books tracing the early history and development of a region, portraits on former owners, printed histories of the inns . . .

Amusing & interesting collections - antique dolls, shoes, & kaleidoscopes, folk art, samplers, hand-cut jigsaw puzzles, stuffed animals . . .

Community involvement - events such as 4th of July celebrations, blueberry or apple festivals, antique car meets, bike or foot races, pumpkin-carving contests, Easter egg hunts, and art shows . . .

Homage to poets - One inn has an Edna St. Vincent Millay Room, where the poet first recited one of her poems: another has many Scottish references, with poems, quotations, and portraits of Robert Burns and Walter Scott and other famous Scots . . .

Miscellaneous - Christmas festivities with huge, festooned trees and all sorts of entertainments and events sometimes including sleigh rides. A 1958 Bentley or a London taxicab for transporting guests to and from the airport . . . **by Virginia Rowe**

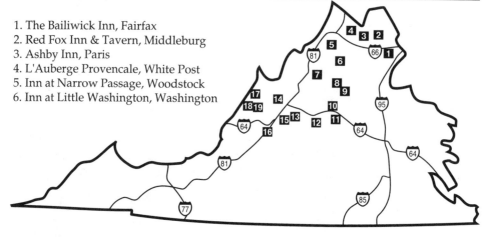

1. The Bailiwick Inn, Fairfax
2. Red Fox Inn & Tavern, Middleburg
3. Ashby Inn, Paris
4. L'Auberge Provencale, White Post
5. Inn at Narrow Passage, Woodstock
6. Inn at Little Washington, Washington

7. Jordan Hollow Farm Inn, Stanley
8. Graves' Mountain Lodge, Syria
9. The Hidden Inn, Orange
10. Silver Thatch Inn, Charlottesville
11. Prospect Hill, Trevilians
12. High Meadows, Scottsville
13. Trillium House, Nellysford

14. The Belle Grae Inn, Staunton
15. Maple Hall, Lexington
16. Alexander Withrow House/McCampbell Inn, Lexington
17. Inn at Gristmill Square, Warm Springs
18. Meadow Lane Lodge, Warm Springs
19. Fort Lewis Lodge, Millboro

ALEXANDER-WITHROW HOUSE/ McCAMPBELL INN

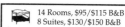
14 Rooms, $95/$115 B&B
8 Suites, $130/$150 B&B

MC, Visa, Discov

All Private Baths

Open Year-round

Children Welcome
No Pets - Kennels
available

Historic Buildings, Museums, fishing, Canoeing, Tennis, Pool, Croquet

Breakfast for houseguests
Dinner at Maple Hall nightly

Limited Smoking

Conference Facilities (15)

16 In southwest Virginia, replete with impressive history and scenery, is the town of Lexington and two gracious and graceful inns, the Alexander-Withrow House, (ca. 1789) and McCampbell Inn (ca. 1809) of Historic Country Inns. Parents of VMI or W&L students as well as business or holiday travelers enjoy the comforts of these inns, within easy walking distance of all attractions.

I-81 or I-64, take either exit for Lexington and continue to town center, Main & Washington Sts. Inn is across from courthouse.
TEL. 703-463-2044
FAX 703-463-7262
11 No. Main Street
Lexington, VA 24450
The Peter Meredith Family, Owners;
Don Fredenburg, Innkeeper

THE ASHBY INN

 10 Rooms, $80/$175 B&B

 Visa, MC

 8 Private, 1/2 shared baths

 Closed Jan. 1, July 4, Dec. 24 & 25

 Appropriate for Children over 10; No Pets

 Antiquing, Vineyards, Bocci, Horseshoes, Horseback Riding, Golf, Tennis, Hiking

Breakfast, Dinner Wed.–Sat.; Sun. Brunch
Wine & Liquor available

No Smoking in guest rooms

 Conference Facilities (20)

From Wash. D.C. Rte 66 (W) to Exit 23 — Rte. 17 (N), 7.5 mi. L. on Rte. 701 for .5 mi. Or Rte. 50 (W) thru Middleburg; 3 mi. beyond Upperville. L. just after traffic light (Rte. 759).

TEL. 703-592-3900

Rte. 1, Box 2A
Paris, VA 22130
John & Roma Sherman, Innkeepers

 This 1829 inn finds its character in the small village of Paris and its heart in the kitchen. The views from guest rooms or dining patio are wonderful in every direction. The menu changes daily, ranging from home-cured salmon gravlaks or local wild mushrooms on toast to jumbo lump crabcakes or duckling with turnips.

THE BAILIWICK INN

13 Rooms, $105/$165 B&B
1 Suite $225 B&B

Visa, MC, Amex

All Private Baths, 2 with Jacuzzis

Open Year round

Children Welcome
No Pets

Mt. Vernon, Gunston Hall, & Woodlawn Plantations. Convenient to Washington, D.C. by metro. Civil War battlefields. Vineyard tours and Antiquing.

Full Breakfast; Afternoon Tea; Dinner
Wine & Beer available
No Smoking

 Conference Facilities (20)

Direct access is via route 123 (Chain Bridge road) 1 mi. (S) of I-66, or via Rte. 50 from I-495 and I-95 to the (E) and (S). Located midway between National and Dulles International Airports.

TEL. 703-691-2266; 800-366-7666; FAX 703-934-2112
4023 Chain Bridge Road
Fairfax, VA 22030
Anne and Ray Smith, Innkeepers

This luxurious, 1800 National Historic Register Inn has rooms patterned after those of famous Virginians, featuring antiques, queen size feather beds, fireplaces and jacuzzis. Afternoon tea and full breakfasts are included in the room rate. Candlelight dinners are available by reservation. The inn has monthly Winemaster Dinners and Murder Mystery Weekends.

THE BELLE GRAE INN

	9 rooms, $65/$95 B&B 5 suites, $85/$135 B&B
	All Private Baths
	Open Year-round
	Appropriate for Children over 12; No Pets
R	Full service Athletic Club, Golf, Tennis, Swimming in/out, Theater, Antiquing, Museums, Historic homes
	Breakfast daily; Lunch & Dinner Wed.-Sun. MAP Rates Available; Wine & Liquor Available Smoking in Some Rooms
	Conference Facilities (50)
	Wheelchair Access

14 With a wide veranda and wicker rockers for chatting and sipping, and graciously furnished rooms with fireplaces, canopied and 4-poster beds and antiques, this group of restored Victorian mansions is in the center of Historic Staunton, near the homes of 4 presidents and numerous museums. Southern-flavored Continental cuisine is served in the Old Inn or in the courtyard cafe.

Exit 222 off I-81. Follow 250 west to center of Staunton. Circle block for off-street parking.

TEL. 703-886-5151

515 W. Frederick St.
Staunton, VA 24401

Michael Organ, Innkeeper

FORT LEWIS LODGE

	7 Rooms, $120/$130 MAP 1 Suite, $135 MAP
	3 Family Suites, $145 MAP Visa, MC
	All Private Baths
	Closed Jan. - Mar.
	Children Welcome Prior Approval for Pets
R	5 mi. private River Fishing, Hiking, Mtn. Biking, Tubing, Swimming, Overnight Campouts, Deer Watching, Golf Course
	Breakfast, Dinner, Picnic Lunch available Beer & Wine available
	No Smoking in Guest Rooms
	Conference Facilities (25)

19 Mountain forests teeming with deer and wild turkey; a glistening river running cool and clear. These are the gifts nature has bestowed on Ft. Lewis. The lodge's large gathering room and guest rooms, with wildlife art and handcrafted furniture, are cozy — downright comfortable. Meals served in the restored Lewis Mill reflect a rare devotion to home cooking.

From Staunton, Rte. 254 (W) to Buffalo Gap; Rte. 42 to Millboro Sprgs.; Rte. 39 (W) for 0.7 mi to R. onto Rte. 678, 10.8 mi. to L. onto Rte. 625, 0.2 mi. to lodge on L.

TEL. 703-925-2314

HCR 3, Box 21A
Millboro, VA 24460

John & Caryl Cowden,
Innkeepers

GRAVES' MOUNTAIN LODGE

   53 Rooms/Cottages
Hotel Rooms $125 AP
Cottages, $90/$160 AP
Visa, MC
Private & Shared Baths

   Closed Dec. to Mar.

Children Accepted; Pets
Accepted in some rooms

Swimming, Tennis,
Nature, Walks, Hiking,
Fishing, Basketball,
Horseback riding

Breakfast, Lunch, Dinner
Wine & Beer available

Smoking allowed in
Designated areas

Conference Facilities (100)

Wheelchair Access (38
Rooms)

From Madison, VA. U.S. Rte. 29, take Rte. 231 (N) for 7 mi. to L. at Greystone Service Sta. Turn L. on Rte. 670 for 3 mi. to Syria Gen'l Store. Continue .5 mi. to lodge on L.

TEL. (703) 923-4231
General Delivery
Syria, VA 22743
Jim & Rachel Graves,
Innkeepers

8 This Blue Ridge Mountain rustic paradise offers complete resort facilities as well as gracious Southern hospitality and good home-cooked food, like country-fried chicken, corn pudding, and hot fudge cake. Many fun things to do, from experiencing great natural beauty to sightseeing and touring or just relax and enjoy the rustic serenity. A few rooms are in the old farmhouse.

THE HIDDEN INN

   6 Rooms $79/$119 B&B
4 Cottages $139/$159 B&B
Visa, MC
All Private Baths;
4 Jacuzzis
Closed Christmas

  Children Accepted
No Pets

Lawn games, Wineries,
Antiquing, Historic Sites,
Biking, Fishing, Boating
Full Breakfast & Afternoon
Tea; Optional candlelight
Picnic; Tues.-Sat. fixed
price Dinner;
Wine & Beer available
No Smoking

Conference Facilities (20)

From Wash., DC, I-66 (W) to Rte. 29 (S) at Gainesville to Rte. 15 (S), Orange exit, to Orange; inn on L. From Richmond, I-64 (W) to Rte. 15 (N), through Gordonsville to Orange; inn on R.

TEL. 703-672-3625; 800-841-1253; FAX 703-672-5029
249 Caroline St.
Orange, VA 22960
Ray & Barbara Lonick,
Innkeepers

9 Lace and fresh-cut flowers accent this romantic Victorian farmhouse, surrounded by seven wooded acres and gardens in the heart of historic Virginia's wine country. Enjoy a cup of tea before a crackling living room fire or sip lemonade on the veranda porch swing. A full country breakfast in the sunlit dining room starts the day, packed with fascinating things to do.

HIGH MEADOWS

7 Rooms, $95/$145 B&B
5 Suites, $105/$145 B&B

Visa, MC, Pers. Checks

All Private Baths

Closed Dec. 24 & 25

Appropriate for
Children over 8;
Prior Approval for Pets

Hiking, Wine-tasting,
Croquet, Vineyard, Ca-
noeing, Tubing, Fishing,
History, Antiquing,
Horseshoes, Monticello

Breakfast & Dinner; Twi-
light Wine-tasting; Sat.
rates MAP, add $35 pp

Smoking restricted

Conference Facilities (20)

12 Romantic flower gardens, relaxing walks on 50 acres of rolling meadows and woods; European supper baskets at the pond, in the gazebo or the vineyard; Breakfasts on the terrace or by the fire; Candlelight dinners after a twilight tradition of Virginia wine tasting are a few of the pleasures that await you at this 19th-century inn (National Register of Historic Places).

I-64 in Charlottesville, Exit 121 to Rte. 20 (S) for 17 mi. After intersection with Rte. 726, continue .3 mi. to L. at inn sign

**TEL. 804-286-2218;
800-232-1832**

Route 20 S., Rte. 4, Box 6
Scottsville, VA 24590

Peter Sushka and Mary Jae
Abbitt, Innkeepers

THE INN AT GRISTMILL SQUARE

8 Rooms, $85/$90 EP
6 Suites, $85/$150 EP

Visa, MC, Discov

All Private Baths

Open Year-round

Children Welcome; Pets
not allowed

Swimming Pool, Tennis,
Sauna, Golf, Horseback
Riding, Hiking, Fishing,
Skiing, Ice Skating

Continental Breakfast &
Dinner; Sun Brunch;
MAP Available

Wine & Liquor available

Smoking Allowed

Conference Facilities (45)

17 On a designated historic site, a 1771 gristmill and a blacksmith's shop are among the cluster of restored 19th-century buildings comprising this handsome inn. Guest rooms are tastefully furnished in both traditional and contemporary decor; many have working fireplaces. Exceptional dining and the many attractions of the Allegheny Mountains & spa country draw visitors from afar.

From (N) on Rte. U.S. 220 turn R. (W) on Rte. 619 (Small state marker) for .3 mi. to inn on R. From (S) on Rte. 220, L. (W) on Rte. 619.

TEL. (703) 839-2231

P.O. Box 359
Warm Springs, VA 24484

The McWilliams Family,
Innkeepers

THE INN AT LITTLE WASHINGTON

 9 Rooms, $230/$420 B&B
3 Suites, $390/$540 B&B

 MC, Visa

All Private Baths

 Open Year-round

Children by special arrangement

 Blue Ridge Mtns., Shenandoah Natl. Park, Luray Caverns, 1 1/2 hr. from Washington, D.C.

Breakfast for inn guests
Dinner
Wine & Liquor available

 Conference Facilities (20)

 Wheelchair Access

From Wash., D.C., (1.5) hrs.) to I-66 (W) to Exit 43A (Gainesville) to Rte. 29 (S) to R. on Rte. 211 (W) (Warrenton). Continue 23 mi. to R. on Bus. Rte. 211 to Washington (W) for 0.5 mi. to inn on R.

TEL. 703-675-3800
FAX 703-675-3100
Middle and Main Streets,
Washington, VA 22747
Patrick O'Connell and
Reinhardt Lynch, Innkeepers

6 In a sleepy village, America's 1st and only 5★ 5◆ inn offers luxurious guest rooms, lavishly furnished in imported English antiques and lush fabrics, some with balcony views of town and countryside. Chef Patrick O'Connell has captured international acclaim with his creative regional cuisine, which, along with the impeccable service, makes a visit here a memorable experience.

INN AT NARROW PASSAGE

 12 Rooms, $55/$95

 Visa, MC

10 Private Baths,

 Closed Dec. 24 & 25

Well-behaved Children welcome; No Pets

Fishing, Canoeing, Vineyards, Antiquing, Hiking, Skiing, Historic Sites, Caverns

Full Breakfast
BYOB

No Smoking in guest rooms

Conference Facilities (20)

From Wash., D.C.; I-66 (W) to I-81 (S) to Exit 283 (Woodstock) and U.S. Rte. 11 (S) for 2 mi.

TEL. 703-459-8000

U.S. 11 South,
Woodstock, VA 22664

Ellen & Ed Markel,
Innkeepers

5 This historic 1740 log inn with five acres on the Shenandoah River is a convenient place to relax and enjoy the beauty and history of the valley. Early American antiques and reproductions, working fireplaces, queen-sized beds, original beams, exposed log walls, and pine floors create a comfortable Colonial atmosphere. Fine restaurants for lunch and dinner are nearby.

JORDAN HOLLOW FARM INN

	21 Rooms, $140/$180 MAP
	Visa, MC, Diners, CB, Discov
	All Private Baths 4 Whirlpools
	Open Year-round
	Well-behaved Children Welcome; No Pets
R	Horseback Riding, Pub/game Rooms, Walking Trails, Hiking, Swimming, Canoeing
	Full Breakfast, Dinner and Box Lunches Wine & Liquor available
	Smoking allowed
	Conference Facilities (34)

7 A cozy 200-year-old restored Colonial horse farm with walking trails and spectacular views, located in the beautiful Shenandoah Valley. Guest rooms have sun porches, rocking chairs, whirlpool baths, and four with fireplaces. The restaurant serves a "country continental" menu. The stable offers trail rides daily and carriage rides by appointment.

Luray, Va. Rte. 340 Business (S) for 6 mi. to L. onto Rte. 624 L. on Rte. 689 over bridge & R. on Rte. 626 for .4 mi. to inn on R.

TEL. 703-778-2285
FAX 703-778-1759
Route 2, Box 375
Stanley, VA 22851
Marley & Jetze Beers,
Innkeepers

L'AUBERGE PROVENÇALE

	10 Rooms, $120/$165 B&B; 1 Suite, $165 B&B
	Visa, MC
	All Private Baths
	Closed January
	Appropriate for Children over 9 No Pets
R	Horseback Riding, Antiquing, Golf, Tennis, Canoeing, Sightseeing
	Breakfast & Dinner Wine & Liquor available
	Smoking Allowed
	Conference Facilities (30)

4 A warm, "south of France" breath blows over this eclectic and sophisticated country inn, with its renowned "cuisine moderne Provençale" by French master- chef/owner Alain Borel, who grows his own vegetables, herbs and spices. Charming guest rooms and the bucolic setting in the hunt country of northern Virginia offer a special experience for discerning guests.

On Rte. 340 (S). 1 mi. (S) of Rte. 50; 20 mi. (W) of Middleburg, 9 mi. (E) of Winchester, VA

TEL. 703-837-1375
800-638-1702;
FAX 703-837-2004
Route 340, P.O. Box 119
White Post, VA 22663
Celeste & Alain Borel,
Innkeepers

MAPLE HALL

 16 Rooms, $95/ $115 B&B
5 Suites, $130/$150 B&B

 MC, Visa, Discov

 All Private Baths

 Open Year-round

 Children Welcome; No
Pets—Kennel 1/4 mile

 Tennis, Pool, Croquet,
Fishing, Walking Paths,
Canoeing, Hiking,
Museums, Historic Sites

 Breakfast, Houseguests
Dinner daily
Wine & Liquor available

 Smoking somewhat
restricted

 Conference Facilities (20)

Wheelchair Access (1
Room)

I-81 Exit 195 to Rte. 11 (N). Inn is (E) of
the Interstate.

TEL. 703-463-2044

11 No. Main St.
Lexington, VA 24450

Peter Meredith Family,
Owners; Don Fredenburg,
Innkeeper

15 A member of the Historic Inns of Lexington, this 1850 plantation home on 56 rolling acres offers guests a lovely place for recreation, exploring historic sites, or just relaxing. There are walking trails, a swimming pool, tennis and fishing. The new Pond House has lovely suites and many of the attractive guest rooms have fireplaces. Historic Lexington is just a short drive away.

MEADOW LANE LODGE

11 Rooms, $90/$115 B&B
3 Suites, $100/$130 B&B

Visa, MC, Amex

All Private Baths,
1 Jacuzzi

Open all Year

Appropriate for Children
over 6; Pets require prior
approval

Tennis, Fishing, Swimming, Croquet, Hiking,
Mtn. Biking, Cascades
Golf Course

Full Breakfast daily for
house guests; Picnic
lunches available by request; Dinner Fri. & Sat.
for house guests; Beer &
Wine available; BYOB

TEL. 703-839-5959

Star Route A, Box 110
Warm Springs, VA 24484

Steve & Cheryl Hooley,
Innkeepers

18 With two miles of a scenic private trout and bass stream rippling through its 1,600 acres of mountain forests and meadows, this is one of the most unusual inns to be found anywhere. Wildflowers, wildlife, birdlife, and domestic animals galore add to the enjoyment of this beautiful, peaceful estate, a rarity in today's rapidly expanding world.

151

PROSPECT HILL PLANTATION INN

🛏	10 Rooms, $180/$230 MAP 3 Suites, $240/$280 MAP
💳	MC, Visa
🛁	All Private Baths, 7 Jacuzzis
💡	Closed Dec. 24 & 25
🐕👧	Children Accepted in some Rooms; No Pets
®	Swimming Pool, Walking Paths, Biking, Golf, Carriage Rides, Antiquing, Ballooning, Peace & quiet
🍽	Breakfast & Dinner daily Wine & Beer available
🚬	Smoking/non-smoking areas
⌐⌐⌐	Conference Facilities (26)
♿	

11 Prospect Hill is a 1732 plantation just 15 miles east of Charlottesville, Virginia. Lodgings are in the manor house and renovated outbuildings featuring working fireplaces, verandahs, Jacuzzis, and breakfast-in-bed. Continental candlelight dinners served daily by reservation. (AAA★★★★ "Best combination food & lodging")

Rte. 29 (S) to Rte. 15 (S) to Zion Crossroads & Rte. 250 (E) 1 mi. to L. on Hwy. 613 for 3 mi. to inn. (Inn is 15 mi. (E) of Charlottesville via Rte. 250; 98 mi. (SW) of D.C.) **TEL. 703-967-0844**
Res. 800-277-0844
FAX 703-967-0102
Route 3 (Hwy. 613) Box 430
Trevilians, VA 23093
Bill, Mireille and Michael
Sheehan, Innkeepers

RED FOX INN & MOSBY'S TAVERN

🛏	15 Rooms, $135/$145 B&B 8 Suites, $155/$225 B&B
💳	Visa, MC, Amex, Diners, Discov
🛁	All Private Baths
💡	Open Year-round
🐕👧	Children Accepted No Pets
®	Manassas Battlefield, Polo, Upperville Horse Show, Nat'l Beagle Trials, Steeplechasing
🍽	Breakfast, Lunch, Dinner Wine & Liquor available
🚬	
⌐⌐⌐	Conference Facilities (250)
♿	Wheelchair Access (4 rms)

2 In one of the oldest incorporated towns in America, Joseph Chinn built his tavern in 1728 and called it Chinn's Ordinary. It has continued, through many changes and reincarnations, to be a popular destination for Washingtonians. Deep in hunt country, this historic inn preserves the feeling of the past along with all the modern amenities and outstanding cuisine. (AAA◆◆◆◆)

From Washington, D.C. * Rte. 66 (W) to Rte. 50 (W) exit for 25 mi. to Middleburg & inn on right.

TEL. 703-687-6301
or 800-223-1728
2 E. Washington St.
P.O. Box 385
Middleburg, VA 22117
The Reuter Family,
Innkeepers

SILVER THATCH INN

 7 Rooms, $105/$125 B&B

 Visa, MC

All Private Baths

Open Year-round

 Well-behaved Children over 5 welcome; No Pets

 Swimming, Tennis, Golf nearby, Horseback Riding, Jogging, Hiking, Biking, Blue Ridge Mtns., Monticello, U. of Va.

Breakfast, houseguests Dinner Tues. — Sat. Wine & Liquor available

No Smoking

Conference Facilities (20)

From (N); U.S. Rte. 29 (S) 1 mi. (S) of Airport Rd. to L. on Rte. 1520 to inn. From(S): U.S. 250 (W) Bypass to U.S. Rte. 29 (N) 5 mi. to R. on Rte. 1520 to inn.

TEL. 804-978-4686

3001 Hollymead Dr.
Charlottesville, VA 22901

Rita & Vince Scoffone,
Innkeepers

10 This historic inn began life as a barracks built by captured Hessian soldiers during the Revolutionary War. It now provides gracious accommodations in antique-filled guest rooms and elegant candlelit dining. The restaurant features modern American cuisine, which changes with the seasons, and a wine list that won the 1992 Wine Spectator Outstanding Wine List Award.

TRILLIUM HOUSE

10 Rooms, $85/$105 B&B
2 Suites, $120/$150 B&B

Visa, MC

All Private Baths

Closed Dec. 24 & 25

Well-behaved Children Welcome; No Pets

Skiing, Golf, Tennis, Swimming, Hiking, Fishing, Horseback Riding, Canoeing, Antiquing

Breakfast; single entree fixed-price Dinner Fri. & Sat.; Reservation required Wine & Liquor available

Non-smoking Dining Room, discouraged in bedrooms
Conference Facilities (25)

Wheelchair access (8 Rooms)

(S) of I-64; (E) of I-81; (W) of Rte. 29. On Rte. 664, which connects Rte. 151 with Blue Ridge Pkwy, between Mile Posts 13 & 14

TEL. 804-325-9126; RES. 800-325-9126; FAX 804-325-1099
Wintergreen Dr., Box 280
Nellysford, VA 22958
Ed & Betty Dinwiddle,
Innkeepers

13 One of the newer country inns, designed and built in 1983 to meet today's standards while retaining the charm of yesteryear. Outstanding library and sunroom. In the heart of Wintergreen's Devil's Knob Village, a year-round 11,000-acre resort, an assortment of recreation available to guests. Mountain country, with trees and birds and a golf course, can be seen from the breakfast table.

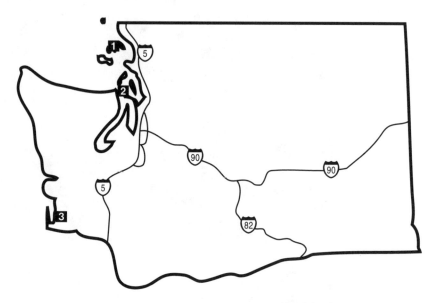

1. Turtleback Farm Inn, Orcas Island
2. Captain Whidbey Inn, Coupeville
3. Shelburne Inn, Seaview

THE CAPTAIN WHIDBEY INN

	29 Rooms, $50/$115 B&B 3 Suites, $125/$175 B&B
	Visa, MC, Amex, Discov, Diners
	Private & Shared Baths
	Open Year-round
	Children Welcome in some Rooms
	Beach, Library, Boats, Bikes, Horseshoes, Walking Trails, Historic Town, Sailing, Charters avail.
	Breakfast & Lunch, Peak Seasons; Dinner daily; Wine & Liquor available
	Non-Smoking areas
	Conference Facilities (44)

From north: I-5 (S) Exit 230 & Hwy. 20 to Coupeville. Turn on Madrona. From (S): I-5 (N) Exit 189, Mukilteo Ferry, Hwy. 525. Hwy. 20. From west: Keystone Ferry, Hwy. 20.

TEL. 206-678-4097; 800-366-4097; FAX 206-678-4110
2072 W. Captain Whidbey Inn Rd.
Coupeville, WA 98239
Capt. John Colby Stone, Innkeeper

2 This romantic and rustic hideaway built in 1907 on the shore of Penn Cove has the feeling of an old-fashioned New England inn. In a wonderful natural setting, where a bald eagle or a great blue heron might be glimpsed, the original inn has a big stone fireplace and quaint guest rooms, with other more modern rooms and cottages.

SHELBURNE INN

 13 Rooms, $85/$125 B&B
2 Suites, $155/$165 B&B

 Visa, MC, Amex

All Private Baths

 Open Year-round

Quiet, well-supervised
Children
No Pets

 Beachcombing, Bicycling,
Golf, Horseback Riding

 Breakfast, Lunch, Dinner
Wine & Liquor available

Smoking restricted

Conference Facilities (35)

Wheelchair Access (1 Room)

From Seattle, I-5 (S) to Olympia Hwy. 8 & 12 to Montesano & Hwy. 101 (S) to Seaview. From OR coast, U.S. 101 across Astoria Bridge L. to Liwaco (N) 2 mi. to Seaview.
TEL. 206-642-2442
FAX 206-642-8904
4415 Pacific Way, Box 250
Seaview, WA 98644
David Campiche & Laurie Anderson, Innkeepers

3 An unspoiled 28-mile stretch of wild Pacific seacoast is just a 10-minute walk from this inviting country inn, built in 1896. Restoration and refurbishing of the award-winning inn has included the addition of Art Nouveau stained glass windows, along with antique furnishings and fine art. Innovative cuisine has brought national recognition to the outstanding restaurant.

TURTLEBACK FARM INN

 7 Rooms, $75/$150 B&B

Visa, MC

All Private Baths

Open Year-round

Appropriate for children over 8; Pets not allowed

Hiking, Salt & Fresh-water Fishing, Sea Kayaking, Golf, Bicycling, Boating, Local Crafts

Full Breakfast, Beverages any time, Sherry and Fruit BYOB

No Smoking

Conference Facilities (15)

Wheelchair Access (3 Rooms)

From Orcas ferry landing, follow Horseshoe Hwy. (N) to first intersection (2.9 mi.). Turn L. to first R. (0.9 mi.). Continue on Crow Valley Rd. 2.4 mi. (N) to inn.
TEL 206-376-4914
Crow Valley Rd., Route 1
Box 650, Eastsound,
Orcas Island, WA 98245
William & Susan C.
Fletcher, Innkeepers

1 On spectacular Orcas Island, this graceful and comfortable inn is considered one of the most romantic places in the country (*L.A. Times, USA Today*). Turtleback is noted for its detail-perfect restoration, glorious setting & award-winning breakfasts. Take a step back in time and experience the quiet comforts of rural surroundings, while nurturing your spirit with a unique peacefulness.

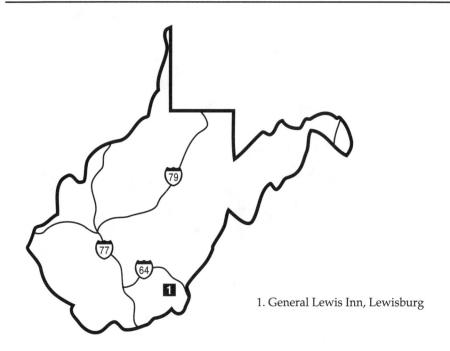

1. General Lewis Inn, Lewisburg

THE GENERAL LEWIS

24 Rooms, $55/$80 EP 2 Suites, $80/$120 EP	
Visa, MC, Amex	
All Private Baths	
Open Year-round	
Children Welcome Pets Allowed	
Garden, Historic Sites, Golf, Swimming, Hiking	
Breakfast, Lunch, Dinner Wine & Liquor available	
Smoke-free Dining Room	

1 Located in a National Register Historic District with over 50 other antebellum buildings, the inn dates from 1834. It is furnished with antiques collected over 60 years by the inn-keeping family. A country garden for summer and a cozy living room for winter make it a relaxing year-round getaway with numerous recreational facilities nearby.

I-64, Lewisburg Exit 169 & Rte. 219 (S) for 1.5 mi. to Rte. 60 (E) for .3 mi. to inn on R.

TEL. 304-645-2600
800-628-4454
301 E. Washington St.
Lewisburg, WV 24901

Mary Hock Morgan,
Proprietor;
Rodney Fisher, Innkeeper

TENNIS ANYONE?

There are usually places to go, things to do, and sights to see in the vicinity of most country inns, and the inns will have suggestions and maps for all sorts of activities, scenic drives, and sightseeing, from nature walks to nearby historic sites to the best outlet shopping. Tennis courts, swimming pools, and sometimes golf courses are standard at resort inns. Many other forms of diversion are offered at various inns. Here is an idea of the kinds of recreation or entertainment you might find on the grounds or under the auspices of a country inn.

Near water there could be fishing, sailing, rowboating, canoeing, kayaking, paddle boating, rafting, waterskiing, and tubing. A couple of innkeepers have Coast Guard captain's licenses and take guests out in their boats. Others have boats for the use of their guests for fishing, excursions, and sightseeing.

In ski country, sometimes there are groomed and marked ski and nature trails leading from front doors into woods, where deer, moose, fox, mink, bobcats, raccoons, or maybe even a bear might be glimpsed. Some inns have their own ski shops with lessons and rental equipment. These might also have tobogganing, sledding, and ice skating.

Western ranches have horses and trail rides, as do a few inns in the South and East. Farms have animals for petting, feeding, and watching; some guests like to flex their muscles at haying time, tossing and stacking bales of hay.

Guided or unguided wildflower, birdwatching, and nature walks might include a picnic beside a forest stream. Some inns provide a basket of goodies for a picnic lunch on a remote beach, by a waterfall, or to break a mountain hike or a bicycle ride on back roads. There are inn-to-inn programs for hikers and bikers.

A couple of inns feature hot-air balloon rides, either from the inn grounds or nearby.

Some on-premises activities include English croquet, shuffleboard, lawn bowling, paddle tennis, pitch 'n' putt golf, volleyball, horseshoes, ping-pong, pool or billiards, fitness centers for aerobic exercise, Nordic track exercisers, stationary bicycles, rowing machines, barre, weights, hot tubs, saunas, spas with mineral springs, massages, and facials.

For rainy days, some inns have VCR's and film libraries, puzzles, board games, and libraries of all sorts of books and magazines. Some inns offer evening entertainment with lovely music programs-musicians playing original instruments and tunes form the 1800s, or chamber music and soloists, or sometimes impromptu recitals by a talented guest who sits down at the baby grand or picks up a guitar. A few innkeepers are accomplished musicians in their own right. A Canadian inn offers local color with films about the area, storytellers, singers and fiddlers, and square dances. Another Canadian inn holds sugaring-off parties in March.

And then there is the inn that has created a sylvan glade where guests can sit and commune with nature. And there are lots of porches with rocking chairs – sometimes all the recreation or entertainment a guest desires is to sit and rock and watch the world go by.

— by Virginia Rowe

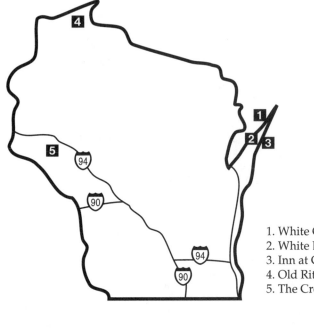

1. White Gull Inn, Fish Creek
2. White Lace Inn, Sturgeon Bay
3. Inn at Cedar Crossing, Sturgeon Bay
4. Old Rittenhouse Inn, Bayfield
5. The Creamery, Downsville

THE CREAMERY RESTAURANT & INN

3 Rooms, $75/$105 B&B
1 Suite, $105 B&B

No Credit Cards

All Private Baths

Closed March

Children - Yes
Pets Discouraged

R Dunn Co. Pottery & Gallery, Red Cedar St. Park, Hiking, Biking, Skiing Historical Museums

Breakfast daily for guests; Lunch, Dinner Tues.-Sun., Sun. Brunch;Wine & Liquor available

Smoking not encouraged

5 This remodeled turn-of-the-century creamery in the hills of western Wisconsin contains four large guest quarters with cherry woodwork, handmade tiles, pottery lamps and concealed TVs. Its sweeping views of the Red Cedar River Valley and hills along with a reputation for exceptional cuisine and fine wines has made this family-run inn well known from Chicago to Minneapolis.

From I-94, Exit 41 at Menomonie; Hwy. 25(S) 10 mi., L. at CTH "C," 1/3 mi. on R. (75 mi. E. of St. Paul, MN.)

TEL.715-664-8354

P.O. Box 22
Downsville, WI 54735

Richard, David, John
Thomas; Jane Thomas
De Florin, Innkeepers

INN AT CEDAR CROSSING

 9 Rooms, $78/$128 B&B

 Visa, MC, Discov

All Private Baths

 Open Year-round

 Older Children Welcome
No Pets

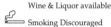 Sailing, Hiking, Skiing,
Beaches, 5 State Parks,
Galleries, Shops, Summer
Theater

 Breakfast, Lunch, Dinner,
Snacks & Refreshments
Wine & Liquor available

Smoking Discouraged

Conference Facilities (30)

Wheelchair access (Dining
Room)

Hwy. 42 or 57 (N) to Sturgeon Bay.
Bus. Rte. 42/57 into town across old
bridge. L. on 4th Ave. 1 blk., then L. on
Louisiana St. to inn.

TEL. 414-743-4200

336 Louisiana St.
Sturgeon Bay, WI 54235

Terry Wulf, Innkeeper

3 Warm hospitality, elegant antique-filled rooms, and creative regional cuisine are tradition at this most intimate Door County inn (National Register of Historic Places). Luxurious whirlpool tubs, cozy fireplaces, and evening refreshments await pampered travelers. Exquisite dining features fresh ingredients, and sinful desserts set in the beauty and culture of Wisconsin's Door peninsula.

OLD RITTENHOUSE INN

 17 Rooms, $89/$129 B&B
4 Suites, $139/$189 B&B

 Visa, MC

All Private Baths;
5 Whirlpools

 Open Year-round; inquire
for Winter weekdays

 Children Accepted

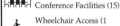 Sailing, Biking, Skiing,
Tennis, Swimming
(indoor year-round)

 Breakfast houseguests
Dinner & Sun Brunch,
public; Wine available

 No Smoking in Dinning
Rooms

 Conference Facilities (15)

Wheelchair Access (1
Room)

Duluth Hwy. 2 (E) for 60 mi. to L. on
Hwy. 13 (N) (just outside Ashland) for
20 mi. to Bayfield

TEL. 715-779-5111

311 Rittenhouse Ave., P.O.
Box 584
Bayfield, WI 54818

Jerry & Mary Phillips,
Innkeepers

4 Three turn-of-the-century homes make up this Victorian inn where hospitality, superior dining, and music blend into a joyous whole. Mary and Jerry Phillips share in the creation of wonderful meals, lovely dinner concerts and other events. Guest rooms are handsomely outfitted with antiques (20 guest rooms have working fireplaces) and the entire inn offers a delightful sojourn.

159

THE WHITE GULL INN

13 Rooms, $64/$116 EP 5 Cottages, $133/$195 EP	
Visa, MC, Amex, Discov, Diners	
Private & Shared Baths	
Closed Thanksgiving Day, Dec. 24 & 25	
Children Welcome in suitable rooms; No Pets	
Golf, Tennis, Swimming, Sailing, Hiking, Biking, XC Skiing	
Breakfast, Lunch, Dinner, Wine & Beer available	
Smoking Restricted	
Conference Facilities (15)	

1 This "New England picture perfect" landmark 1896 white clapboard inn is tucked away at the quiet end of the peninsula. Guests love the country-Victorian antiques and fireplaces that create a warm, comfortably hospitable atmosphere. Known for its food, the inn is particularly famous for the unique, traditional Door County fish boils, cooked outside over an open fire.

Milwaukee I-43 for 98 mi. to Green Bay, then R. on Rte. 57 (N) for 39 mi. to Sturgeon Bay; (N) on Rte. 42 for 25 mi. to Fish Creek. L. at stop sign for 3 blks. to inn.

TEL. 414-868-3517
FAX 414-868-2367
4225 Main St., P.O. Box 160
Fish Creek, WI 54212
Andy & Jan Coulson,
Innkeepers

WHITE LACE INN

14 Rooms, $66/$125 B&B 1 Suite, $150 B&B	
Visa, MC	
All Private Baths, 7 Whirlpools	
Open Year-round	
Older Children welcome No Pets	
Gardens, Beaches, Sailing, Shopping, XC Skiing, Hiking, Golf	
Breakfast & Snacks	
10 No-smoking Guest Rooms	
Wheelchair Access (1 Room)	

2 Romance begins as you follow a winding garden pathway that links this charming inn's 3 historic homes. Guest rooms are furnished with exceptional comforts, period antiques, oversized whirlpool tubs, and inviting fireplaces. A warm welcome awaits as guests are greeted with lemonade or hot chocolate. Located in the resort area of Door County, the inn is close to many delights.

Hwy. 57 (N) to Sturgeon Bay & Bus. Rte. 42-57 into town. Cross downtown bridge to L. on 5th Ave.

TEL 414-743-1105

16 No. 5th Ave.
Sturgeon Bay, WI 54235
Dennis & Bonnie Statz,
Innkeepers

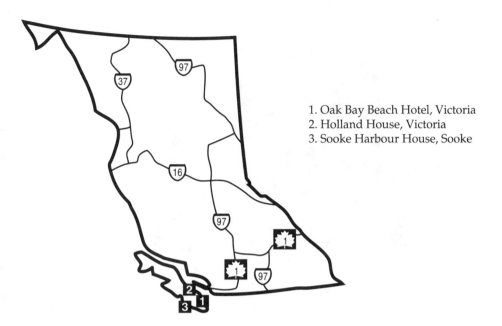

1. Oak Bay Beach Hotel, Victoria
2. Holland House, Victoria
3. Sooke Harbour House, Sooke

HOLLAND HOUSE INN

🛏	10 Rooms, $80/$175 Can. B&B
💳	Visa, MC, Amex, Diners
🛁	All Private Baths
🎭	Open Year-round
🐕	Children Accepted; No Pets
☀R	Golf, Fishing, Cycling, British High Tea, Butchart Gardens, Royal B.C. Museum, Antiques, Beacon Hill Park
🍷	Full Gourmet Breakfast Beverages at any time. Wine Available; BYOB
🚭	Non-Smoking Environment
⌨	Conference Facilities (20)
♿	Wheelchair Access (1 Room)

From Hwy. 17; (S) to Belleville St., L. on Government St. for 2 blocks (S) to corner of Government & Michigan.

TEL. 604-384-6644

595 Michigan St.
Victoria, B.C. Canada
V8V1S7

Lance Austin-Olsen &
Robin Birsner, Innkeepers

2 This unique small hotel, where fine art and unequalled comfort are combined, creates an atmosphere of casual elegance — luxurious rooms, some fireplaces, queen-size beds, goose-down duvets, antique furnishings and delightful small balconies. The Gallery Lounge, where you may relax by the fire or browse in the art library, showcases original works by premier artists of Victoria.

161

OAK BAY BEACH HOTEL

46 Rooms, $65/$220 Can. B&B; 5 Suites, $265/$395 Can. B&B

Visa, MC, Amex, Diners

All Private Baths

Open Year-round

Children Welcome
No Pets

Yacht Excursions, Fishing, Lunch/Dinner Cruises, Jogging. Also: Golf, Tennis, Pool. Recreation Center nearby.

Breakfast or Lunch Cruise Included; Dinner, High Tea; Wine & Liquor avail.

Some Non-Smoking Rooms

Conference Facilities (140)

Follow Patricia Bay Hwy.

1 This prestigious family-owned hotel in the residential area of Oak Bay is a significant part of the history and heritage of the city of Victoria. Magnificent lawns and gardens rolling to the ocean, islands, mountains in the distance, provide wonderful views. The Tudor-style architecture is complemented by antiques and period pieces. Meals, service and hospitality are the best.

to Hillside (E), which becomes Lansdowne. Continue to R. on Beach Dr. to Hotel.

TEL. 604-598-4556

1175 Beach Dr.
Victoria, B.C. Canada
V8S 2N2

Bruce R. Walker, Innkeeper

SOOKE HARBOUR HOUSE INN

13 Rooms, $100/$223 B&BL (includes lunch)

Visa, MC, Amex

All Private Baths, 7 Jacuzzis

Open Year-round

Children Welcome; Well behaved Pets Accepted

Botanical & Garden Tours Wind Surfing, Scuba Diving, Salmon & Steelhead Trout Fishing, Hiking

Breakfast & Lunch for Houseguests; Dinner for Public; Wine & Liquor Available

Non Smoking Areas

Conference Facilities (50)

Wheelchair Access (1 Room)

3 Cozy and homelike, consistently rated one of Canada's top ten restaurants, this charming inn by the sea offers such luxuries as a bathtub for two with a fireplace, aesthetically designed guest rooms with fireplaces, gardens and porches. Sophisticated cuisine uses freshest produce from the organic vegetable and herb gardens. There are fabulous views of ocean and mountains.

Victoria, B.C., Hwy. 1 (W) to Hwy. 14 & Sooke Village. Through Stoplights, 1 mi. to L. on Whiffen Spit Rd. for .5 mi. to inn.

TEL. 604-642-3421

1528 Whiffen Spit Rd.
R.R. #4, **Sooke, B.C.,**
Canada V0S 1N0

Fredrica & Sinclair Philip,
Innkeepers

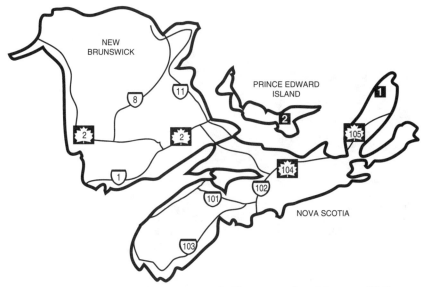

NEW BRUNSWICK

PRINCE EDWARD ISLAND

NOVA SCOTIA

1. Normaway Inn, Margaree Valley
2. Shaw's Hotel, Brackley Beach

NORMAWAY INN

28 Rooms, $150/$200 Can. MAP

Visa, MC, Amex

All Private Baths

Closed mid-Oct. to mid-June

Children Accepted; Pets by prior Arrangement

Tennis, Hiking, Biking, Lawn Games, Recreation Barn, Canoeing, Salmon Fishing, Cruises, Beaches

Breakfast & Dinner; Packed Lunches; Wine & Liquor Available

No Smoking in Dining Room

Conference Facilities (50)

Wheelchair Access (2 Rooms)

Trans Canada Hwy. Jct. 7 at Nyanza (N) on Cabot Trail. 17 mi. Between Lake O'Law and N.E. Margaree turn at Egypt Rd. 2 mi. to inn.
TEL. 800-565-9463 or 902-248-2987
(Off season 902-564-5433)
Box 138, Margaree Valley
N.S. Canada B0E 2C0
David M. MacDonald, Innkeeper

1 On 250 acres in the hills of the famed Margaree River Valley, near the beginning of Cape Breton's spectacular Cabot Trail, this homey, informal inn offers rooms in the lodge, cabins — most with woodstove fireplaces, some with jacuzzis — superb food, service, and choice wines. Guests often relax by the fire after dinner and enjoy films of traditional entertainment.

SHAW'S HOTEL

27 Rms., $130/$185 Can. MAP; 18 Cottages, $175/$230 Can. MAP

Visa, MC, Amex

Private & Shared Baths
2 Jacuzzis

Closed Oct. 1 to June 1
Cottages open year-round

Children Welcome
Pets in Cottages only

Sailing, Canoeing, Walking Paths, Golf, Ocean Swimming, Tennis

Breakfast, Dinner
Wine & Liquor available

Smoking allowed

Conference facilities (60)

2 The Shaw family turned their original 1793 pioneer farm into an inn in 1860. It served a real need in this popular resort area, with its wild seascapes, breathtaking views, and one of Canada's finest national parks. Robbie Shaw says there is much to do here for both children and adults, and meals are good and plentiful for hearty appetites.

Take ferry or plane to P.E.I. Trans Canada Hwy. (Rte.1) to Charlottetown. Follow signs to airport and Rte. 15 for 10 mi. to Brackley Beach.

TEL. 902-672-2022
Brackley Beach,
Prince Edward Island,
Canada COA 2HO
Robbie and Pam Shaw,
Innkeepers

WHO ARE THE INNKEEPERS?

Innkeepers who can lay claim to being the third or fourth generation of an innkeeping family are a rare breed, indeed. They have had the advantage of growing up in an inn and becoming thoroughly conversant and comfortable with the intricacies of innkeeping. There are only a very few of these younger innkeepers who are able to draw on a wealth of past experience.

Since the mid-1970s, more and more people have followed their dream of owning a lovely country inn, enjoying a slower-paced lifestyle and the opportunity to be creative and independent far away from urban pressures and the "fast track."

This dream has brought into the world of innkeeping such diverse types as advertising executives, bankers, school teachers, airline stewardesses, management consultants, engineers, interior decorators, social workers, architects, political speech writers, and many others who have left successful careers. Some innkeepers came out of training in large hotel chains, many are graduates of hotel management schools and culinary institutes. A few are master chefs.

As is so often the case, the reality does not live up to the dream in all respects. Innkeeping is a hard taskmaster — the hours are long, the demands on time, energy, patience, perseverance, humor, and cash are great. However, the rewards, too, are great. There is the pride of accomplishment in creating an independent way of life, and in seeing the results of hard work, ingenuity, and creativity paying off.

Beyond the satisfaction of operating a successful inn is the sense of the personal pleasure in knowing that guests truly enjoy themselves and appreciate the atmosphere of the inn.

Innkeepers sometimes develop long-standing friendships with guests who return for visits over many years. In fact, just as there are a few third-and fourth-generation innkeepers, so there are a few third and fourth-generation guests. This is more likely to happen at resort-type inns, where families spend their vacations year after year.

Innkeepers or their assistants have many kinds of personal interactions with guests, sometimes sharing a recipe for a particularly favored dish, tracking down a baby sitter or the location of some esoteric antiques dealer, finding lost eyeglasses, mapping out a scenic drive, verifying a quotation in a book, recommending a doctor, a mechanic, a jeweler, or.....Making reservations at restaurants, reserving tickets for concerts and the theater, and calling taxis are among the more usual services in metropolitan areas.

This is just a glimpse at the kind of dedicated, intelligent and friendly people who are keepers of country inns. — **by Virginia Rowe**

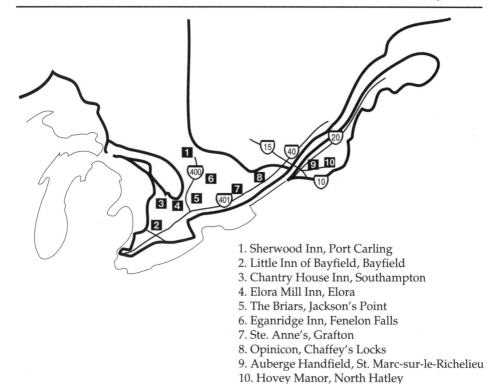

1. Sherwood Inn, Port Carling
2. Little Inn of Bayfield, Bayfield
3. Chantry House Inn, Southampton
4. Elora Mill Inn, Elora
5. The Briars, Jackson's Point
6. Eganridge Inn, Fenelon Falls
7. Ste. Anne's, Grafton
8. Opinicon, Chaffey's Locks
9. Auberge Handfield, St. Marc-sur-le-Richelieu
10. Hovey Manor, North Hatley

THE BRIARS

78 Rooms, $98/$139 Can. AP; 14 Suites & Cott., $130/$150 Can. AP

All Private Baths

Open Year-round

Fun-filled Children's program
Pet Kennels nearby

Golf, Tennis, Swimming, Boating, Summer Theatre, nature Trails, Fireplaces, Solarium Pool, Whirlpool, Sauna & Game Rooms. Breakfast, Lunch, Dinner Wine & Liquor available

No pipes/cigars in dining room

Conference Facilities (75)

Wheelchair access (14 rms.)

Toronto Hwy 404 (N) to Davis; R (E) to Woodbine; L (N) 20 mi on hwy to Sutton; L (N) on Dalton to Jackson's Pt; R (E) on Lake Drive .6 mi to Hedge Rd & Briars.

TEL 800-465-2376
55 Hedge Rd., R.R. #1
Jackson's Point, Ontario, Can. LOE 1LO
John & Barbara Sibbald, Innkeepers

This enchanting, historic inn is an oasis of traditional hospitality in acres of lush lawns, gardens & trees beside sparkling Lake Simcoe. 1840 Regency manor has newer wings, lakeside cottages. Challenging Scottish Woodlands golf course, tennis, nature walks, year-round recreation. Social and children's programs in season. Country-fresh gourmet fare. AAA Four-Diamond Award.

165

CHANTRY HOUSE INN

🛏	2 Rooms, $75/$95 Can. B&B; 3 Suites, $95/$150 Can. B&B
💳	All Major Credit Cards
🛁	All Private Baths
🕯	Open Year-round
🐕	Well-supervised Children Kennel for Pets nearby
R	Boardwalk, Beaches, Lake Huron, Golf, Tennis XC Skiing, Bird Sanctuary, Historic Lighthouses
🍽	Breakfast for houseguests Dinner by reservation Wine & Beer licensed
🚬	Designated Smoking areas
⊢▪▪⊣	Conference Facilities (12)
♿	

3 This restored, award-winning inn (1859-1885) is in the lake port of Southampton (pop. 2,000). The Synders are descendants of Joseph Schneider from Lancaster, PA, founder of Kitchener, Ontario. Historic family recipes from 1563 to the present time influence their menu. Enjoy modern comforts, warm hearts and food that *Schmecks*.

On Hwy. 21 between Port Elgin & Owen Sound. Gateway to toll ferries connecting with upper MI.

TEL. 519-797-2646
FAX 519-797-5538
118 High Street
Southampton, Ontario,
Canada NOH 2LO
David & Diane Snyder,
Innkeepers

EGANRIDGE INN & COUNTRY CLUB

🛏	5 Cotts., $140/$175 Can. B&B; 6 Suites, $120/$140 Can. B&B
💳	Visa MC
🛁	All Private Baths
🕯	Closed Nov. - Apr.
🐕	Children Accepted No Pets – Kennels nearby
R	Private Golf, Tennis, Beach, Boating, Antiquing, Theater, Galleries, Shopping
🍽	Lunch, Dinner, Room Service; MAP Rates available Wine & Liquor available
🚬	Some Non-smoking areas
⊢▪▪⊣	Conference Facilities (45)
♿	Wheelchair Access (4 Rooms)

6 Overlooking a spectacular vista across Sturgeon Lake, in a setting of pine and stone, this inn includes Dunsford House, one of North America's finest preserved examples of 2-story, hand-hewn log home architecture, built in 1837. Challenging golf, award-winning continental cuisine, and the ultimate in luxurious accommodations fulfill guests' highest expectations.

From Toronto, (E) on Hwy. 401 to Exit 436. Hwy. 35. R. on Hwy. 121 to Fenelon Falls. R. on County Rd. 8 for 9 km to inn signs.

TEL. 705-738-5111
RR#3, Fenelon Falls
Ontario, Canada, K0M IN0
John & Patricia Egan,
Innkeepers

ELORA MILL INN

29 Rooms, $90/$140 Can. B&B; 3 Suites, $140/$200 Can. B&B

Visa, MC, Amex En Route

All Private Baths

Open Year-round

Children Welcome
No Pets

Golf, Tennis, Squash, Hiking, XC Skiing, Canoeing, Crafts & Antiques Shopping, Mennonite tours, Music & Highland Fest.

All Meals
MAP Rates available
Wine & Liquor available

Non-smoking Dining Room

Conference Facilities (120)

Wheelchair Access (Public Rooms)

From Hwy. 401, Exit 295 (N) on Hwy. 6 (Guelph Bypass) for 2 mi. (N) of Guelph. Turn L. on Elora Rd. for 9 mi. to flashing light. Turn R. & follow signs to Elora center.

TEL. 519-846-5356
FAX 519-846-9180
77 Mill St. West, **Elora,**
Ontario, Canada N0B 1S0
Timothy & Kathy Taylor,
Innkeepers

4 This converted 19th-century grist mill is perched on the spectacular Grand River Falls in the quaint village of Elora. With heritage guest rooms and a fireside dining room and lounge, the historic country inn serves Canadian specialties with a Continental flair. Guests can enjoy the diversions of Ontario festival country or while away the hours in the inn's out-of-the-way nooks.

THE LITTLE INN OF BAYFIELD

20 Rms, $65/$160 Can. EP; 11 Sts, $100/$190 Can. EP; 10% disc. w/theatre fest. tickets

Visa, MC, Amex, EnRoute,

All Private Baths

Open Year-round

Children Welcome
Pets by prior arrangement

Lake Huron, Beach, Golf, Tennis, Marina, XC Skiing, Hiking, Skating, Specialty Shops, Stratford Theatre, Blyth Festival

All Meals, afternoon Tea Sun. Brunch; MAP avail.
Wine & Liquor available

Non-smoking dining area

Conference Facilities (62)

Wheelchair access (5 Rooms)

From Port Huron, MI> Hwy. 402(E) to Hwy. 21(N) to Bayfield. From Toronto, Hwy. 401(W) to Hwy. 8(W) to Seaforth; follow signs to Bayfield.

TEL 519-565-2611
FAX 519-565-5474

Main Street, Bayfield,
Ontario, Canada N0M1G0

Patrick & Gayle Waters,
Innkeepers

2 Originally a stagecoach stop, this inn has welcomed guests to picturesque Bayfield on the the sandy shores of Lake Huron since 1830. The designated heritage Ontario building is replete with fireplaces, books and games, and suites with large whirlpool baths. There is much to do at any time of the year. Fine dining has long been a tradition with superb meals and imaginative menus.

THE OPINICON

🛏	18 Rooms, $53.50/$72.50 21 Cott./Suites $65/$82
💳	Pers. Checks Accepted
🛁	All Private Baths
🕯	Closed mid-Nov. to early Apr.
🐕	Children Accepted Pets in Cottages Only
⚡R	Swimming Pool, Fishing, Boating, Tennis, Badminton, Hiking, Marine Dock & Yacht Basin, Horseback Riding & Golf in area
🍽	Breakfast, Lunch, Dinner, MAP available
🚬	
⊢╫╫⊣	Conference Facilities (110)
♿	Wheelchair Access (27 Rooms)

8 Offering a restful and relaxing holiday to guests of all ages and pursuits, this 19th-century respected resort-inn is a destination for sportsmen, nature-lovers and loungers. The cheery, informal atmosphere, hearty meals, and attractive rooms make guests feel at home. The beautiful grounds, the lake, and recreational facilities provide endless opportunities for fun and relaxation.

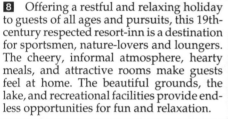

Hwy. 15 (N) to Chaffey's Locks Rd. for 6 mi. to lock station & inn.

TEL. 613-359-5233

Chaffey's Locks, R.R. #1
**Elgin, Ontario, Canada
KOG 1CO**

Al & Janice Cross,
Innkeepers

AUBERGE HANDFIELD

🛏	55 Rooms, $55/$115 Can. EP; 3 Suites, $145/$205 Can. EP
💳	Visa, MC, Amex, EnRte, Disc
🛁	All Private Baths, 11 Jacuzzis
🕯	Open Year-round
🐕	Children Accepted No Pets; Kennel nearby
⚡R	Swimming Pool, Ping-pong, Skating, Theater, Sugaring-off parties, Bicycle Ride, Boating, Golf, Tennis, Health Club
🍽	Breakfast, Lunch, Dinner Wine & Liquor available
🚬	Smoking Allowed
⊢╫╫⊣	Conference Facilities (130)
♿	Wheelchair Access (20 Rooms)

9 Quintessentially French is this inn on the Richelieu River in an ancient French-Canadian village, where French is universally spoken. The rustic decor of this venerable 160-year-old mansion is complemented with antiques and crafted furnishings. A marina and resort facilities, including a health club, along with outstanding cuisine make this a most enjoyable experience.

From Hwy. 20 Exit 112 (Beloeil/St.Marc) turn L. on Rte. 223 (N) for about 10 km. to inn.

**TEL. 514-584-2226
FAX 514-584-3650**
555 Chemin du Prince
**St. Marc-sur-Richelieu
Quebec, Canada J0L 2E0**
M. & Mme. Conrad
Handfield, Innkeepers

HOVEY MANOR

 35 Rooms, $90/$150 Can. MAP (tips incl.)

 Visa, MC, Amex, Diners, EnRoute

All Private Baths, 8 Jacuzzis

 Open Year-round

 Young Children Discouraged; No Pets

 Beaches, Water Sports, Heated Pool, Tennis, XC Ski trails, Skating Rink, Ice Fishing on-site. Alpine Skiing, Golf, Riding nearby.

Breakfast, Lunch, Dinner Wine & Liquor available

Non-smoking Dining area

Conference Facilities (75)

Wheelchair Access (2 Rooms)

VT. I-91 (N) to border. Continue on Rte. 55N for 29 kms. to No. Hatley Exit 29 & Rte. 108 (E) for 9 kms. to No. Hatley & Hovey Manor signs.

TEL. 819-842-2421
FAX 819-842-2248
Hovey Rd., P.O. Box 60,
No. Hatley, Quebec,
Canada J0B 2CO
Steve & Kathryn Stafford,
Innkeepers

10 Formerly a private estate modeled on Mt. Vernon, this gracious manor abounds with antiques and flowers in a romantic, lakeside setting. Individually decorated rooms feature fireplaces, private balconies and whirlpool tubs. Acclaimed cuisine and a full range of year-round recreational facilities make Hovey a destination in itself, only 20 minutes from Vermont. (AAA◆◆◆◆)

SHERWOOD INN

 26 Rooms, $134/$196* MAP - $99 B&B

2 Suites, $196/$204* MAP
Visa, MC, Amex, Diners

Private & Shared Baths

 Open year-round

 Children Welcome: No Pets

 Tennis, Hiking, Mountain Bikes, Health Spa & Water Sports on site, Golf nearby, XC Skiing, 16 kms of trails.

 Breakfast & Lunch, Dinner available Wine & Liquor available

Conference Facilities (90)

2 Hrs from Toronto, via hwy. 400 N, to hwy. 69 N to Foot's Bay. Turn R. to 169 S & travel 10 kms. to the Sherwood Rd; turn L. just before the junc. of hwy 118.

TEL. (705) 765-3131
800-461-4233
FAX (705) 765-6668
Sherwood Road
Glen Orchard, ONT P0B IJ0
John & Eva Heineck,
Innkeepers

1 Set amongst towering pines on the edge of Lake Joseph, tranquil Sherwood Inn offers atmosphere, impeccable service and gastronomic excellence, complimented by an outstanding wine cellar. Attentive staff anticipate guest's needs with quiet efficiency and genuine friendliness. Most of all, Sherwood is a place where guests may relax and rediscover the finer qualities of life.

STE. ANNE'S INN

🛏	10 Rooms, $150/$180 AP $440/$500 Spa Weekends
💳	Visa, MC, Amex, Enroute
🛁	All Private Baths
🛋	Open Year-round
🐕🧒	Not suitable for Children No Pets
Ⓡ	Tennis, Swimming Pool, Hot Tub, Walking Trails, Victoria Hall, The Northumberland Players, Antique Hunting, Full Spa
🍽	Breakfast, Lunch & Dinner available for guests; BYOB
🚭	No Smoking
⊢▥⊣	Conference Facilities (20)
♿	

7 Rest, relax, rejuvenate . . . savor the sweet smell of fresh country air, drink pure spring water, enjoy a candle lit dinner. Pamper yourself with a massage, or maybe a facial. All this can be found in this English style "Castle" nestled on 560 acres in the hills of Northumberland County, one hour from Toronto. Mid week and weekend spa getaways provide a mix of rest and relaxation.

Hwy. 401 to Grafton. Exit @ 487. N towards Centreton on Aird St. for 1.5 km, to Academy Hill Rd. 1.5 km, L. to stone wall.

TEL. 416-349-2493
FAX 416-349-3106
Massey Road, R.R. 1
Grafton, Ontario,
Canada K0K 2G0
Jim Corcoran, Innkeeper

The IIA Gift Certificate

A Lovely Gift for Someone Special

The gift of an overnight stay or a weekend at a country inn can be one of the most thoughtful and appreciated gifts you can give your parents or children, dear friends, or valued employees for Christmas, a birthday, an anniversary, or any special occasion. Innkeepers and other employers are discovering this is an excellent way of rewarding their employees, while at the same time giving them some much needed rest and relaxation.

An IIA gift certificate means that you can give the gift of a stay at any one of over 250 member inns from Kennebunkport, Maine to Southern California; from Quebec, Canada to Key West, Florida: from Martha's Vineyard, Massachusetts to Seaview, Washington. We have inns in the Blue Ridge Mountains, on ranches in the western desert, near state parks and forests and nature preserves, in restored villages in historic districts, on lakes and by the sea. Choose your pleasure.

An IIA gift certificate is good for two years, and may be purchased through the IIA office by personal check or Mastercard or Visa. With each gift certificate, we send along a brand new copy of the *Innkeepers' Register*. For further information call **800-344-5244.**

A five dollar ($5) postage and handling fee will be added to all gift certificate purchases.

Recommended Inns
in the United Kingdom

Following is a list of selected country house hotels, B&B's, traditional inns, manor houses, farmhouses, and small hotels in England and Scotland. Their inclusion in this book is a step by the IIA in exploring the possibilities of forging a closer relationship with selected British inns.

Rates are approximate for two people for one night and include breakfast. It is well to inquire about added tax and/or gratuities and also about reservation and cancellation policies. In most cases baths are private and the inns are open year-round.

LONDON

THE BEAUFORT
33 Beaufort Gardens, London SW3 1PP

In a peaceful square, 100 yards from Harrods. Run like a private house, the Beaufort provides privacy and personal attention. Guests are provided with a key to let themselves in and out. Each bedroom is individually decorated and the hotel has a large collection of original floral watercolors. A truly prodigious number of complimentary services and features are available.

TEL: 071 584 5252
FREE FAX 1-800-548-7764
Diana Wallis
From £170 • 28 rooms

WEST COUNTRY

SOMERSET HOUSE
35 Bathwick Hill, Bath BA2 6LD

Former restauranteurs Malcolm and Jean Seymour have created a family atmosphere in this 1829 classical Regency house in a quiet residential area of popular Bath, with its many attractions. Bedrooms are well proportioned with private baths. Dinner in the 36-seat restaurant includes freshest produce and homemade dishes. The large garden features a model railroad.

TEL: 0225 466451
Malcolm & Jean Seymour
From £40 • 10 rooms

SOUTH/SOUTHEAST ENGLAND

CHEDINGTON COURT
Chedington, Nr. Beaminister, Dorset DT8 3HY

Jacobean Style Manor. Renowned for food and wine. One of the most spectacular views in Southern England. Splendid 10 acre gardens, massive sculptured yew hedge, grotto, water garden, ponds, lawns, terraces. Welcoming interior, fine Persian rugs, antiques, stone fireplaces, atmosphere of distinctive informality and relaxation. 9–Hole Par 74 golf course on beautiful parkland. Excellent center for seeing Dorset, Devon, Somerset and many country houses and gardens, antique shops, and Thomas Hardy country.

TEL: 0935 891265; FAX 0935 891442
Philip & Hilary Chapman
From £70 • 10 rooms

CHEWTON GLEN
New Milton, Hampshire BH25 6QS

An attractive house in beautiful grounds. A Georgian manor world-famous with a reputation envied by most country house hotels. A warm welcome from professional staff. Bedrooms are luxurious. The Marryat Room provides gourmet food, fine cheeses and 600 bins of wine, elegant decor and subtle lighting complete a perfect experience. Indoor and outdoor swimming and tennis; golf, croquet and snooker. A new Health and Beauty Club with complete gym and 34 kinds of treatments is now available.

TEL: 0425 275341; Toll free: 800-344-5087; FAX 0425 272310
Martin Skan
From £178• 58 rooms

FIFEHEAD MANOR
Middle Wallop, Stockbridge, Hampshire SO20 8EG

A friendly family atmosphere attracts guests regularly to this convenient hotel managed by Margaret Van Veelen, who speaks French, German and Dutch. The oldest part of the house is 11th century but modern large bedrooms look out onto the attractive garden. Convenient, on main route west from London airports.

TEL: 0264 781565
Mrs. Margaret Van Veelen
From £75 • 16 rooms

SOUTH/SOUTHEAST ENGLAND

HOWFIELD MANOR
Chartham Hatch, Canterbury, Kent CT4 7HQ

Dating from 1181, The oldest part is the restaurant, which was a chapel. The menu offers fresh ingredients with imagination and flair. A new wing has been added with a new bar area, but beams and nooks abound. Bright bedrooms are in both the old and the new part, and have their own sitting areas. Acres of gardens include an English rose garden. Convenient for Canterbury and the Cathedral.

TEL: 0227 738294
Martin Towns
From £80 • 13 rooms

LANGSHOT MANOR
Gatwick (Horley), Surrey, RH6 9LN

A beautifully restored Grade II Elizabethan manor house, tucked away down a quiet country lane, offering the warmest welcome and old-fashioned hospitality. Log fires, excellent, hearty food. . . a resting place, a perfect stopover for Gatwick Airport, 8 minutes away. Jaguar courtesy car to airport and rental car depots, an ideal base from which to explore London and the southeast of England.

TEL: 0293 786680; FAX 0293 783905
Geoff & Christopher Noble
From £83 • 5 Rooms

MERMAID INN
Rye, Sussex TN31 7EU

This famous Elizabethan inn provides hospitality in a unique atmosphere. It has historic associations of French invasions and the traditions of the Cinque Ports. Bedrooms are up-to-date, yet most have interesting connections with historic episodes. Low ceilings, beams and panelling characterize public rooms. The open hearth in the bar adds to the appeal of being in such a unique place.

TEL: 797-233788; Toll free: 800-843-1489;
FAX 797- 226995
M.K. Gregory
From £90 • 30 Rooms

CENTRAL/EASTERN ENGLAND

KNIGHTS HILL HOTEL
South Wootton, King's Lynn, Norfolk PE30 3HQ

With its origins firmly rooted in history — growing from a hunting lodge in the King's Chase to large working farm and hub of the local community — Knights Hill has evolved, through sympathetic renovation into a well-appointed, three-star hotel with a choice of bedroom styles, restaurants, a traditional country pub and extensive leisure center. Close to the royal estate at Sandringham, guests have a comfortable base from which to explore the coastal and rural beauty of West Norfolk.

TEL: 0553 675566; FAX 0553 675568;
TELEX 818118 Knight G
Bernard Ducker, Howard Darking
From £70 • 58 Rooms

LE STRANGE ARMS HOTEL
Old Hunstanton, Norfolk PE36 6JJ

A Victorian building located on the North Norfolk coastline with lawns sweeping down to the beach. Near to Hunstanton Golf Course and within easy reach of many of the local wildlife reserves and places of historical interest such as Sandringham and Hokham Hall. The hotel has been sympathetically developed over the years, whilst still retaining the atmosphere of a Country house with good food and friendly, professional service.

TEL: 0485 534411; FAX 0485 534 534724
Robert & Anne Wyllie
From £90 • 38 rooms

MAISON TALBOOTH & LE TALBOOTH RESTAURANT
Dedham, Colchester, Essex CO7 6HN

John Constable country, with this unique combination of a hotel and restaurant 10 minutes walk apart. Gerald Milsom started this business nearly 40 years ago and has achieved fame with Pride of Britain Hotels, which he started. Maison Talbooth is elegant with luxurious bedrooms, some quite glamorous. Le Talbooth is very attractive with Tudor white and black half-timbers overlooking the garden and river Stour, with an appropriate high standard of food.

TEL: 0206 322367; FAX 0206 322752
Gerald Milsom
From £102·50 • 10 rooms

ORTON HALL HOTEL
The Village, Orton Longueville, Peterborough PE2 ODN

A former stately home, this magnificent 17th Century building is one of Peterborough's finest Hotel and Conference Centres, set in twenty acres of glorious mature parkland in the heart of the conservation village of Orton Longueville, Peterborough. Excellent base from which to visit the rich assortment of local culture and history, in Peterborough, Cambridge, Oundle and Stamford — the latter being the home of Burghley House. Traditional English and Scottish fare. Fifty luxury bedrooms — many with four poster beds.

TEL: 0733 391111; FAX 0733 231912
Barry Harpham
From: £69 • 50 Rooms

NORTH COUNTRY

THE MILL
Mungrisdale, Penrith, Cumbria CA11 OXR

At the foot of the Skiddaw Range in the Lake District is a charming white house by a stream. Here Richard & Eleanor Quinlan have established a good reputation for individual hospitality. Homemade bread and a mouth-watering range of puddings are featured alongside main courses which include vegetarian dishes as well as game, beef and lamb. Most people return again and again. The cluster of farms and the church nearby with the great fells towering around never cease to appeal.

TEL: 07687 79659
Richard & Eleanor Quinlan
From £55 • 9 Rooms

PARROCK HEAD FARM
Slaidburn, Clitheroe, Lancashire BB7 3AH

Just an hour's drive from Manchester airport this 17th-century Dales farmhouse is in a world apart. Surrounded by rolling fells. Centrally placed for the lakes and dales of northern England; an ideal place to relax after your flight or visits to busy tourist centers. A warm welcome awaits U.S. visitors from Richard and Vicky Umbers. All rooms en suite, lounge and library furnished with antiques, and a restaurant with a growing reputation.

TEL: 0200 6614
Richard Umbers
From £55 • 9 rooms

WHITE MOSS HOUSE
Rydal Water, Grasmere, Cumbria LA22 9SE

Wordsworth once owned this attractive house overlooking Rydal Water. A very intimate atmosphere has been created by Susan and Peter Dixon, that has so many comforts and good food. The reputation of the restaurant is well deserved and one should stay for at least two nights in this central area of the Lake District, with so much to see and such excellent walking in every direction.

TEL: 05394 35295
Susan & Peter Dixon
From £100 • 7 rooms

SCOTLAND

BALLATHIE HOUSE HOTEL
(Nr. Perth) Kinclaven, by Stanley, Perthshire PH1 4QN

A haven of tranquility 1-1/4 hrs. north of Edinburgh and 15 min. NE of Perth. Ballathie is a turreted Victorian baronial mansion within its own estate on the River Tay – Idyllic! Comfortable bedrooms range from a cozy cottage style to grand. Varied rates reduce for 3-7 nights. Well cared for and unpretentious, the house has a lived-in feel with many thoughtful extras. Open fires. Award winning cuisine (A.A. 2 rosettes). Ballathie has also earned these awards; S.T.B. 4 Crown De Luxe, Michelin, and Karen Brown's guide to Country Hotels. Near Scone Palace, Glamis Castle, golf nearby and an easy touring base.

TEL: 0250 883268; FAX 0250 883396
David J. A. Assenti
From £100 • 27 rooms

KILDRUMMY CASTLE HOTEL Kildrummy,
by Alford Aberdeenshire AB33 8RA

A converted country mansion house set amidst acres of planted gardens, in the heart of the Grampian Highlands, 35 miles west of Aberdeen and close to the royal family's Scottish retreat — Balmoral Castle. All the facilities of a modern first-class hotel with the original turn-of-the-century interior — carved oak paneling, wall tapestries, oak ceilings — the perfect base from which to explore Scotland's Castle Trail, discover the Malt Whiskey Trail, and enjoy the northeast's fine natural produce.

TEL: 09755 71288; FAX 09755 71345
Thomas & Mary Hanna
From £96 • 16 Rooms

COUNTRY INN ARCHITECTURE

Country inns are probably more often found in Victorian buildings than in any one other style of architecture; however, that includes such a variation in styles as Queen Anne, Edwardian, Carpenter Gothic, and Italianate. Showy and flamboyant, these buildings have great eye-catching appeal with their cupolas, chimneys, gables, shingles, widow's walks, and capacious wraparound porches. The sometimes rather unusual combinations of exterior paint colors can be a little shocking to the modern eye, but were de rigueur for the Victorians. Understandably, as the country expanded westward in the 19th century, building followed the current architectural styles, and consequently there are more inns in Victorian buildings in the Midwest and Far West than in the East and South.

In New England will be found the more pristine and classic pre-Revolutionary, Federalist, and Georgian Colonial buildings. White clapboard or red brick, black shutters, two or more chimneys, "6 over 6" or "12 over 12" double-hung windows (infrequently with the original hand-blown wavy glass), and a fanlight over the door most often characterize the exterior of Colonial buildings. The very earliest have low, beamed ceilings and great fireplaces, sometimes with a blackened crane, that provide a cozy, welcoming setting for guests.

Beyond those two predominant styles, country inn architecture takes off in all directions. Rustic log houses with bark still covering the beams, 19th-century red brick mansions or brick factory buildings and small Midwestern hotels reflecting opulent early days, Greek Revival, English Tudor, Bavarian hip-roofed buildings with balconies, French Mediterranean, Spanish haciendas with flower-laden courtyards, classic, simple Shaker buildings — country inns offer hospitality in these and many other kinds of buildings. Many of them are listed on the National Register of Historic Places.

In the South, there are inns in "shotgun" or "single" houses, built sideways to the street with open piazzas along the side, for privacy, allowing cool breezes to blow through the house. Imposing Southern Colonial mansions with graceful 2-story Grecian pillars house several inns, although there are a few of these transplanted to other parts of the country, too. Some inns have been built in more contemporary styles, and these are usually found in very natural forest or mountain settings, utilizing local woods and stone and other materials.

A few buildings have been designed by famous architects, such as Cass Gilbert, Charles Bulfinch, and Walter Martens. Many American country inns are reminiscent of the country house hotels of Britain.

— by Virginia Rowe

United States

Upper New England
Maritimes and Quebec

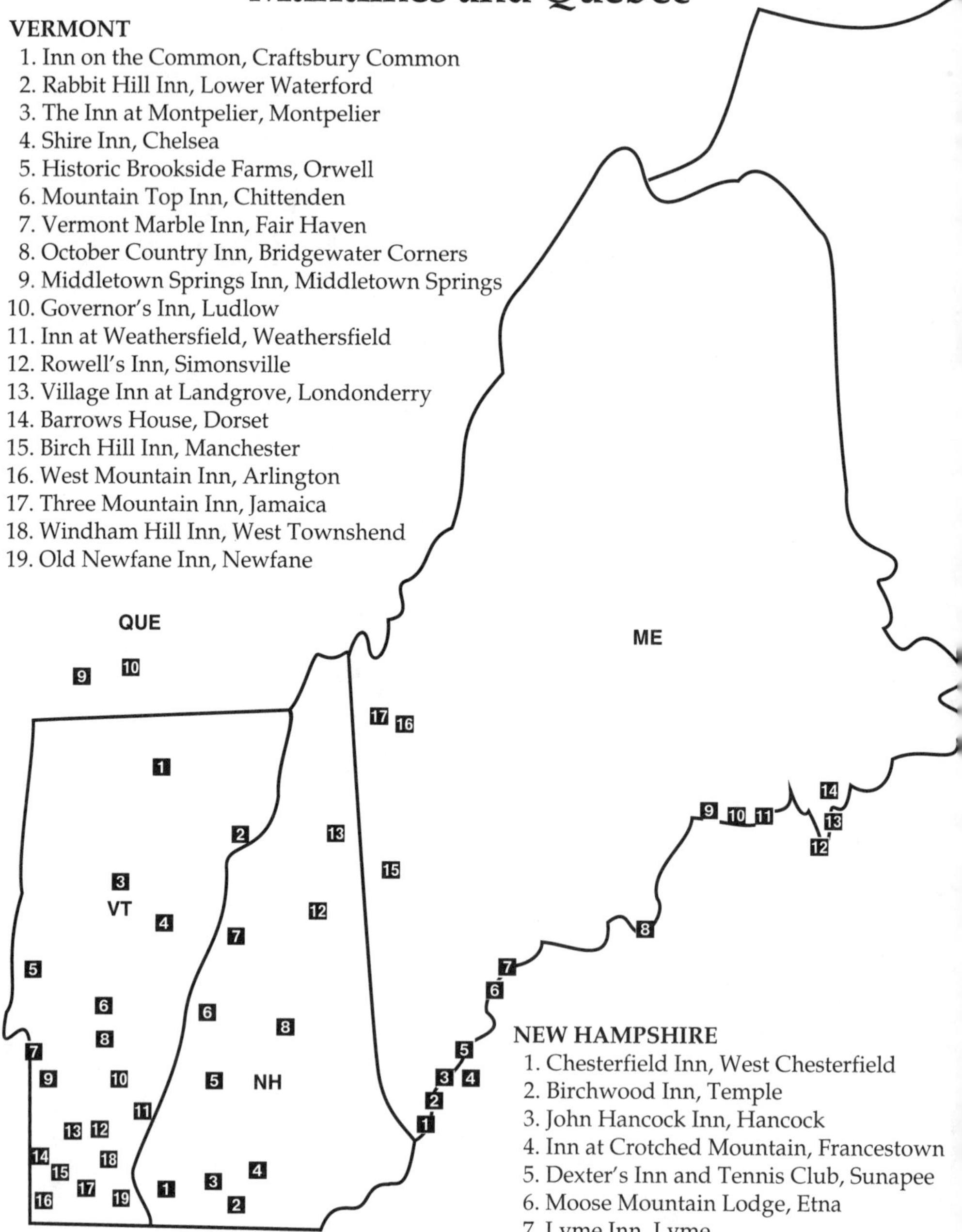

VERMONT
1. Inn on the Common, Craftsbury Common
2. Rabbit Hill Inn, Lower Waterford
3. The Inn at Montpelier, Montpelier
4. Shire Inn, Chelsea
5. Historic Brookside Farms, Orwell
6. Mountain Top Inn, Chittenden
7. Vermont Marble Inn, Fair Haven
8. October Country Inn, Bridgewater Corners
9. Middletown Springs Inn, Middletown Springs
10. Governor's Inn, Ludlow
11. Inn at Weathersfield, Weathersfield
12. Rowell's Inn, Simonsville
13. Village Inn at Landgrove, Londonderry
14. Barrows House, Dorset
15. Birch Hill Inn, Manchester
16. West Mountain Inn, Arlington
17. Three Mountain Inn, Jamaica
18. Windham Hill Inn, West Townshend
19. Old Newfane Inn, Newfane

QUE

ME

VT

NH

NEW HAMPSHIRE
1. Chesterfield Inn, West Chesterfield
2. Birchwood Inn, Temple
3. John Hancock Inn, Hancock
4. Inn at Crotched Mountain, Francestown
5. Dexter's Inn and Tennis Club, Sunapee
6. Moose Mountain Lodge, Etna
7. Lyme Inn, Lyme
8. Hickory Stick Farm, Belmont
9. Corner House Inn, Center Sandwich
10. Stafford's in the Field, Chocorua
11. Darby Field Inn, Conway
12. Christmas Farm Inn, Jackson
13. Philbrook Farm Inn, Shelburne

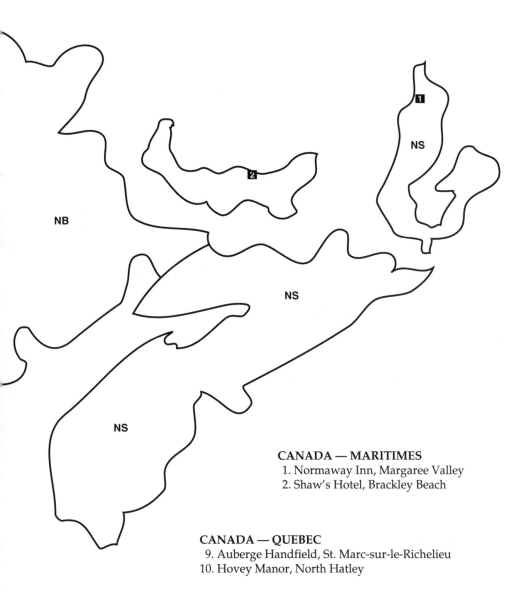

CANADA — MARITIMES
1. Normaway Inn, Margaree Valley
2. Shaw's Hotel, Brackley Beach

CANADA — QUEBEC
9. Auberge Handfield, St. Marc-sur-le-Richelieu
10. Hovey Manor, North Hatley

MAINE
1. Dockside Guest Quarters, York
2. Hartwell house, Ogunquit
3. Captain Lord Mansion, Kennebunkport
4. Old Fort Inn, Kennebunkport
5. Black Point Inn, Prouts Neck
6. Squire Tarbox Inn, Westport Island
7. Newcastle Inn, Newcastle
8. Whitehall inn, Camden
9. Pentagoet Inn, Castine
10. Goose Cove Lodge, Deer Isle
11. Pilgrim's Inn, Deer Isle
12. Claremont Hotel and Cottages, Southwest Harbor
13. The Inn at Canoe Point, Hulls Point
14. Crocker House Country Inn, Hancock Point
15. Waterford Inne, East Waterford
16. Rangeley Inn, Rangeley
17. Country Club Inn, Rangeley

Southern New England

MASSACHUSETTS
1. Village Inn, Lenox
2. Red Lion Inn, Stockbridge
3. Inn at Stockbridge, Stockbridge
4. Weathervane Inn, South Egremont
5. Longfellow's Wayside Inn, South Sudbury
6. Hawthorne Inn, Concord
7. Lenox Hotel, Boston
8. Yankee Clipper Inn, Rockport
9. Ralph Waldo Emerson, Rockport
10. Isaiah Jones Homestead, Sandwich
11. Charles Hinckley House, Barnstable
12. Bramble Inn, Brewster
13. Captain's House Inn, Chatham
14. Queen Anne Inn, Chatham
15. Charlotte Inn, Edgartown, Martha's Vineyard Island
16. Jared Coffin House, Nantucket Island

CONNECTICUT
1. Bee and Thistle Inn, Old Lyme
2. Griswold Inn, Essex
3. Homestead Inn, Greenwich
4. Silvermine Tavern, Norwalk
5. West Lane Inn, Ridgefield
6. Boulders Inn, New Preston
7. Under Mountain Inn, Salisbury

RHODE ISLAND
1. Inn at Castle Hill, Newport
2. The Inntowne, Newport
3. Larchwood Inn, Wakefield
4. Hotel Manisses, Block Island
5. 1661 Inn, Block Island

PENNSYLVANIA
1. Inn at Starlight Lake, Starlight
2. The Settlers Inn, Hawley
3. Cliff Park, Milford
4. Sterling Inn, South Sterling
5. The French Manor, South Sterling
6. Crestmont, Eagles Mere
7. Pine Barn Inn, Danville
8. Glasbern, Fogelsville
9. 1740 House, Lumberville
10. Barley Sheaf Farm, Holicong (Lahaska on maps)
11. Whitehall Inn, New Hope
12. Smithton Inn, Ephrata
13. Cameron Estate Inn, Mount Joy
14. Hickory Bridge Farm, Orrtanna
15. Century Inn, Scenery Hill
16. The Tavern, New Wilmington
17. Tara, Clark
18. Gateway Lodge, Cooksburg

Upper Mid-Atlantic

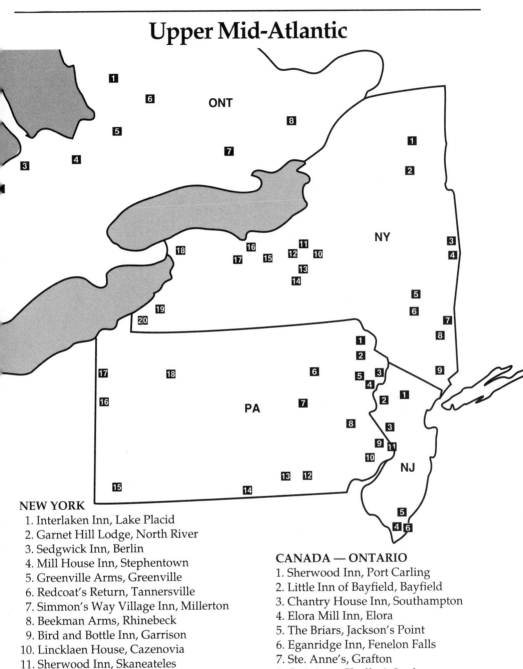

NEW YORK
1. Interlaken Inn, Lake Placid
2. Garnet Hill Lodge, North River
3. Sedgwick Inn, Berlin
4. Mill House Inn, Stephentown
5. Greenville Arms, Greenville
6. Redcoat's Return, Tannersville
7. Simmon's Way Village Inn, Millerton
8. Beekman Arms, Rhinebeck
9. Bird and Bottle Inn, Garrison
10. Lincklaen House, Cazenovia
11. Sherwood Inn, Skaneateles
12. Springside Inn, Auburn
13. Ben Conger Inn, Groton
14. Rose Inn, Ithaca
15. Morgan-Samuels B&B Inn, Canandaigua
16. Oliver Loud's Inn, Pittsford
17. The Genesee Country Inn, Mumford
18. Asa Ransom House, Clarence
19. White Inn, Fredonia
20. William Seward Inn, Westfield

CANADA — ONTARIO
1. Sherwood Inn, Port Carling
2. Little Inn of Bayfield, Bayfield
3. Chantry House Inn, Southampton
4. Elora Mill Inn, Elora
5. The Briars, Jackson's Point
6. Eganridge Inn, Fenelon Falls
7. Ste. Anne's, Grafton
8. Opinicon, Chaffey's Locks

NEW JERSEY
1. Whistling Swan Inn, Stanhope
2. Inn at Millrace Pond, Hope
3. Stockton Inn, "Colligan's," Stockton
4. Mainstay Inn & Cottage, Cape May
5. Manor House, Cape May
6. The Queen Victoria, Cape May

Lower Mid-Atlantic

MARYLAND
1. Antietam Overlook Farm, Keedysville
2. Inn at Buckeystown, Buckeystown
3. Robert Morris Inn, Oxford

WEST VIRGINIA
1. General Lewis Inn, Lewisburg

VIRGINIA
1. The Bailiwick Inn, Fairfax
2. Red Fox Inn & Tavern, Middleburg
3. Ashby Inn, Paris
4. L'Auberge Provencale, White Post
5. Inn at Narrow Passage, Woodstock
6. Inn at Little Washington, Washington
7. Jordan Hollow Farm Inn, Stanley
8. Graves' Mountain Lodge, Syria
9. The Hidden Inn, Orange
10. Silver Thatch Inn, Charlottesville
11. Prospect Hill, Trevilians
12. High Meadows, Scottsville
13. Trillium House, Nellysford
14. The Belle Grae Inn, Staunton
15. Maple Hall, Lexington
16. Alexander Withrow House/McCampbell Inn, Lexington
17. Inn at Gristmill Square, Warm Springs
18. Meadow Lane Lodge, Warm Springs
19. Fort Lewis Lodge, Millboro

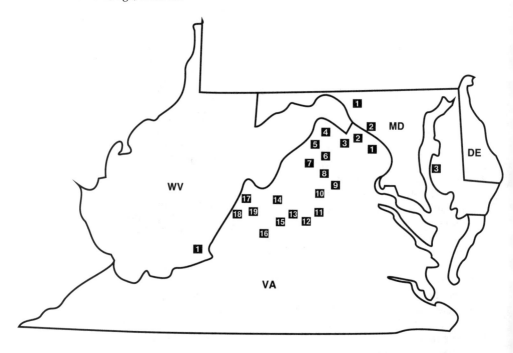

South Atlantic

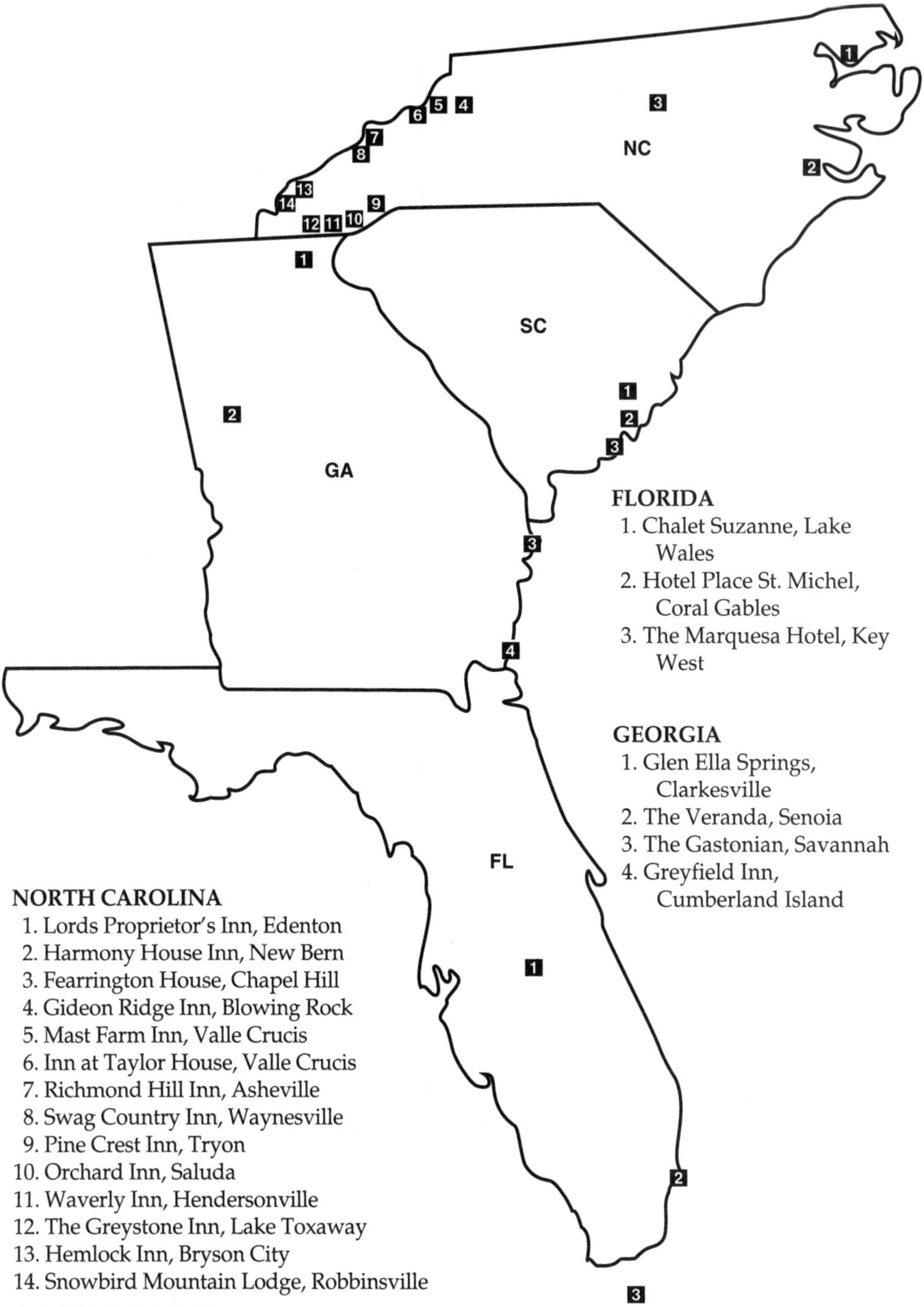

NC

SC

GA

FL

FLORIDA
1. Chalet Suzanne, Lake Wales
2. Hotel Place St. Michel, Coral Gables
3. The Marquesa Hotel, Key West

GEORGIA
1. Glen Ella Springs, Clarkesville
2. The Veranda, Senoia
3. The Gastonian, Savannah
4. Greyfield Inn, Cumberland Island

NORTH CAROLINA
1. Lords Proprietor's Inn, Edenton
2. Harmony House Inn, New Bern
3. Fearrington House, Chapel Hill
4. Gideon Ridge Inn, Blowing Rock
5. Mast Farm Inn, Valle Crucis
6. Inn at Taylor House, Valle Crucis
7. Richmond Hill Inn, Asheville
8. Swag Country Inn, Waynesville
9. Pine Crest Inn, Tryon
10. Orchard Inn, Saluda
11. Waverly Inn, Hendersonville
12. The Greystone Inn, Lake Toxaway
13. Hemlock Inn, Bryson City
14. Snowbird Mountain Lodge, Robbinsville

SOUTH CAROLINA
1. Two Meeting Street, Charleston
2. John Rutledge House Inn, Charleston
3. Rhett House, Beaufort

West and South

ARKANSAS
1. Dairy Hollow House, Eureka Springs

COLORADO
1. The Lovelander Bed & Breakfast Inn, Loveland
2. River Song, Estes Park
3. Castle Marne, Denver
4. Hearthstone Inn, Colorado Springs
5. Abriendo Inn, Pueblo

MISSISSIPPI
1. The Burn, Natchez
2. The Duff Green Mansion, Vicksburg

NEW MEXICO
1. Grant Corner Inn, Santa Fe

OKLAHOMA
1. Harrison House, Guthrie

TENNESSEE
1. Adams Edgeworth Inn, Monteagle

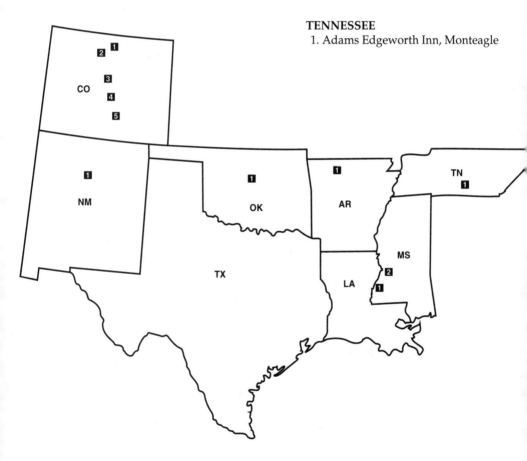

Midwest

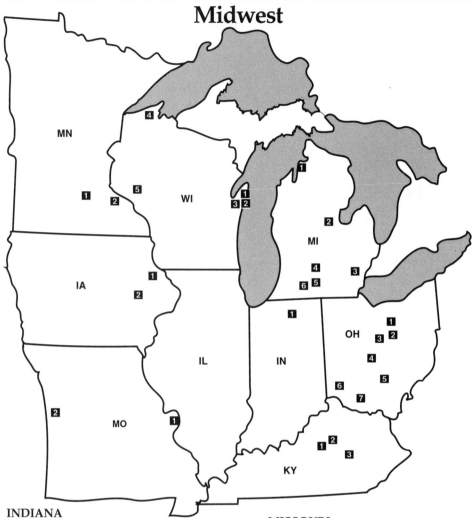

INDIANA
1. The Checkerberry Inn, Goshen

IOWA
1. Redstone Inn/Stout House, Dubuque
2. Die Helmat Inn, Homestead

KENTUCKY
1. Beaumont Inn, Harrodsburg
2. Inn at Pleasant Hill, Shakertown
3. Boone Tavern Hotel, Berea

MICHIGAN
1. Stafford's Bay View Inn, Petoskey
2. Montague Inn, Saginaw
3. Botsford Inn, Farmington Hills
4. Dusty's English Inn, Eaton Rapids
5. National House Inn, Marshall
6. Victorian Villa, Union City

MINNESOTA
1. Schumacher's New Prague Hotel, New Prague
2. St. James Hotel, Red Wing

MISSOURI
1. Boone's Lick Trail Inn, St. Charles
2. Southmoreland On The Plaza,
   Kansas City

OHIO
1. Wooster Inn, Wooster
2. Inn at Honey Run, Millersburg
3. White Oak Inn, Danville
4. Buxton Inn, Granville
5. Inn at Cedar Falls, Logan
6. Golden Lamb, Lebanon
7. Murphin Ridge Inn, West Union

WISCONSIN
1. White Gull Inn, Fish Creek
2. White Lace Inn, Sturgeon Bay
3. Inn at Cedar Crossing, Sturgeon Bay
4. Old Rittenhouse Inn, Bayfield
5. The Creamery, Downsville

Far and Northwest

ARIZONA
1. Rancho de Los Caballeros, Wickenburg
2. Lodge on the Desert, Tucson
3. Tanque Verde, Tucson

CALIFORNIA
1. Carter House, Eureka
2. Gingerbread Mansion, Ferndale
3. Benbow Inn, Garberville
4. Grey Whale Inn, Fort Bragg
5. Harbor House, Elk
6. Madrona Manor, Healdsburg
7. Wine Country Inn, St. Helena
8. Pelican Inn, Muir Beach
9. Mountain Home Inn, Mill Valley
10. Babbling Brook, Santa Cruz
11. The Inn at Depot Hill, Capitola
12. The Martine Inn, Pacific Grove
13. Sandpiper Inn at-the-Beach, Carmel-by-the-Sea
14. Vagabond's House, Carmel-by-the-Sea
15. Inn at Petersen Village, Solvang
16. Seal Beach Inn and Gardens, Seal Beach

OREGON
1. Columbia Gorge Hotel, Hood River
2. The Johnson House, Florence
3. Steamboat Inn, Steamboat
4. Tu Tu' Tun Lodge, Gold Beach
5. Jacksonville Inn, Jacksonville
6. Winchester Inn, Ashland

WASHINGTON
1. Turtleback Farm Inn, Orcas Island
2. Captain Whidbey Inn, Coupeville
3. Shelburne Inn, Seaview

CANADA — BRITISH COLUMBIA
1. Oak Bay Beach Hotel, Victoria
2. Holland House, Victoria
3. Sooke Harbour House, Sooke

Index

The dot indicates those inns that may be booked through your travel agent. Your travel agent should contact the inn directly for specific commission rates and restrictions.

Index

Index

NOTES

Help us help our members maintain the standards of excellence that the IIA upholds by answering the questions below and mailing the card directly to the IIA office. Your signature below is not necessary; however, we would be pleased to know who you are. Please rate each item on a scale of 1 to 5, with 1 being "least satisfactory" and 5 being "nearly perfect."

Name of the inn: _____

_____ 1) Were you greeted and served with a spirit of hospitality throughout your stay?

_____ 2) Was the guest room equipped with your comfort and safety in mind?

_____ 3) Did the inn evidence high standards of housekeeping and maintenance?

_____ 4) Was the food/service (or the area's food/service) of high quality?

_____ 5) Was the feeling of individuality in the personality or character of the inn aesthetically pleasing and consistent?

_____ 6) Did you receive value for your dollar?

_____ 7) Would you return to this inn?

Additional comments: _____

_____

Name and address of other inns you would like to recommend:

_____

_____

Your name and address (optional) _____

_____

Help us help our members maintain the standards of excellence that the IIA upholds by answering the questions below and mailing the card directly to the IIA office. Your signature below is not necessary; however, we would be pleased to know who you are. Please rate each item on a scale of 1 to 5, with 1 being "least satisfactory" and 5 being "nearly perfect."

Name of the inn: _____

_____ 1) Were you greeted and served with a spirit of hospitality throughout your stay?

_____ 2) Was the guest room equipped with your comfort and safety in mind?

_____ 3) Did the inn evidence high standards of housekeeping and maintenance?

_____ 4) Was the food/service (or the area's food/service) of high quality?

_____ 5) Was the feeling of individuality in the personality or character of the inn aesthetically pleasing and consistent?

_____ 6) Did you receive value for your dollar?

_____ 7) Would you return to this inn?

Additional comments: _____

_____

Name and address of other inns you would like to recommend:

_____

_____

Your name and address (optional) _____

_____

Independent Innkeepers' Association
P.O. Box 150
Marshall, MI 49068

Independent Innkeepers' Association
P.O. Box 150
Marshall, MI 49068